Advertising

ADVERTISING

Ray Wright

An imprint of PEARSON EDUCATION

Harlow, England · London · New York · Reading, Massachusetts · Menlo Park, California · Toronto · Don Mills, Ontario · Sydney
Tokyo · Singapore · Hong Kong · Seoul · Taipei · Cape Town · Madrid · Mexico City · Amsterdam · Munich · Paris · Milan

Pearson Education Limited
Edinburgh Gate
Harlow
Essex
CM20 2JE

and Associated Companies around the world

Visit us on the World Wide Web at:
www.pearsoned-ema.com

_____

First published 2000

ISBN 0 273 63289 2

British Library Cataloguing-in-Publication Data
A CIP catalogue record for this book can be obtained from the British Library.

Library of Congress Cataloging-in-Publication Data
Wright, Ray.
    Advertising / Ray Wright.
        p. cm
    Includes bibliographical references and index.
    ISBN 0–273–63289–2 (alk. paper)
    1. Advertising. I. Title.
HF5821.W745 1999
659.1--dc21

99–25716
CIP

10 9 8 7 6 5 4 3 2 1

Typeset by 30 in Stone Serif 9.5pt.
Printed in Great Britain by Henry Ling Ltd., at the Dorset Press, Dorchester, Dorset.

Contents

Preface

Advertising makes a major contribution to the successful functioning of market economies in both national and global economies in almost every part of the world. There is hardly any country where advertisements for products and services cannot now be seen. From sophisticated and well-established markets in Western Europe, Japan, USA and Australia to developing markets in South America, China, Siberia and Africa, adverts for Coca-Cola, Pepsi-Cola, McDonald's and Marlboro exhort consumers to satisfy their needs by purchasing these brands. TV, radio, newspapers, magazines and billboards cry out across the world with messages promising all types of enticing benefits if particular products and services are bought, used and re-purchased. As potential markets grow both in size and geographical spread, and as existing customers become more demanding and worldly-wise, exciting new information technology methods are allowing advertisers, agencies and media owners to be at the cutting edge of advertising corporate and product brand benefits, and so gain competitive advantage. In fact, in many areas, it could be argued that it is partly this explosive technological development that is driving and enhancing this market growth.

In this book we look at all aspects of advertising, and attempt to gain an insight into this fascinating, ever-changing area of the communication mix. The Internet and World Wide Web have a significant presence in the book, with addresses of relevant and interesting web-sites liberally sprinkled throughout every chapter. Further addresses and references given at the end of each chapter allow the reader the opportunity to explore varied and almost unlimited data offerings and gather up-to-date information from organisations involved in advertising worldwide.

Each chapter finishes with a case study based on an article about a 'live' advertising event, written by both advertising practitioners and involved commentators. Although different sources are used, most of the articles are taken from the *Financial Times* web reference archives, and source channels are given for further exploration. The questions at the end of each chapter allow students to probe deeper into the chapter material and discuss it further. Examples of common practice are given throughout, including information about prices and methods. Readers should be aware that these are only examples: the market is changing so rapidly that many will be overtaken by current events. Up-to-date sources can always be consulted if prevailing examples are needed. Once again, source points are given.

The book begins by taking a brief look at the history and background to advertising, moving on to examine the myriad of ways advertising can be used by various types of practitioners. The role that advertising plays within both the marketing mix and the promotional mix is then identified, emphasising the need for integration into the whole marketing planning process at every stage and level. The relationship between advertising and all areas of the promotional mix are discussed in further detail, including: sales promotions, merchandising, packaging, direct response, the Internet, public relations, publicity, personal selling, sponsorship and exhibitions.

The major players in the advertising industry, the advertisers, advertising agencies and media owners are described – names and contact addresses supplied – and the part that each group plays in the overall process of advertising is examined in some detail. Both traditional and contemporary areas are covered, and future direction is discussed. The vital importance attached to the need for reliable information linked to national and global markets and audiences, both business and end consumer, is recognised, and two chapters are dedicated to this area. One examines the types of advertising information needed and methods used for collection and analysis, and the other looks at understanding audience and customer thought processes, needs and wants.

The advantages and disadvantages of advertising methods identified in an earlier chapter are analysed and compared with examples of current practice. The advertising process is then examined in more detail, and creativity, innovation and presentation are discussed – again with examples given of common usage. The advertising planning process is described, including the reasons why an organisation needs to plan, and where the plan sits within the overall corporate and marketing plan and the strategic and tactical advertising plan itself. Progressive diagrams are used throughout this chapter to aid reading and ease of learning. Finally, the last chapter attempts to look into the future and discuss where advertising might be going on both a national and global level.

Ray Wright (www.raynetmarketing.com)
March 1999

Part 1 Advertising today – setting the scene

1 The growth of advertising and advertising methods
2 Society and advertising
3 Advertising – internal and external communications
4 Advertising and marketing

The International Advertising Association: The case for advertising

There are people who actually believe that the world would be a better place without advertising. And unfortunately, many of those people hold powerful and influential positions in our governments. The others, we suspect, haven't thought about the benefits that advertising brings to their daily lives.

The Campaign for Advertising is the IAA's response to both groups of people. Launched in 1992, the Campaign is the first ever global pro-bono media effort illustrating the vital roles of advertising. Created in response to continuing legislative threats to commercial free speech and unfavourable consumer attitudes towards advertising, the Campaign has gathered more than $310 million in pro-bono media time and space. The Campaign's commercials and print ads have appeared in 210 countries around the world. Viewers will not need English to understand the Campaign's message. The IAA Chapters (members) around the world will adapt the material into native languages for satellite transmission. Translated versions of the commercial include, Arabic, Hindi, Mandarin, Spanish and Korean.

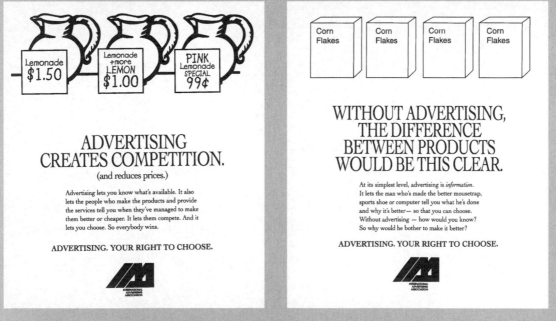

Fig. 0.1 The IAA spreads the gospel *Source:* International Advertising Association (www.iaaglobal.org)

(The mission of the IAA is to preach the advantages of advertising around the world whilst combating counter, denigrating arguments. The IAA represents advertisers, agencies and media owners in over 88 countries.)

Advertising is a global activity and no other business activity is able to harness the explosive technological growth of multimedia more than advertising. In the first four chapters of this book we look at the meaning and use of advertising, its growth, the part that it plays in society, its relationship with marketing and the elements of the promotional mix, and how the organisation can maximise its potential.

1 The growth of advertising and advertising methods

OBJECTIVES

By the end of this chapter the reader should be able to:

1. Describe and evaluate the role that advertising plays in society.

2. Describe the ways that advertising might be categorised.

3. Identify and analyse the different ways that advertising is used.

4. Evaluate changes that are taking place.

INTRODUCTION

The simplest definition of advertising, and the one that will probably meet the test of critical examination, is that advertising is selling in print.

(Daniel Starch, *Principles of Advertising*, 1923)

Advertising is everywhere. Never a day passes without some kind of advertising message impinging on human activity. It is as much a part of daily life as sleeping, eating, working and following leisure pursuits. There are very few places left on planet Earth where we are able to escape its ubiquitous (some say insidious) presence. Adverts hit us in every conceivable way, from every imaginable position and from every possible angle. On land, in the sky, on the highest mountain, at sea, on the sides of the highest buildings, from north to south and east to west, advertisements trumpet their persuasive messages. Scale the heights of Everest, trek through the Amazon rain forest, sail down the Ganges, sweat across the Sahara Desert, and evidence of the pervasive influence of advertising abounds. Stories have even circulated (one hopes with tongue in cheek) about using laser technology to bounce company logos off the face of the moon. Like it or hate it, advertising is as much a part of the market economic system as the entrepreneur, the marketplace and the freedom to buy and sell products and services at will.

The background to advertising

History, progress, new ideas, innovations, new ways of approaching concepts come about through human interaction – by people talking and arguing with one another, by the presentation of one approach, discussed, refuted and refined by others, leading to other approaches and even better ways of doing things. This has applied in all different areas of human progress – painting, sculpture, writing, architecture, biology, zoology, physics, chemistry – with great thinkers in one generation building on the ideas from other generations in a progressive spiral from antiquity through the middle ages and the Renaissance to the modern world and the portals of the twenty-first century. At the very centre of the process is the ability and the need to communicate, to interchange and spread ideas, to exchange and barter artifacts, to improve methods of growing food, to build vast infrastructures and develop sophisticated political and economic systems that can be passed on, culturally, from one generation to another.

Advertising benefit messages

Advertising, communicating messages to existing and potential customers, has been a part of the process as long as individuals and groups have wanted to make it known that they had products and services (this includes a definition of 'products and services' in its widest sense meaning anything, a person, idea, concept, tangible or intangible, that somebody is prepared to put a value to) that they wished to sell or wanted to purchase. In modern society most advertising is paid for and takes place through large intermediary media companies, TV, newspapers, magazines and so on, and the vast substance of this book will be looking at this area. At the heart of advertising is the wish to influence people and persuade them to take action of some sort, usually purchase of a product or service, and so inevitably advertising messages will contain benefit messages aimed at particular groups of people. Although anything from religious and political beliefs to government and charitable services can be advertised, by far the largest amount of money spent around the world is on corporate and manufacture brand advertising by such global giants as Procter & Gamble, Nestlé, Nike, McDonald's, Coca-Cola, Marlboro, Toyota, Kodak and General Motors, to name but a few.

| DEFINITION | Advertising is 'making it publicly known that an individual or an organisation has benefits, usually products and services, it wishes to offer to an identified target audience in return for some other benefit, usually money'. |

Advertising as part of a greater promotional mix

Advertising is only one part, albeit a very important part, of the promotional mix of communication tools available to an organisation. Other complementary techniques available include sales promotions, PR, publicity, personal selling, exhibitions and sponsorship. Many different tools exist to achieve different objectives as the advertiser attempts to move the customer through the communication process from a state of unawareness to one of awareness, interest, desire and eventual purchase. The way advertising works with complementary techniques is shown in Fig. 1.1.

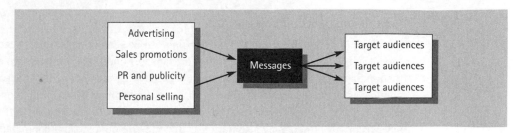

Fig. 1.1 Advertising and complementary techniques

Characteristics of advertising

- It is communicating benefit messages to target audiences.
- It is used by profit and non-profit organisations in both private and public sectors.
- Most advertising is paid for and takes place through TV, print, outdoor, radio, cinema and direct mail channels owned by companies other than the advertisers.
- Although anything can be advertised, most advertising worldwide is concerned with ultimately selling products and services and will often go through a process including creating awareness, affecting attitude and then persuading people to purchase.
- Most advertising is used for corporate and product brand advertising.
- It is an intricate part of an organisation's promotional mix and complements sales promotions, PR, publicity, and personal selling.

'Above the line' and 'below the line' advertising

All advertising can be classified as either 'above the line' or 'below the line'.

'Above the line' advertising

This is the main media advertising (often known as the 'media mix') for which commission is paid to an advertising agency; this will include advertising in the press, magazines, directories, and TV (by far the largest areas), and radio, cinema and outdoor media.

'Below the line' advertising

This includes almost all other forms of advertising, including direct mail; merchandising (e.g. retail posters, banners, show cards, carrier bags, gifts, display stands); sponsorship advertising (e.g. on the sides of racing cars, on football shirts, hot-air balloons and dirigibles); the Internet; and any other area where advertising can be seen other than those classified as 'above the line'.

'Through the line' advertising

'Through the line' advertising is a combination of both 'above the line' and 'below the line' advertising. Kellogg's advertising on TV both its cornflakes (above the line) and a sales promotion giveaway (below the line) is an example.

> ### Advertising at its most basic
>
> Travelling in developing countries, advertising can be seen in its simplest sense. In Vietnam the bicycle is still the predominant form of transport and there are over two million on the road in Saigon alone. This universal usage has spawned many dependent services, the most ubiquitous being the widespread need for puncture repair services. And so on virtually every major street corner there sits a local entrepreneur offering this instant service and advertising his presence by a solitary used bicycle tyre on a stick, predominantly displayed by the side of the road and instantly recognised by needing customers. In the Mekong Delta, in the south of the country, everyday life is conducted by the side and on the many thousands of rivers and tributaries. The floating market is central to this activity and every day small manually propelled boats arrive from the countryside, to congregate in known parts of the water where their occupants buy and sell all manner of locally grown produce. On many of the boats can be seen tall poles with string tied from one to the other similar to a washing line. Attached to the line, and able to be seen from a distance, will be different fruits or vegetables advertising the wares offered by that particular vendor on that particular day.
>
> (Baily, B. *Advertising in Developing Countries*, 1997)

Market and media growth

Initially the advertising task would have been local and a great deal simpler than it is now. The services supplied by the butcher, baker and blacksmith would have been communicated by word of mouth, by signs outside the place of work, by the local town crier and by notices displayed at a general meeting place in the village or the town. Feedback would be almost immediate and alterations and adjustments could be made to match the mood of the consumer. As economic and social activity expanded so markets became larger and people were prepared to travel greater distances to buy and sell produce.

Word of mouth and posters

The communication process became more difficult. Bill posters were employed to travel around outlying districts informing all of forthcoming attractions; people with sites in prominent positions began to charge for poster display. Experience proved that the more relevant and attractive the poster was to the desired audience the more publicity it caused, and so experts on poster creation and design came into being, eventually turning it into a serious contribution to the process and even a collectable art form.

Print

The invention of the printing press and the widespread growth in the ability to read saw the development of information sheets, newspapers and magazines reaching ever wider and larger audiences. At the same time the commercial potential in reaching so many people was recognised, and print owners began offering advertising services, often pulling in more money in this way than through the newspaper or pamphlet cover price. Advertising in the print media developed nationally as mass production techniques expanded markets and producers became ever more detached from the end consumer. A product, produced in Scotland, might now be sold anywhere in the UK and consumers needed to be informed of its availability and persuaded to purchase. As economic activity created mass consumption markets expanded from national to international, followed by the need for mass communication, and advertising on a global scale.

Mass production ⟶ Mass distribution ⟶ Mass communications ⟶ Mass consumption

Direct mail, leaflets and pamphlets

The growth and development in print technology also made possible the production of pamphlets and advertising and sales letters that could be delivered inexpensively from door to door either by special delivery or included as a loose insertion within the delivered daily newspaper. Over the last twenty years there has been an enormous leap in direct mail usage with the spectacular progress made in information technology and computer development leading to ever more sophisticated marketing and customer information database capabilities. In the UK the Post Office offers advertisers a complete service including target customer identification, customised advert design, letter delivery and feedback and control options. The major UK grocery supermarket chain, Tesco, is able to write and send up to 20 000 different personal letters advertising individual customised product offers. This form of advertising is seen as a crucial driver in the development of relationship marketing.

Cinema and television

The 1930s saw the invention, introduction and widespread development of other entertainment media, particularly in the US followed by the UK, Europe and the rest of the world. First came the cinema, then radio and then all-pervasive TV. It was with the coming of TV that a perfect media for mass communication came into being. Now bought and watched in virtually every household in the Western world, many having two, three or more, and fast reaching the same levels in developing nations, TV is an ideal way for advertisers to get over benefit messages to the bulk of consumers in the privacy of their own homes. The concept of TV as mass in-house entertainment and advertising medium was pioneered and driven by commercial interest in the US (unlike the UK, where public broadcasting was the original driving force). The US has always had a great many commercial TV channels with both advertising and programme sponsorship. In fact the term 'soap opera' came about through the big soap manufacturers' sponsorship of these sorts of programmes. As with other media forms, TV as an advertising media refuses to stand still and we are now witnessing more dramatic changes and exciting opportunities.

Technology and media developments

Large national and multinational organisations have grown and expanded by marketing and selling to mass markets at home and around the world. They have been able to use the mass media, notably TV, to do this. Satellite and cable technology have enabled first radio signals and then pictures to be beamed almost anywhere in the world, and in real time, opening up for the first time an international market covering every continent in the world. The Americas, Europe and the Far East can all be reached from one centralised location with one basic message simultaneously reaching consumers whether they be in Shanghai, Chicago, Sydney or Rome. Print technology now allows words and pictures to be digitised, downloaded on a linked computer, and instantaneously sent in the same way as TV signals, from one corner of the earth to another for reprinting into a magazine or newspaper. The use of digital image manipulation to correct, clean up and combine photographs has become so commonplace that hardly any of the images we see in magazines or on billboards depicts reality as the camera saw it. We are now experiencing even greater changes with the growth of the Internet and the World Wide Web, at present accessed mainly on computer monitors but soon to be available on television screens. This will open the way for an explosion in advertising opportunities – but not before advertisers undergo a steep learning curve to understand the advantages and disadvantages of this exciting new communications channel.

Media and change

As we move into the new millennium, organisations have a bewildering array of media vehicles to use to communicate messages to their different stakeholders, and to make matters more complex technological development is causing the whole scene to change on a month by month and year by year basis. This change is happening in an exponential manner making it ever more difficult for advertisers to keep abreast of what is happening as conventional media vehicles change in the benefits offered and new methods spring up with untried and unproved opportunities. The onset of digital technology is opening up the airways to hundreds of new TV and radio stations, typing and print technology is making it much easier to produce newspapers and magazines, and information technology has opened up undreamed-of worldwide opportunities through the use of the Internet. As well as creating opportunities the explosion of channels and of new methods is disrupting, reshaping and irrevocably altering conventional ways of reaching the target market, creating some disharmony and confusion in its wake.

Media fragmentation

An enormous problem for mass advertisers with the development of so many more media vehicles is the accompanying fragmentation of existing methods, particularly TV. Until recently a company could reach a mass market segment through one media channel, but many might now be needed as more options now become available. There is some consolation for the mass advertiser, however, as usage in the US shows that despite the enormous proliferation of TV channels most American viewers still watch the major channels. The reason for this is that many of the newer channels tend to be specialised and for minority tastes and cannot offer the same consistent quality of programming as the old, well established stations with their economies of scale. An interesting development caused by TV media fragmentation is the need for channel owners to promote individual programmes through media other than their own TV channel, so that adverts for forthcoming programmes such as soaps, dramas and films appear on outdoor posters and in newspapers and magazines.

Change and risk

The present degree of change and uncertainty makes it very difficult, if not dangerous, for advertisers and advertising managers because mistakes made, the wrong media chosen, target audiences not reached and communication objectives not achieved can mean millions wasted and, in some cases, jobs lost as shareholders and senior management react angrily to wasted money by inviting those responsible to find employment elsewhere. This explosion of advertising methods has put a tremendous amount of pressure on advertising executives jolted out of past certainties and having now to learn about new methods and to consider new opportunities. This fear of the unknown can cause advertising managers to stick conservatively with tried and tested advertising methods, seeing safety in convention rather than attempting to gain competitive advantage by trying different, innovative approaches. Alternatively it might lead them to use the services of an advertising agency, feeling that buying outside media services in times of such change would be safer left to the professional rather than risking the process themselves. Such change has also put added obligation onto media owners, forcing them to come up with more objective benefit criteria for users or risk business loss to more farsighted competitors.

Media choice in the UK

TV Land-based; Cable; Satellite
   Possibility of 3000–4000 stations by 2002. Local; regional; national; international
Radio Local, regional, national, European, international
   Possibility of 200 stations by 2002
The World Wide Web Available opportunities by the year 2002 uncertain and unlimited
   TV link
The press Newspapers, magazines. Local, regional, national, European, global
   Options by 2002 may be 7,500 magazines and newspapers
Outdoor Options available by the year 2002: movement, 3D, innovative sites
Cinema Multiplex entertainment centres

Advertising objectives

Advertising exists to fulfil the communication needs of every type of industry, organisation, product, brand and service. In very basic terms it is used to educate, to inform and to persuade. Breaking this down further, it can be used in all the following ways:

- to create awareness at the industry, corporate and brand level;
- to inform, educate and entertain;
- to reinforce, maintain, remind, and alter opinions and attitudes;
- to create favourable images;
- to manipulate and persuade;
- to induce the trial of products and services;
- to encourage repurchase on a continuous basis;
- to support other media methods;
- to counter damaging happenings;
- to motivate inquiries;
- to provide sales leads for the sales force – but chiefly
- to help sell products and services.

It is used to appeal to the rational, the emotional and the instinctive aspect of human nature. Some objectives are more difficult to define, measure and control than others but effort must always be made.

Advertising objectives and accountability

I know that 50% of my advertising works, I'm just not sure which 50%.

(Lord Leverhulme)

The case for setting clear measurable objectives for advertising will be visited and revisited throughout the book because of the need for accountability and the imperative to justify all marketing and promotional spend if competitive advantage is to be maintained. The difficulty with advertising is that, much as many marketing managers would like to set objectives in terms of sales, this is not always possible. Rather, behavioural objectives, identified above, such as creating awareness or reinforcing attitude, have to be used. This is not a problem as long as it is clearly understood by all involved what the communication objectives of the particular media are and adequate measurement and control mechanisms are installed to monitor progress and outcomes. It would be unrealistic to think that in practice advertising campaigns are always conducted with this amount of rigour, but the argument must be made that adherence should be as close as possible especially as organisational resource allocation becomes ever more stringent and accountability ever more demanded.

Business/advertising objectives should be **SMART**:

- Specific,
- Measurable,
- Achievable (agreed),
- Realistic, and
- Time-based.

Advertising and marketing research

Advertising should never be undertaken without some form of marketing research being used to establish such things as target markets, customer profiles and benefits demanded, media availability and characteristics, message content and so on. Research will be undertaken at the beginning, during and after any promotional campaign.

The power of advertising

Research carried out by TSMS and Taylor Nelson AGB found that people who watch the most TV were the most responsive to adverts on the box and even light viewers were influenced by commercials. Adverts shown repeatedly during peak time had the biggest impact, as did adverts shown three days before a shopping trip. It was found that they still had an effect up to fourteen days after the first showing. High-tech monitoring devices were attached to TV sets in 750 carefully selected, representative homes to discover which adverts were seen and which where not. This was then matched to a record of FMCG purchases (items were logged by participants when they arrived home using a hand-held bar code scanner) from the same household to see if the adverts had influenced purchases. Research investigators found that adverts seen matched many products bought and that there was a direct connection.

Advertising as a science

There are a lot of great technicians in advertising; and unfortunately they talk the best game. They know all the rules . . . but there's one little rub. They forget that advertising is persuasion, and persuasion is not a science but an art. Advertising is the art of persuasion.

(William Bernbach)

Having just strenuously argued the case for a quasi-scientific approach to advertising it would be disingenuous not to put the opposite side of the argument. In practice many agency staff work as much by intuition and gut reaction (admittedly based on some experience) as they do by a reasoned approach. This is especially true when looking at the creative process involved with message and image associated with advert production. There are many examples of successful adverts that have happened, not because of extensive consumer research, but because the agency creative staff had a 'feeling' for success. Similarly it should be said that many have also failed and probably a balanced approach to the problem is the most satisfactory answer.

Types of advertising

Advertising can be categorised in many different ways, by industry, by company type, product or service, media used, message objectives, target audience and so on; no set method can be deemed to be 'correct' or to 'fit' organisational purpose and policy. Some of the methods used are described below.

Corporate advertising

It is often said that people will not buy products from companies unknown to them. Any salesperson trying to sell in this situation will probably sympathise whole-heartedly with this aphorism as they have door after door closed in their face by prospects unwilling to meet sales representatives from unfamiliar organisations. This problem can be often be rectified and an interview and presentation granted by corporate advertising establishing credibility and legitimacy in the eyes of the buyer.

Corporate image

All organisations, small, medium and large, have an identity and this will be reflected by some kind of corporate image in the minds of the various interested stakeholders. This image might be good, bad or indifferent, probably depending on the level of stakeholder involvement. The organisation might be very well known at regional, national and international level, or it might only be known within very limited geographical or specialised markets. A company will have a corporate image whether it undertakes formal corporate advertising or not. It will be known by its employees and their families and by local communities because of its particular location. It will generate an image because of its production methods, the products and services it produces and how it behaves generally in its environment as a corporate citizen.

Why corporate advertising?

Realising the importance of corporate image, more and more companies are taking control of the process and instigating social audits to discover how they are seen by their customers and the general public. They then use public relations, publicity, and corporate or institutional advertising to try to maintain, control and continually improve the way the company is seen by all interested stakeholders. Empirical evidence has shown that customers are concerned about corporate image and this will eventually have an effect on long-term company sales performance. We only have to look at the mission statements of some of the great global companies to see how strategically important they consider corporate image to be. They abound with commitments to safeguard the environment, to treat all peoples with respect and only to produce products that are acceptable to all areas of society.

Product, service and brand advertising

The most widely used form of advertising around the world is product and service brand advertising. The importance of brands, on a global basis, cannot be overestimated as the evidence is now incontrovertible. Customers trust and buy brands they recognise, and they will continue to use them as long as they come up to expectations. Because product brand leaders in most markets can command higher sales and a higher price and make more profit, the value to the company of its brands can outweigh all other considerations. Crucial to brand recognition is the need to keep the brand name continuously in front of the consumer and advertising, in all its many complex forms, plays a dominant part in this.

One of the problems with brand advertising is that money spent now can take some time, months and even years, to filter through into brand recognition, acceptance and purchase. In times of hardship this can sometimes persuade senior management to cut advertising budgets because of the gap between the immediate expense involved and the resultant benefits obtained.

Some organisations choose not to use their own brand and produce products for others, usually retailers, to brand under a retail name. 'Own' label brands are advertised either under the corporate name, for example Tesco, Sainsbury or Walmart, or under a retail sub-brand name such as Sainsbury's Novo washing powder or Dixons' Saisho electrical products. In the case of own label products the cost (and of course the benefits that accrue from brand exposure) of advertising is taken by the retailer.

Some brand advertising strategies

- Advertising an overarching corporate umbrella brand used on all products and services. An example would be Sony or Heinz who use the one name on all products produced.
- Advertising separate brand names for individual products. Procter & Gamble and Unilever both adopted this strategy with such well-known brands as Bold, Ariel, Tide, Daz, Lenor, Omo and Persil although recently the corporate logo has become more visible.
- Advertising both the corporate and individual brand together. This brand strategy is used by Kellogg with such products as Kellogg's Rice Krispies, Kellogg's Coco Pops, Kellogg's All-Bran, Kellogg's Frosted Flakes.
- Advertising separate family names for product categories. For example, Granada (www.granada.co.uk) prefers to maintain separate brand names for its various hotel chains including Travelodge, Posthouse, Heritage and Le Meridien.

Advantages and disadvantages of corporate brand umbrella

- Corporate strength and advertising will benefit all brands.
- Individual product brand advertising can be diluted.
- Individual brand benefits not focused enough.

Advantages and disadvantages of separate brand/family names

- Aids tight segmentation: each brand can develop its own USP for each market.
- Competition must attack many brands rather than one.
- Bad publicity with one brand will not necessarily spread to other brands.
- Family brands can have hard-won reputations not to be squandered.
- Corporate advertising not optimised across all brands.
- Advertising can be costly as each brand must have its own campaign.

Advertising approaches

There are many different advertising approaches used to accommodate many different needs. Some of these are described below.

Generic advertising

Organisations will often come together, usually through their trade association, to use generic advertising and promote the industry as a whole rather than individual companies or brands. As companies are in competition with one another so one industry will be in competition with another. Examples are the wool industry urging us to use their product rather than man-made fibres, the beef industry pushing their product over lamb or chicken, and the Milk Board extolling the benefits from the intake of more of their product. Individual companies will promote the benefits of their own company and the company brands but this could be taking place whilst the industry as a whole is in decline and under threat from other alternative generic products and services. At the time of writing the International Advertising Association (www.iaaglobal.org) is running a generic TV advertising campaign selectively across the world emphasising the need for brand advertising spend to be maintained (especially during an economic downturn) and money not cut or siphoned off into sales promotions so that long-term brand attractiveness is not lost. Generic campaigns such as these will be paid for by member contributions.

Co-operative advertising

Co-operative advertising is joint advertising along the distribution chain, with manufacturers and retailers agreeing to fund a joint campaign hoping to gain market synergy. This might involve two complementary manufacturers with each recommending the other – for example, a soap powder manufacturer and a washing machine manufacturer (Persil and Whirlpool) – or a manufacturer and a retailer, with the manufacturer recommending the retailer as an outlet to purchase the product – for example, Sony and Dixons. Who will pay the lion's share in the partnership will depend on expectations of the value to be obtained.

Direct response advertising

Advertisements often appear in the press with a direct response box asking the customer to fill in details and either send for more information or purchase the product itself. Direct response type adverts are now increasingly appearing on TV, radio and the Internet.

Comparative advertising

Sometimes called 'knocking copy', comparative advertising is arguing for the superiority of one's own product against that of a competitor. Its use was slightly frowned on in the past, being viewed by some as somehow not quite decorous. It was also argued that disparaging the competitor's product could be counterproductive, not being believed by the customer and casting suspicions about the honesty of the advertiser. These past reservations, however, seem gradually to have dissipated and we can often now see this type of advert, with the benefits of one car listed against the similar model of a close competitor, one financial service package against another or the prices in one large supermarket group shown against another. Of course the claims made must be truthful and sustainable, otherwise complaints will be made to the Advertising Authority and/or legal action for misrepresentation instigated through the law courts.

Advertising by sector

Once considered inappropriate by some organisations, the need to advertise now encompasses every possible kind of industry whether profitmaking or non-profitmaking.

Business to business advertising

Although seemingly less glamorous when compared with consumer advertising, a huge amount of advertising takes place in the business to business marketing sector (nearly one-third of all advertising in the UK). Business to business marketing is one business marketing to another and is defined as one business selling products to another for the company's own use rather than to sell on to the retailer. Trade advertising is used to create corporate and product awareness, to build loyalty, to introduce and reinforce the sales operation, to inform on new product and service developments and, of course, to ultimately sell products.

Derived demand

Although business to business advertising is concerned with advertising products to another business (capital equipment, components that might go into the finished products or services that help in running of the business), derived demand works on the premise that all demand is eventually determined (derived) by the end consumer. It might therefore be profitable for a business, for example a computer chip manufacturer, both to advertise to manufacturers, through the trade press, to buy the chip and to advertise to the end consumers, through TV, to buy more computers.

Business to intermediary

A great deal of advertising takes place between producer and retailer. This tends, again, to build corporate and brand awareness and to encourage product listing and stocking. Target audience and media factors are similar to those identified above in business to business advertising. Retailers will often be persuaded to purchase if they know that the producer is going to initiate an advertising campaign (as well as a trade campaign) to encourage retail visits and consumer purchase.

Business to consumer

By far the largest amount of advertising effort and money is put into advertising to the end consumer, and this is the element of advertising that has the highest profile. We only have to look through a newspaper in the morning, pick up a magazine at work, or switch on the TV when we come home in the evening to be assailed by messages and images exhorting us to buy motor cars, soap powder, coffee, financial service packages and holidays. Consumer advertising might be for the long term, for example to build corporate and brand awareness, to reinforce and maintain interest, to reassure and generate loyalty, or it might be more for the shorter term, for example to persuade people to purchase and repeat purchase and to encourage, through the consumer, stocking of products by the retailer. Consumer targeting and segmentation of markets has reached extremely sophisticated levels and media choices have grown to match advertisers' continually demanding needs.

Retail advertising

Retail advertisements are placed in both the national and local press, and retail advertising is by far the largest business to consumer method. The national press is usually used to reinforce corporate brand image and the local press to advertise brands, prices and special offers to encourage customer traffic.

Business to business and consumer advertising

Business to business advertising is different to consumer advertising in both the approach taken and the weight given to the various elements of the communication mix. This is because the products and services offered and the nature of the target audiences are basically different.

Target audience

In business to business the purchase is for company use whilst in consumer markets customers purchase for themselves or for close relatives or friends. In the first case reason tends to drive the purchase and in the second it is predominantly emotion. This will greatly affect both advert structure and message content.

People involved in the purchase decision

In business to business the number of buying points will be significantly less than in consumer markets and, because of the possible importance to the company of the purchase and the amount of people it might affect, the number of people involved in any one decision (the decision-making unit or buying centres) will inevitably be greater.

Media used

All the above will have a fundamental influence on both the style and content of the message and the choice of media used. Advertising tends to be in the trade press, trade directories, direct mail, through trade shows and exhibitions and, the most widely used (especially if the product or service is very complex and needs detailed explanation) by personal contact rather than through the main media because experience has shown that this is the most effective way to reach the desired selected target audiences.

Business to other stakeholders

Every business has many audiences, other than the customer, with some type of interest in its activities that might need to be sent tailored messages at some time or another. Stakeholders will be both internal and external to the organisation. Depending on the organisational type, internal stakeholders may include employees, the family of employees, the board of directors, and governors; external stakeholders may include, amongst others, regulators, pressure groups, journalists, city financiers, suppliers, intermediaries, competition, local communities, and politicians. The media used will vary according to the audience targeted and the message to be delivered. Different stakeholders demand different benefit messages (see Fig 1.2).

National and local government, and public organisations

National governments are big advertising spenders intermittently running campaigns to educate, inform or sell to sections of the general public and businesses about such things as the dangers of smoking, welfare entitlements, services available, policy development and changes, legal requirements, tax responsibilities, gilt-edge shares and so on. An enormous amount of money was spent by the Conservative

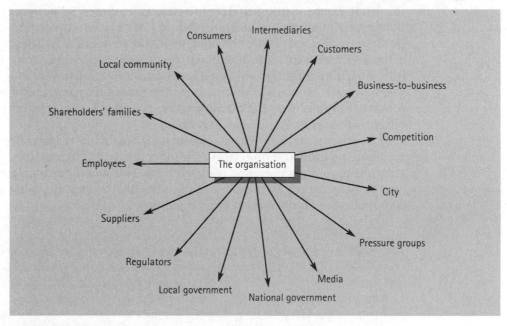

Fig. 1.2 The range of stakeholders

government advertising privatisation shares in industries such as the railways, water, electricity and gas. Local government will advertise information about the availability of local services, usually through the local paper but now venturing onto local TV and even the Internet. Departments that make use of advertising include the National Information Office, Defence, Social Welfare, the Office of National Statistics, Parks and Highways, Planning, the Treasury, Heritage and Tourism.

Public organisations that might advertise from time to time include the National Health Service and General Practitioners, the Post Office, the Metropolitan Police, the ambulance service, the fire service, public tourist offices and so on.

Advertising objectives for the above might include health and safety information, public relations activities, and performance indicator attainment. Target audiences will include taxpayers, ratepayers, voters, tourists, and welfare recipients.

Individual to individual

Anybody can advertise, and most people will do so at some time or another. When this happens it will probably be by a classified ad in the local newspaper. In the UK there are 1351 regional and local newspapers accounting for 20 per cent of all advertising billings. Classified columns are used to advertise everything from vacuum cleaners and houses to possible marriage partners and health cures; and to announce births, weddings and deaths.

Advertising in the not–for–profit sector

The not-for-profit (nfp) sector consists of charities, associations, political parties, clubs, religious groups, pressure groups, mutual societies, and all types of organisation that exist for other than profitmaking commercial activities. It used to be thought by many that advertising should not be used in promoting some not-for-profit activities, especially charities, as it was in some way distasteful to mix the commercial with the altruistic. It was also argued that people contributing to charities would be unhappy to see large amounts of charity money going on TV or press adverts. Nowadays there are less reservations particularly when it can be proven that money spent on advertising is cost-effective and can be more than offset by the resultant increase in revenue.

The nfp organisation will use advertising for many reasons depending on the corporate mission and objectives. The biggest spend is by charities, predictably, on attempting to attract revenue contributions. The spend has increased dramatically over the last decade as the amount of charitable organisations has multiplied and competition for limited resources has increased.

There are now over 187 000 registered charities in the UK and the figure is increasing by over 3000 a year. In 1997/98 income reached £18.3 billion pounds and 85 per cent of this income was received by 5 per cent of the charities. Strict rules and regulations exist on what a charity can and cannot do. The Charity Commission (www.charity-commission.gov.uk) is the controlling body in the UK.

In the same way as the commercial company, the nfp organisation will have many different clients and customers in both the business and the consumer sectors and will need to tailor messages to meet clearly the need of the targeted audience. They will also use advertising for reasons other than revenue contributions, including attracting new members, volunteers and helpers and attempting to change government policy and laws.

As with other specialised areas nfp advertising agencies exist to offer professional help and advice.

Why people give to charities

It must be understood when developing creative advertising messages that individuals and organisations give to charities in return for some form of benefit similar but subtly different to benefits people want in return for buying products and services. Research has shown that we might give for one or more of the following reasons:

- to obtain a feel-good factor;
- to alleviate feelings of guilt or embarrassment;
- to demonstrate to others our caring nature;
- to demonstrate to others how wealthy and successful we are;
- to help others (including animals) less fortunate than ourselves;
- to pave our way to the next life.

Message competition

Many organisations fall into the trap of thinking that what they consider is important will carry the same magnitude of concern for all others, especially customers. An advertisement is constructed and its style and content is applauded by company personnel agency alike. It should be realised, however, that the company's product is only one of many thousands that might be purchased at any one time and its existence is very low down in consumer levels of thinking. This revelation will also apply to the advertisement that will have been put together in such a painstaking and costly fashion. Add this to the fact that thousands of competitors will also be attempting the same exercise and the frightening size of the task advertising has to achieve becomes transparently apparent. If the message is not seen, if attention is not grabbed, then all that follows, despite its value, will be a complete waste of time. The first and dominant task of the advertiser, therefore, is to be noticed and seen by an apathetic audience amidst the clutter of innumerable competitors all driven by the same advertising imperative.

Factors with an effect on advertising

The following factors will all have an effect on the advertising process and will need detailed consideration when developing an advertising programme:

- the task to be achieved and the advertising objectives;
- the budget;
- the market segment and target audience;

- the product/service;
- the message content;
- the medium chosen;
- other complementary promotional methods chosen;
- the competition;
- the method of control.

CONCLUSION

Advertising is now an intricate and indissoluble part of everybody's life. Whether this be through the main media or by one of the thousands of other methods we cannot escape the incessant clamour of companies wanting to sell products and services to customers all around the world. If we look back historically we can see an inevitable growth in the use of advertising and advertising media concurrent with the growth in the economy and the wealth of nations. Advertising is used by all that want to sell products and services both from one business to another and from the business to the end consumer. In the process of selling it can be used to inform, educate, reinforce, and persuade customers about the attractiveness of generic products and services as well as corporate, product and service brands. It can be used in the private and public sector and, in the profit and not-for-profit sectors. Inevitably advertising will be used with other elements of the communication mix such as sales promotions, publicity and personal selling, moving the customer in a process from unawareness to purchasing the product on a regular basis. It is crucial that clear quantifiable objectives be set for every technique used so that results can be measured and accountability can be designated.

CASE STUDY

FT

Moving out of the shadows

In stamping its presence on KitKat and other chocolate, cereal and dairy products, Nestlé (www.nestle.com) is one of several international consumer brand owners that have been moving their names out of the shadows. Besides adding the corporate name to some products, it has renamed some brands, such as the yoghurt brand Chambourcy, as Nestlé and put a smaller Nestlé 'seal of guarantee' on other types of products. Peter Brabeck, Nestlé's chief executive, explains the strategy: 'Nestlé is a brand in its own right. If we want to be perceived as the world's leading food company, we have to offer consumers an increasing amount of products that they can identify as Nestlé's.' The approach is a shift away from traditional marketing wisdom: the argument used to be that an organisation that owned a number of diverse product brands should remain firmly in the background, rather than get in the way of the individual brand's communication with consumers. There was also the argument that companies could have more than one brand in a category. Dave Allen, chief executive of Enterprise IG (www.entergroup.com), the branding identity group, says: 'The old thinking was to keep company names out of the picture, so that you could have competing brands. I think that is a bit outdated now. Over the last twelve months, we have seen some very large brand owners starting to look at what the role of the parent company should be.'

Even at Procter & Gamble (www.pg.com) the mood has changed. The food, household and personal products group is the world's largest advertiser but has also been renowned for

▶

keeping a low corporate profile. Paul Polman, general manager of Procter & Gamble in the UK, says: 'The company is now a bit more flexible about corporate branding than it was five or ten years ago when we would have said that promoting our [individual] brands globally was the best solution for creating value. In some countries such as Japan, Russia or India we have taken a different approach and used the corporate umbrella of P&G for creating value.'

Richard Block, global planning director at J. Walter Thompson (www.jwtworld.com), the advertising agency, says that one of the original factors behind the growth of corporate branding was to combat the rise of 'own label' supermarket products fifteen to twenty years ago. 'Brands were ill-equipped to respond individually to the attack of the retailers: the corporation had to take responsibility for the quality of its products.' Since then, he adds, inflation in the cost of marketing and advertising means it has become uneconomic for an organisation to support all its product brands equally. Brian Boylan, chairman of Wolff Olins (www.wolff-olins.com) corporate identity consultancy, agrees that the need to use resources efficiently is one of the reasons organisations turn to corporate branding. 'Marketers are under pressure to leverage their brands over a larger number of products and services in order to justify the investment in brand building,' he says.

Making more use of the corporate brand can also be a way of coping with the growing number of audiences that consumer companies want to address and their increasing demands for information. In many markets – Mr Polman gives the example of Japan – consumers want to know more about the company behind the products they buy. Mr Block says that shareholders in a company may be reassured by visible reminders that the organisation in which they have invested is behind successful products. Linked to this there is, he believes, an element of 'corporate hubris', especially among US corporations, in the need to make their presence more strongly felt on their products. According to Mr Boylan, employees are another demanding audience. He says that promoting a corporate brand has a role in attracting and keeping staff. And as consumers, investors and staff overlap, the case for projecting a single image of the parent company becomes stronger.

However, there can be dangers in raising the parental profile. 'The big risk has always been that if one of your brands has a problem then the corporation is tainted and it takes every other brand down with it,' says Mr Allen. The most quoted example of the perils of linking products through the parent brand is that of Persil Power. This was the storm that engulfed Unilever's Persil and Omo soap powders in 1994, after the manganese crystals added to enhance cleaning power were found also to damage certain fabrics. If Unilever had marked its ownership of these detergents and its other brands, the fall-out could have badly affected the company's other cleaning products and its foods and personal products. Some say there may be a risk to the corporate brand itself if a company adopts a high profile but does not put into practice the values it seeks to represent and impart to its individual products. 'It's too easy to get wrapped up in huff and puff,' says Mr Boylan. 'The brand has to deliver what it promises.'

These risks are seen by many consumer companies as issues to be dealt with rather than reasons for not developing the corporate brand. However, instead of a single new orthodoxy to replace the traditional relationship between product brands and their parents, it looks as though companies will increasingly adopt a flexible approach in how far they step into the spotlight. In some cases this will mean a higher profile for the corporation. But for companies whose products span many types of goods it may mean developing 'category' brands to support individual products in, for example, baby care or household cleaning.

Source: Alison Smith, *Financial Times*, 5 June 1998. Used with permission.

Case study questions

1. Discuss the argument for and against corporate umbrella branding and individual brand advertising. What do you think is meant by 'category advertising'?
2. How important is advertising to both corporate and brand development? How would you justify spending large amounts of money on brand advertising with no immediate affect on sales levels?

CHAPTER QUESTIONS

1. How might advertising be different when used in the not-for-profit sector compared with the commercial? Similarly, how will consumer advertising be different from business to business advertising?
2. Discuss how new technology might affect advertising in the new millennium. What other changes might have a strategic effect?
3. It is argued that as more media methods come on-line the ability to easily reach mass audiences will be threatened. Do you think that this will be the case and if so how might the problem be overcome?
4. Advertising can be used to achieve many things. Identify and discuss the different objectives in terms of how realistic they might be and how the results can be measured.
5. What are the factors to be considered when advertising at the local, national and international level? How might identified problems be overcome?

REFERENCES

Baily, B. (1997) *Advertising in Developing Countries*, Lexden Press, Colchester, Essex.

Bernbach, W., quoted in Stephen Fox, *The Mirror Makers* (1984), Vintage Books, New York, p. 257.

Charity Commission (www.charity-commission.gov.uk)

Electronic Telegraph (www.telegraph.co.uk)

Financial Times (www.ft.com)

The International Advertising Association (www.iaaglobal.org)

Procter & Gamble (www.pg.com)

Starch, D. (1923) *Principles of Advertising,* A.W. Shaw Company, Chicago.

UK Advertising Association (adassoc.org.uk)

Ray Wright (www.raynetmarketing.com)

FURTHER READING

Bovée, C.L. et al. (1995) *Advertising Excellence,* McGraw-Hill, London.

Hutt, M.D. and Spey, T.W. (1998) *Business Marketing Management,* Dryden Press, London.

Lauffer, A. (1984) *Strategic Marketing for Not-for-Profit Organizations,* Free Press, NY.

Nevett, T.R. (1982) *The History of Advertising,* Heinemann, London.

2 Society and advertising

OBJECTIVES

By the end of this chapter the reader should be able to:

1. Describe the nature of advertising and evaluate its pervasive influence on society.

2. Identify and analyse the environmental issues confronting the advertising industry.

3. Describe and evaluate the ways that the advertising industry is regulated and controlled.

INTRODUCTION

Contrary to what self-appointed protectors of the consumer so loudly proclaim, advertising does not cause people to buy bad products. Nothing will put a bad product out of business faster than a good advertising campaign. Advertising causes people to try a product once, but poor quality eliminates any possibility of a repeat purchase.

(Morris Hite)

With the development and increase in information technology and media forms the amount of advertising hitting the individual increases month on month and year on year. This explosive growth of advertising continues apace throughout the world spreading to Eastern Europe, Africa, South America and the Far East. China, with over 1.2 billion consumers, one-fifth of the world's population, holds almost limitless lucrative possibilities for advertisers and advertising agencies in the development of corporate and product brands. Many commentators, however, are concerned about this unremitting pressure on society and its institutions and seek to control the process in some way or another. Similarly, advertising practitioners are aware that they have to keep pace with environmental demands and call for change if they are to maintain competitive advantage.

The advertising environment

Advertising takes place within a greater, wider environment that will include political, economic, social and technical factors (see Fig. 2.1). Advertisers, advertising agencies and media owners will ply their business interacting with consumers whilst operating within a shifting, changing, dynamic market that will be affected by economic and demographic factors, pressure and interest groups, local, national and international government policies, laws and regulations, social and cultural patterns and technical and informational developments.

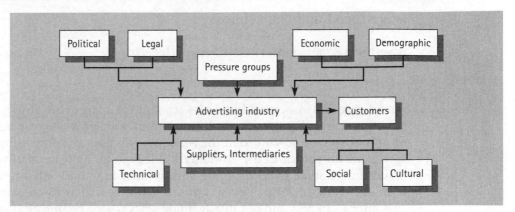

Fig. 2.1 Environmental factors affecting the advertising industry

The organisation will be able to influence some of these factors whilst others will be uncontrollable. Having information and being aware of the surrounding world as it changes will allow proactive advantageous arrangements to be made.

Advertising and political and legal issues

All governments will have some form of policy that will have an effect on the role of advertising in society. At one extreme this might be the imposition of regulation and laws that monitor and control all media advertising (autocratic) whilst at the other extreme it might be to leave the industry totally alone to regulate itself (laissez-faire). In a modern democracy the level of interference tends to sit somewhere between these two extremes (see Fig. 2.2) but there will always be those that will hassle for change in one direction or another.

Pressure groups

Pressure groups, or interest groups, come into being to promote particular causes in any way that might further their interest. Many exist in all areas of society and the advertising industry, because of its high profile, attracts the attention of more than most – pressure groups that want less advertising, pressure groups that want more, groups that want more government involvement and groups that want less. FOREST and ASH are examples of two interest groups with diametrically opposed objectives, with FOREST promoting the interest of the tobacco industry and ASH promoting the concerns of the anti-smokers (the anti-smokers appear to be winning). Many pressure groups will employ the professional services of public relations or lobbyist agencies.

Fig. 2.2 Levels of government involvement

Advertising and the economy

Advertising is the lubricant for the free-market economy.

(Anon)

Advertising and associated industries account for a large part of the economy both at national and global level and the contribution they make is increasing. As with most industries, a downturn in the economy will lead to a downturn in advertising spend and an upturn in the economy will lead to an increase in advertising spend. Practitioners argue that corporate and product brand advertising is for the long term and should continue even during a downturn so as to consistently reinforce customer awareness and not disadvantage sales when the upturn happens.

Beneficial effects of advertising on the economy

- It provides information to customers allowing them to make informed judgements about company and product reputation on a worldwide basis.
- More choice leads to greater competition and thence to increased productivity and falling prices.
- Falling prices increase the customer's ability to purchase; this translates eventually into mass production, mass consumption and an overall increase in economic activity.
- The advertising industry accounts for billions of dollars and employs millions of people around the world.

Harmful effects of advertising on the economy

- Powerful organisations with media spend capabilities are able to dominate the global market controlling both the price and channels of distribution.
- It adds to the cost of the product and pushes up the price of brands allowing less to be sold.
- It spawns an industry of waste creating mountains of unnecessary discarded byproducts associated with advertising, branding and packaging eating into finite environmental resources.

Advertising and demographics

Advertising is self-evidently dependent on people seeing and acting on messages emanating from the various media. Accepting the need for tight targeting and the presence of many different niche markets, the bulk of advertising is dependent on the ability to reach large numbers of people. Knowledge of demographic numbers, movement, age, gender and income is critical to effective advertising. This information is more reliable in some countries and regions than in others and care must be taken when spending promotional money on campaigns based on ill-based demographic statistics. To be unaware of the potential audience in China (1.2 billion), India (950 million), or Brazil (165 million) is to be strategically unprepared for future, explosive, global advertising opportunities.

Advertising and the competition

Advertising takes place within a competitive arena, with one company attempting to gain competitive advantage over another by trumpeting louder and more effectively than those with the same or similar products. Some markets, however, are more competitive than others and many argue that the large advertising budgets of the global giants restrict others entering the market. Imagine attempting to go head-to-head with Procter & Gamble or Coca-Cola who spent, worldwide, over £5 billion and $1.4 billion respectively on advertising in 1996 generating indestructible brand franchise and consumer loyalty. Others argue that advertising allows newcomers to enter a market where advertising plays an important part. They must, of course, have the financial muscle to sustain a prolonged and expensive campaign. McDonald's was able to straddle the world in little over thirty years through intensive corporate advertising ($1.6 billion in 1996) and now has a universal empire of over 22 000 outlets. It should be remembered that advertising will only work if the promised value and benefits are inherent within the purchased product as an unhappy customer will not only not repurchase but will tell others about their disappointment. Many of today's top brands – Mars, Tide, Kellogg, Bovril, Mercedes – have been market leaders for decades through a combination of good product and continuous advertising.

Advertising, suppliers, manufacturers and retailers

Severe global competition is forcing companies to work closer together along the distribution chain. To gain and maintain competitive advantage in many industries it is now realised that all players, suppliers, producers, retailers, involved in bringing the end, value added, product to the customer must act co-operatively in concert so that the whole process becomes efficient, effective and economic from beginning to end. Of course the most powerful in the 'value' chain will dominate discussions and have the major say in policy. Joint, co-operative advertising should focus tightly on clearly researched consumer needs ensuring that all channel members are 'singing off the same song sheet'.

'Other business' strategic alliances

The growth of loyalty cards has spawned the growth in 'other business' strategic marketing alliances and jointly run advertising campaigns. Large retail supermarket chains now work in close relationship with such diverse businesses as petrol stations, airlines, financial institutions and fast food restaurants, advertising together to offer consumers a universal loyalty card able to be used wherever they shop within the alliance. All businesses involved gain as consumers purchase specifically from alliance members as well as from 'other business' corporate brand association.

Voluntary buying groups

Groups of small retailers now join together to form large strategic operating and buying groups such as Londis, Happy Shopper and Electronix. Group advertising is then used both to promote an image for the corporate whole and to give recognised brand identity (with all the attendant advantages) to 'own label' products.

The size of the campaign should generate economics of scale and experience curve savings and make the whole advertising planning process more productive.

Advertising and franchising

Franchising has enjoyed tremendous growth over the last 25 years and now accounts for over one-third of all retailing in the major industrial countries. The advantage of franchising, allowing individuals to buy into their own business, relies heavily on the corporate brand attraction of the parent company. Organisations such as McDonald's, KFC, Herts Rental, Seven/Eleven and Body Shop are attractive to franchisees because they are such well known and well supported companies. Group advertising is crucial to the offering both at the corporate and product/service level as the franchisee sees this as an essential part of the bought-in package. Complaints will proliferate if it is felt that the franchiser is scrimping on this vital ingredient.

Influences on the consumer, and ethical issues

History will see advertising as one of the real evil things of our time. It is stimulating people constantly to want things, want this, want that, there is no end to it.

(Malcolm Muggeridge)

The argument that advertising can be socially damaging

Some advertisements are up front, explicit and undeniably 'in your face' whilst others are much more laid back, implicit and unobtrusive. Whatever the type of advertising there are many in society who are concerned about its role and influence in a civilised society, see it as potentially damaging and seek in some way or another to control and regulate both its geographical and media spread and the substance and the timing of the content. It is argued that advertising can be damaging for the following reasons:

- It reinforces unhelpful and harmful stereotypes such as that a woman's place is in the home cooking and cleaning, a man's place in the workplace bringing in the money.
- It uses images, especially sexual, that have the potential to dehumanise women and objectify the female body. The same accusation is beginning to be made in the same way about the sexual portrayal of men.
- It seeks to make people unhappy with existing material possessions.
- It encourages addictive, obsessive, and acquisitive behaviour.
- It manipulates people into buying products that they do not really need and do not really want.
- It distorts the language and encourages bad usage and incorrect spelling.
- It encourages consumers, especially children, to want products and brands that they cannot afford causing feelings of inadequacy when these are not obtained.

- It uses images that encourage consumers to buy products and brands that have the potential to be unhealthy, such as cigarettes and alcohol.
- It encourages unnecessary production and consumption (for example, of cars) thereby depleting the world's resources and despoiling the environment.

As if this list is not enough, advertising is also held, by some, to be partly responsible for a general decline in overall social, moral and educational standards.

The Ford motor company has driven into a row about changing black faces to white on a company brochure. Black workers were happy to appear in an advertising photograph with white colleagues to promote the multi-ethnic nature of the company's workforce. They were not so happy to discover that their black faces had been replaced by white ones on the brochure when it resurfaced in an Essex showroom. Fords apologised and paid the workers compensation.

According to a National Food Alliance report, junk food accounts for almost three-quarters of food advertisements screened during children's viewing time, three to four times more than adult adverts. This undermines parental authority and goes against government health guidelines.

'Advertising does have an effect', say young smokers – a research survey carried out by Exeter University studied the lives of more than 37 000 children aged 9 to 16 and found that over 70 per cent who described themselves as occasional smokers said they were swayed by advertising. The report will intensify the debate about sponsorship and tobacco advertising.

The counter argument

Advertising is an instrument in the hands of the people that use it. If evil men use advertising for base purposes, then evil can result. If honest men use advertising to sell an honest product with honest enthusiasm, then positive good for our kind of capitalistic society can result.

(Anon)

Many, especially practitioners, would argue that advertising has an innocuous influence, that the words and images used to put over messages only reflect the good or bad intentions of the advertisers themselves, and that there are good or bad practitioners in all areas of business whether this be in the field of human relations, finance, the law or advertising. It is further argued that images and stereotypes used in adverts only reflect the ideas, beliefs and attitudes that already exist in society, that in fact adverts follow rather than lead social and cultural developments. The cause of human dissatisfaction with what many might consider to be adequate material possessions and the incessant drive to acquire more is

blamed on capitalism and the market system. As with all things the answer probably lies somewhere between the two arguments.

Advertisers dispute the contention that they can manipulate customers into
buying products they do not need or want. In all affluent societies, consumers buy
products that at a very basic level are not 'needed' (cars, holidays, fizzy drinks and
so on) but it is this that fuels the market economic system. Advertisers may induce
customers to the store but they would question their ability to persuade the purchase of brands that are of an inferior value, are the wrong colour, or do not
provide the benefits wanted. They go on to say that consumers (even children) are
too questioning, sceptical and sophisticated not to know that an advert is one-sided
and is attempting to sell a particular company's products. Far from being helpless in
the face of unremitting advertising they are able to ignore it, turn off the TV, zap or
zip the commercial, leave the room, turn over the page, or turn down the radio.
Overall they are able to rationalise what is going on and act accordingly.

Harmful environmental effects of advertising

Defenders of advertising believe that it is demand created by our economic way of
life that creates the harmful effects on the environment, weakening of the ozone
layer, the destruction of the rain forests etc., and not advertising which is merely
an innocent purveyor of product information. The powerful nations in society
have the ability to pass laws and to make adjustments to the social and economic
system to protect against environmental vandalism and, as with any other business discipline, advertising will work within these parameters.

Role stereotyping

If we look back at the history of the style and content of the TV advert we can clearly see a
reflection of cultural beliefs, attitudes and stereotypes concerning gender. In the Persil
soap powder adverts it was always the woman that was in the home, cooking breakfast
and seeing the children off to school and the husband off to work. She might then appear
in the evening preparing dinner using Oxo, or tea using Hovis, for her husband and
children when they appeared in the evening. It was always the woman in the kitchen
washing her husband's and children's shirts, or washing floors. She would appear in the
bathroom pouring Domestos down the pan or using Flash to clean the bath; the man never
did these things. He might be seen playing football or taking the children along to watch;
he might be seen at work supervising the construction of a building. It was a time when
male and female social stereotypes were well established. If the advertisers had reversed
the role models and shown men washing and ironing the clothes and cooking the dinner
whilst the women were taking the children to a football match or were seen at work, the
advert would not have seemed credible to the woman of the house (who this type of
advert was aimed at as she actually bought most of the products) and the product might
then not have sold. Gradually, as society has changed, advertisers were able to follow and
change role images and we now see adverts with men washing up, washing the clothes
and cleaning the bathroom.

Evidence has shown that when this role reversal has been attempted before a change in
cultural gender thinking the advert has failed.

Ethical advertising

There are both advertisers and advertising agencies that take a publicised ethical approach (often expressed in their mission statement) both to their business and to their advertising. An ethical advertising agency will offer, as a benefit to its customers, the assurance that it will not work for companies marketing unacceptable products (cigarettes) or work in countries generally considered to have despotic or undemocratic governments. They guarantee that their advertisements will be honest and truthful as opposed to unscrupulous and misleading, and that they will not exploit the weak and the vulnerable. Many companies now adopt this approach, wanting to be seen as good corporate citizens that care about the way that they undertake their business. The gracious observer might argue that this is because of philanthropic, intrinsic concerns about environmental and moral issues whilst the more cynical might argue that companies will only pursue this policy if that is what their immediate customers want and it makes good business sense.

Advertising in developing countries

Although it may be good sales practice, it must be questionable from a moral and ethical standpoint for an organisation to adopt an advertising approach in a developing country when the same approach is banned by law or restricted by an industry code of conduct in the home country of the manufacturer. One of the most famous brands of cigarettes in the world is Marlboro, owned by the US-based company J.R. Reynolds. Under extreme threat in the US from legislation attacking the safety of its product it has had to go to other countries around the world, to maintain sales volume. In the US as well as the UK cigarette advertising is banned from TV and advertising in the other media severely curtailed in terms of advert content, message and image portrayal. Journey to the third world, however, and on posters, in newspapers and on TV Marlboro images from the past have been resurrected with a vengeance. Immediately on arriving at Vietnam Airport you are inundated with colour, back-lighted posters of the Marlboro Cowboy in familiar romantic, 'Wild West' representations. Posters with the same images abound everywhere you go, on the main highways and in the side streets, in cafes and bars and in shops and restaurants. A TV advert, shown unremittingly whilst I was there, was a real 'blast from the past' with its fanciful, visual images of cowboys riding snorting, cavorting stallions across the cactus-filled plains, splashing through rivers, climbing snow-capped mountains whilst driving spirited and excitable cattle and in the evening sitting around the campfire in 'male bonding' mode drinking coffee from a tin mug and smoking a well-earned Marlboro cigarette. Insidious, beguiling and harmful, semiotic messages I had imagined were long since dead and buried.

(Baily, B. *Advertising in Developing Countries*, 1997)

Regulation and control

Because of the concerns discussed above, the pervasive nature of advertising and its potential to influence the way people act and think, all governments in both developed and developing societies will involve themselves to a greater or lesser extent in attempting to influence both the content of advertising and the way in which it reaches the general customer. They might do this by enacting laws and regulations and setting up overseeing regulatory and control bodies, by persuasive pressure for control through self-regulation (either by individual companies or, more usually, through trade and professional bodies), or by using direct interference and lobbying on the offending party.

Laws and regulations

On 28 June 1996, Guernsey became the first place in the British Isles to impose a complete ban on tobacco advertising. Cigarettes can now not be advertised on poster sites, in newspapers and magazines, on the radio or on TV. All forms of tobacco sponsorship are now also banned.

All countries have laws and regulations on what can and cannot be advertised. These might be very specific and relate to a particular area, such as cigarette advertising, or they might be encompassed within some specific piece of consumer legislation such as the Trade Descriptions Act, the Sale of Goods Act, the Consumer Protection Act, or the Misleading Advertisement Act. In different countries across the world some laws are more stringent than others and the case for more or less government legislation and control is discussed below. Membership of the European Union has thrown up problems where European law is different to individual country law: many sales promotions are illegal in Germany; advertising to children is banned in Norway; alcohol advertising is forbidden in Sweden. This can cause enormous concern for companies that advertise around the world as what might be legal in one country could well be illegal in another. This could be a reason to use advertising agencies with specialised local knowledge. In the UK the government relies on public and industry bodies (identified below) to police and enforce its advertising legislation.

Global control of advertising

The media's ability to transgress national borders has created many problems for those that want to see the regulation of the media and to be able to control advertising output. The problem becomes practically insurmountable because of the impossibility of enforcing the law when the medium is in one country and the receiver is in another. Satellite TV and the Internet can both be picked up anywhere in the world if the sophisticated receiver equipment is purchased. There have been attempts to harmonise laws around the world through bodies such as OECD and the

UN but national interests have tended to thwart meaningful co-operation. The UK government can ban tobacco sponsorship of Formula One Racing cars in the UK but it will have real difficulty with control if it continues in Brazil and the pictures are beamed back to UK viewers (although technology is being developed that can selectively 'blank out' unacceptable adverts from the TV screen in specific countries where they might be banned). The discussion at international level continues as governments attempt to keep abreast with the astonishing, phenomenal pace of media and advertising development. Interested readers can visit many web sites to keep themselves up-to-date with what is happening.

Control of the main media

All developed countries have well-seated laws and rules in place, incrementally built up over the decades, to control the activities of TV, the press, radio, outdoor, cinema and direct mail advertising. All countries will have overseeing regulating bodies to oversee compliance and the major UK ones are identified below. As with all man-made agencies change will happen as social pressure for a different approach builds up and gathers powerful support. The exponential growth in new technology is throwing up regulatory problems in certain areas and two, packaging and the Internet, are discussed below.

The law, advertising and packaging

Packaging advertising is an essential part of marketing the product, especially in FMCG self-service markets. Manufacturers are under continuous legal pressure to make certain that the advertising on their package conforms to regulations both at home and abroad and heavy fines have been imposed on companies that make misleading and exaggerated claims. There is also pressure to add more and more information on contents with regard to health and safety and environmental issues.

In 1997 the EU attempted to push through legislation banning any chocolate that contained vegetable fat being advertised as 'milk chocolate'. This ruling, if passed, meant that Cadbury would not be able to call Dairy Milk, Fruit and Nut and Whole Nut Bars 'milk chocolate'. Cadbury argued that the move was political with companies such as Nestlé, Jacobs-Suchard and Ferraro all fighting to gain market share in the billion-pound industry from the UK and six other EU companies that use vegetable fat. This problem underscores the need to have industry specific lobbyists sitting permanently in Brussels protecting the interests of the UK chocolate business from over-zealous and politically motivated EU Commission law-makers.

Packaging and the retailer

Some large manufacturers have been unhappy about retailers that develop 'copy-cat' own label products with packing and brand names that are similar to their own and have formed a brand protection association. They argue that they have spent a fortune in advertising and building brand values and that it is manifestly unfair for retailers to reap unearned benefits by fooling customers into thinking they are buying the real thing. In the past companies such as Kellogg and Coca-Cola have insisted that Tesco and Sainsbury re-package own label cereals and cola on the grounds that they look too much like their own brands. Legal proceedings were ruled out because of relationship damage that would be caused; they preferred to rely on the Institute of Grocery Distribution industry code that commits signatories to not producing lookalike products. Kellogg took out advertisements in national newspapers emphasising and pushing the differences with the strapline 'If it doesn't say Kellogg's on the box it isn't Kellogg's in the box'. On the other hand United Biscuits did take Asda supermarkets to court over the close resemblance between their chocolate biscuit brand 'Penguin' and the Asda own label 'Puffin'. A compromise was reached. Adjustments to patent laws now allow packaging shapes, sizes, colours and even smells to be registered.

Regulation and advertising on the Internet

Regulation of global TV is child's play when compared with control of the Internet. At least with terrestrial TV the media is owned by known large organisations with a public image to maintain and a reputation to uphold. Practically anybody can set up a web site and a web-site company able to use and sell advertising and able to sell products and services. In the UK action can be taken provided the company that sold the goods is in the UK. In some cases the police are involved. Some civil liberties groups are unhappy at this, and the Association of Chief Police Officers is drawing up a 'memorandum of understanding' to give them access to copies of e-mail and details of users' activities from UK Internet Service Providers (ISP) serving 8 million users. The 1984 Data Protection Act also allows the police access to electronic data if it is 'needed for the prevention of crime'. Under the Brussels Convention protection is also given with companies based in other countries of the European Union. If products are bought from countries outside Europe practically no protection exists. Discussion is taking place at a world level but no realistic method of control has yet been found except to appeal to self-regulation or industry body regulation.

Methods of regulation and control

There are three major ways in which advertising is regulated and controlled in most societies: by the government, by industry self-regulation and by companies' own codes of conduct.

Government

All societies have legal regulatory and control agency bodies to oversee and monitor the advertising industry and the main UK ones are identified below. (Most countries will have equivalent organisations with similar powers.)

The Office of Fair Trading (OFT, UK) (www.oft.gov.uk) is headed by the Director General of Fair Trading with the remit of protecting the economic welfare of consumers and enforcing United Kingdom competition policy. With regard to advertising activity it will usually refer complaints to the Advertising Standards Authority, the Independent Television Commission or the Broadcasting Complaints Commission. If the offender persists it has the power to investigate misleading adverts and to stop by law any form of practice it considers to be harmful to the consumer.

All local councils have a local Trading Standards Office with the express purpose of promoting a 'fair, safe and equitable trading environment'. They have the power to prosecute where they feel that consumers have been duped and the law has been broken.

FT

Internet salesmen warned on 'miracle cures'

Internet purveyors of a soap that promises to 'wash away fat in seconds' and of an American herbal remedy that claims to cure cancer in 10 to 14 days were warned recently that their activities might not be legal. These Internet advertisements, along with others that include a toffee-like hair restorer that boasts of being the only one that 'actually works' and books said to contain cures for all cancers, all diseases and AIDS were picked up during a co-ordinated global sweep of the Internet by 60 law enforcement agencies in 20 countries to look for potentially misleading health claims and miracle cures. The Office of Fair Trading, which was part of the sweep, said the sites were warned that they might be subject to legislation regulating their activity and were told where to find the information. The search is being co-ordinated by the OFT's Australian counterpart which will collate what was found and pass the information on to the relevant country.

John Bridgeman, director general of the OFT, said 'People must beware of miracle cures and medical offers on the Internet. If something sounds too good to be true, it probably is.' Consumer protection legislation varies from country to country, making consistent enforcement of advertising and sales standards on the Internet impossible. By collating information, however, the agencies hope that they can point out violations of existing law and codes to each other for enforcement, thereby reducing the amount of misleading information on the net. 'This exercise has been an example of international co-operation aimed at maintaining an enforcement presence on the net and educating site operators about existing legislation,' Mr Bridgeman said.

Source: Nicholas Timmins, *Financial Times*, 12 September 1998. Used with permission.

Industry self-regulation

Whilst some restrictions are backed by the force of law, others are policed by an overseeing industry body and rely on methods other than the law to force conformity. The following organisations exist in the UK to oversee and police the advertising industry covering advertisers, advertising agencies and media owners. The degree of power invested will vary from country to country and will usually reflect the intensity of concern. The globalisation of advertising has led to the call for international organisations to monitor and control the process both at European (in the case of the European Union) and world level. Below we can see a selection of UK regulatory institutions with a brief description of their responsibilities; similar bodies exist throughout the world. Readers are urged to visit the various web sites to acquire greater information.

- The *Advertising Standards Authority* (ASA) (www.asa.co.uk) deals with advertising and sales promotion complaints in newspapers, magazines, videos and video games but not TV and radio. It was set up in 1962 to make sure that non-broadcasting advertisements in the UK are legal, decent, honest and truthful. The authority attempts to protect the public by ensuring that the rules in the British Codes of Advertising and Sales Promotion are followed by everyone who prepares and publishes the adverts. The ASA is an independent non-profitmaking body and is funded by a levy on display advertising. This is collected by a separate body, the Advertising Standards Board of Finance. Although its powers are mainly non-legal it has the ultimate sanction of referring persistent offenders to the OFT for prosecution.

> The ASA has specific rules on alcohol advertising, spelling out that alcohol advertising should not be directed at 'people under 18; show people who look under 25 drinking in adverts; feature real or fictitious characters that would appeal to people under 18. It should not portray drinking as sexy, glamorous, exciting, challenging or brave. It should not be shown to enhance mental, physical, or sexual capabilities, popularity, attractiveness, masculinity, femininity, or sporting achievements' . . . and so on. We can all use our own research to evaluate how closely this code of practice is observed by advertisers.

- *The Independent Television Commission* (ITC) (www.itc.org.uk) is the public body responsible for licensing and regulating commercially funded television services provided in and from the UK. These include Channel 3 (ITV), Channel 4, Channel 5, public teletext and a range of cable local delivery and satellite services. It has the power to take the licence away from recalcitrant media owners. They do not include services provided by the BBC which has its own regulatory body.
- *The Radio Authority* (RA) (Holbrook House, 14 Great Queen Street, London WC2B 5DG) is responsible for licensing and regulating all Independent Radio services. It also sets down codes of practice covering programme content, advertising and sponsorship. The 36-member committee is an independent body appointed, and answerable to, the Department of Heritage. It is financed from the licence fee and this covers all operating costs. It is responsible for national, local, cable, national FM sub-carrier, satellite and restricted services. 'Restricted services' include all short-term, special event type radio and local permanent services such as hospitals and student radio. The Authority can apply sanctions to licensees who break the rules of ownership. Sanctions include broadcast apologies and/or corrections, fines and the shortening or revocation of licences.
- *The Press Complaints Commission* (1 Salisbury Square, London EC4Y 8AE; 0171 353 1248) deals with complaints about newspaper and magazine editorial.
- *The Broadcasting Complaints Commission* (PO Box 333, London SW1 OBS; 0171 630 1966) is an independent body that deals with people who feel that they have been treated unjustly or disrespectfully by a television or radio programme.

- *The Broadcasting Standards Council* (7 The Sanctuary, London SW1P 3JS; 0171 233 0544) invites complaints about violence, sexual conduct, decency and taste in TV and radio programmes and advertisements.

Codes of conduct

Many companies now produce their own codes of conduct on how they will run their business and the ethical framework within which they will conduct their advertising. This is often articulated through the mission statement or company philosophy. Many examples can be seen by looking through company web sites. Also, many companies now realise the importance of self-regulation with regard to product information and advertising, recognising the general demand from both governments and customers for a socially responsible attitude to advertising.

An example of a company advertising codes of conduct and self-regulation

Our advertising philosophy says that all our advertising, anywhere around the world, should be healthy, wholesome, and not give gratuitous offence to any individual, group or national body. It should be truthful and not misleading to consumers. Our advertisements should only be seen in programmes that communicate the same standards of good taste and fair practice that guide all our corporate actions.

More specifically, all our adverts should comply with the relevant laws and regulations, including the self-regulatory guidelines of recognised advertising associations and relevant representives bodies such as children, women and ethnic protection groups.

All our adverts should avoid advertising themes that include excessive and/or unwarranted acts of violence, or the acting-out of anti-social behaviour which easily encourages imitation. They should avoid advertising themes that belittle any group based on its social, racial, ethnic or religious traits, or any person because of his or her age, sex or handicap.

Self-regulation or more government regulation and control?

Many associations have a major role in discussions with interested bodies about the level of involvement and government interference in overseeing and regulating the media industry. The ubiquitous nature of TV, the press, radio etc. and the use that advertising makes of the media has, understandably, an extremely high profile and almost every member of the public has something to say on the influence or otherwise of 24-hour unremitting advertising messages pervading the environment attempting to persuade consumers to purchase from one company rather than another, one brand rather than another or one product rather than another. Public and pressure group concerns tend to centre around such factors as the amount of advertising allowed, the acceptability of the content and whether some advertising should be allowed at all. The industry, and the various associations acting on behalf of the industry, recognise these concerns as legitimate but question the need for rules and regulations and the level of government interference, arguing that self-regulation is better.

Free markets

It is argued that with the fall of the Russian empire and the collapse of the concept of the planned economy it is now widely accepted that a market economy with the free interaction of market forces is a necessary condition for prosperity in the modern world. Company will be in competition with company to produce products and services in a marketplace where no one organisation dominates and the customers will decide which products they want to buy and which they reject. Since no organisation has a monopoly, a consumer encountering products of an unsatisfactory level will be able to go elsewhere. This forces uneconomical and inefficient companies and those making the wrong products to either improve and offer what the market demands or go out of business. So the economy as a whole becomes more efficient and more productive driven by consumer power to choose or reject as the needs and wants come about.

Consumer information and freedom of choice

Consumers will not be able to make these buying judgements unless they have sufficient and relative information about competing corporate and brand benefits. This is the part that the advertising industry has to play in the process. Advertising, in all its many forms, becomes the vital conduit between producer and consumer putting over the advantages and disadvantages of competing products so that informed choices can be made. No other group has the motivation or the means to do this in the same way and with the same results. No marketer is going to spend time, effort and money on innovation, design and new technological development if they are unable to communicate this to existing and potential customers. To do this successfully, the argument continues, there has to be freedom allowed for competing advertisers to talk imaginatively to customers, through the very many different media forms, and argue the case in a way that experience has shown is effective. Whilst accepting that government involvement in the process might be necessary to protect the young and the less able in society, this role should be kept to a minimum in the context of an overarching framework legislation that defines the parameters in which self-regulation can take place. Advertising content is often a matter of relative good taste and shifts with public perceptions, and direct control would reflect the unattractiveness of the 'nanny state' rather than good government.

The argument for self-regulation

The advertising industry argues for self-regulation through overseeing bodies such as the Advertising Standards Authority rather than statutory regulation enacted through parliament and a government-appointed body because it feels that self-imposed codes of conduct engender consensus and will be adhered to in the spirit as well as the letter of the law because members have discussed and agreed on their implementation. It also argues that self-regulating principles about what should be advertised, to whom and when as well as a consumer right to reply, advertiser response and an enforcement mechanism can be more easily and quickly policed and paid for by the industry itself than by an outside bureaucratic authority with little or no knowledge of the complexities and workings of the industry. It argues that overseeing bodies have worked successfully and that existing, non-legislative mechanisms are adequate in enforcing compliance to codes of conduct. It is further argued that the industry is more aware than people outside the industry of areas of difficulties, and that the industry is mature and responsible enough to face up to what must be regulated and what can safely be ignored. Government inter-ference, because of its nature, would be bureaucratic and slow, would constrain innovation, and would reflect the views of so many diverse and extreme opinion leaders and pressure groups that progress would be hampered and advertising development suffer.

To summarise, those in favour of self-regulation believe that leaders within advertising are mature enough to recognise, over those outside the industry, the areas that should and should not, and can and cannot, be regulated, and that self-regulation encourages compliance and enforcement amongst practitioners rather than evasion; that existing mechanisms work and are fast, flexible and can keep pace with developments as they happen; and that self-regulation is cost-effective and can be more easily policed and enforced.

Conversely, statutory regulation

- encourages involvement by many different opinion leaders and pressure groups leading to extreme, unworkable and unnecessary legislation;
- could lead to evasion by advertising practitioners unhappy with too astringent and restrictive limitations affecting competitive advantage;
- is slow, cumbersome and reactive;
- is expensive, bureaucratic, difficult to enforce and against the principles of a free society.

The argument against self-regulation

There are many who argue that the advertising industry is unable to adequately regulate itself because commercial pressures, the need to sell products and services, will always take precedence over greater concern for the common good. The adver-tising of cigarettes and alcohol, encouraging under-age smoking and drinking are cited as examples of poor behaviour and they point to examples where advertisers and agencies have overstepped the mark in using unacceptable themes, images and stereotypes to get over messages and ideas. This includes the brouhaha over cigarette sponsorship of Formula One motor racing, the controversy over 'alcopops' (alcoholic lemonade aimed at under-age drinkers), general advertise-ments incessantly aimed at children and the continuous, gratuitous use of sexual images. These are all given as examples of an industry unable to regulate itself. Finally the self-regulatory bodies are attacked for having little or no real power other than moral and peer group sanctions which advertisers can choose to ignore with impunity.

Against self-regulation, it is argued that

- a commercial industry will never be able to regulate itself because commercial interest will always outweigh concern for wider society issues;
- change affecting freedom of action will always be reactive as it is not in the industry's interest to moderate its approach in a way that will satisfy public opinion but may adversely affect its members;
- members of an overseeing body will inevitably be drawn from the industry itself and will look sympathetically at infringements especially if the miscreant is known.

CONCLUSION

There are many external environmental factors that will influence and be influenced by the advertising industry. Some factors are controllable whilst others are not. Anticipation, realisation and understanding by advertisers that there are factors out in the marketplace that might be profitably utilised or might cause problems either at the present time or in the future are essential if strategic promotional planning is to be successful. Lobbying or public relations might be used to prevent or soften potentially damaging legislation or publicity; contingency plans might be drawn up to prepare for, for example, a downturn (or an upturn) in the economy; demographic changes or cultural shifts that might throw up advertising opportunities; competitive activities which could threaten present and future campaigns; and technological advancement which could offer potential productivity savings and enhanced benefits to offer the customer. Most governments around the world recognise the importance and all-pervasive nature of the mass media with its potential to communicate, manipulate and influence and will legislate to protect the citizens of the state in areas that have the potential to affect the general well-being.

CASE
STUDY

European and UK interference in advertising

Advertising and the European Union

There have been attempts by some MEPs across the European Union to standardise the approach taken to television advertising so that what might be banned in one country will also be banned in all the rest. The current EU 'without frontiers' directive allows any commercial to be transmitted throughout Europe as long as it is legal in the country of origin. The European Association of Advertising Agencies argues that this is a fundamental principle of the common market and that to change this would have the potential to distort the market and create an unfair advantage for some companies over others.

Prime movers behind the move to restrict are Sweden, which will not allow any advertising for children's products, and Greece, which has banned toy companies from advertising before 10 o'clock. There are some within the European Parliament who would like to ban all advertising, and by extension the shopping channels, because of the 'pernicious' effect they have on the well-being of the general public. A Europe-wide ban on tobacco advertising has already been agreed and over the next five years all such advertising on posters, in newspapers and in magazines will go, followed by tobacco sponsorship, except on world-level sports such as motor racing which would be given eight years. By 2006 no cigarette advertising at all will be allowed in the EU except in tobacconists' shops and in specialist tobacco magazines. Alcohol may be next in line as some are unhappy with existing industry codes of conduct.

Many see the call for more controls over the use of advertising as part of a wider attack on the amount of foreign programme imports coming into the EU particularly from the US. It is argued that an incessant diet of American films, chat shows and sit-coms undermines the social and cultural heritage of individual countries and that a quota system should be implemented. They also point to a trade deficit of nearly $4 billion caused by this unequal relationship.

(Baily, B. *Advertising in Developing Countries*, 1997)

FT

Advertisers set to oppose 'nanny state'

Some of the UK's largest companies have warned the government to stop meddling in the way they advertise, and vowed to fight to defend the principle of 'commercial free speech'. In a strongly-worded attack, the companies claimed that ministers are attempting to impose a 'nanny state' on the £10 billion advertising industry.

Coming soon after a pro-hunting march, the concern adds to claims that the government is attempting to intervene in areas previously left to individual free choice. John Hooper, director-general of the Incorporated Society of British Advertisers, claimed: 'No sector is safe from the government having a go at it. New Labour says it is business-friendly, but it should understand that advertising is critical to business success.' ISBA, which represents 300 of Britain's biggest advertisers, fears the government could soon try to restrict the way alcohol, snack foods and children's products are sold.

The society's annual conference heard warnings that the laissez-faire attitude of the previous Conservative administration had been replaced by a 'meddling' approach from government. Malcolm Earnshaw, director of Pedigree Pet Foods, opened the conference with a plea to ministers to allow the industry to regulate itself. 'For the government to meddle further is to sacrifice the principle of free speech,' he said. 'We have a duty to defend our liberties and our freedoms vigorously.' Advertisers worry that the new Food Standards Agency might attempt to restrict advertising of certain products, such as sweets and chocolates, during children's television programmes. They believe a threat hangs over the ability of drinks manufacturers to sell their products, while cars and children's toys could also be affected. There is also a fear that the marketing industry itself could face new controls. Within weeks of taking office, Nigel Griffiths, the consumer affairs minister, warned that the government was ready to act in areas where self-regulation appeared to be failing, as he expressed concern about companies or sectors that repeatedly broke the voluntary codes on advertising.

Jim Murphy, a Labour MP, told the conference that the 'freedom of commercial speech is not a moral absolute', and that the government must retain the right to be a regulator of last resort. Mr Murphy, whose views are in line with government thinking, said: 'The government has a responsibility to the community at large, particularly the vulnerable and the young.' He said that if self-regulation failed, the government would have no hesitation in intervening.

Source: George Parker and Alison Smith, *Financial Times*, 5 March 1998. Used with permission.

Case study questions

1. Discuss the arguments for and against official interference at both national and European level. How would you resolve the competing demands of different nations?
2. 'There should be no ban on anything on the TV screen as all censorship is dangerous and wrong and people can always turn off the TV set'. Discuss.

CHAPTER QUESTIONS

1. Discuss the role that advertising plays in society. Do you think that it is a force for evil, a force for good or that it sits somewhere between the two?
2. Dissect and analyse the argument for and against self-regulation in the advertising business. Do you think that government involvement in the process is good or bad?

3. Do you think that products thought to be harmful to individuals or the environment such as tobacco, alcohol or petrol should be advertised? How do you think the argument might be affected by national barrier-breaking media capabilities and international concerns?
4. Discuss the role of stereotyping in advertisements and how this might have changed over the years. Why do you think that sex and gender plays such an important part in message delivery?
5. Discuss how advertising is influenced by the following external forces:
   a. competition;
   b. suppliers and intermediaries;
   c. pressure groups;
   d. cultural development;
   e. technology.

REFERENCES

Advertising Standards Authority, Advertising and Sales promotions (www.asa.org.uk)

Baily, B. (1997) *Advertising in Developing Countries*, Lexden Press, Colchester, Essex.

Broadcasting Complaints Commission, PO Box 333, London, SW1 OBS 0171 630 1966.

Broadcasting Standards Council, 7 The Sanctuary, London, SW1P 3JS, 0171 233 0544.

Hite, M. (1988), *Morris Hite's Methods for Winning the Ad Game,* E-Hart Press, Dallas, TX.

Independent Television Authority, TV Regulations and Codes of Conduct (www.itc.org.uk)

Kelloggs (www.kelloggs.com)

Office of Fair Trading (OFT, UK) (www.oft.gov.uk)

Press Complaints Commission, 1 Salisbury Square, London EC4Y 8AE, 0171 353 1248.

The Radio Authority (RA), Holbrook House, 14 Great Queen Street, London WC2B 5DG.

FURTHER READING

Advertising Age, US (www.adage.com)

Clark, E. (1988) *The Want Makers: Inside the World of Advertising*, Penguin Books, London.

Packard, V. (1991) *The Hidden Persuaders*, Penguin Books, London.

3 Advertising – internal and external communications

OBJECTIVES

By the end of this chapter the reader should be able to:

1. Describe and analyse the basic process of business and individual communications.

2. Identify and evaluate the process of internal communications.

3. Identify and evaluate the process of external communications at both the corporate and product levels.

INTRODUCTION

If your advertisement goes unnoticed, all else is academic.

(William Bernbach)

It should never be forgotten (but often is) that communications, sending and receiving relevant information, are at the very heart of advertising. All adverts are concerned with putting messages over to identified target audiences and no matter how complex the process might get, it is this basic concept that is behind the multi-billion-dollar industry. If the advert becomes so creative, so clever, so subtle that its message is misunderstood, misinterpreted or just not seen then, no matter how much money has been spent, the advertising campaign will be deemed to be a failure. If messages are sent and no feedback received then, again, it must be considered a failure as measurement, accountability and evaluation are critical to the success or otherwise of all promotional activity. In classical marketing fashion the target audience must be clearly identified, needs identified and messages shaped and tailored to meet these needs. Simplicity of message should be the watchword and creativity and design used only where research (or experience) has shown that this will improve the chances of the message being seen and understood.

Internal and external stakeholders

The marketing and promotions department will want to communicate, talk and listen, to very many stakeholders both internal and external to the organisation. Some groups, notably customers, will be more important than others, and the importance of other groups will fluctuate according to environmental and market circumstances. These stakeholders can be seen as internal and external to the organisation.

Internal stakeholders will include, amongst others, employees and family, middle and senior management, trade unions, shareholders, and boards of governors.

External stakeholders will include, amongst others, customers and consumers, intermediaries, suppliers, local communities, pressure groups, city financiers, journalists, local and national governments and the competition.

Internal communications

If internal communications are unhealthy or distorted in some way then all areas and processes within the company can be severely affected so that its final customer offering is less beneficial than is expected and competitive advantage will be lost. How can a company 'get it right with the customer' when they cannot 'get it right' within their own organisation? When looking at internal communications the following factors should be considered.

Customer care

If marketing is to be successful the idea of care for the customer must permeate the whole of the organisation. Every department and every employee, no matter where they are, must be aware that individual productive effort should focus clearly towards the well-being of the company's customers. This is particularly important where there is some type of customer–employee personal contact, face-to-face, on the telephone, e-mail, fax, in a retail outlet, in the car park, at the firm's entrance foyer, in the customer's home and so on. This takes on an added importance in the service industries where the employee becomes the 'product', the corporate 'brand ambassador', and every contact made is registered and measured in the consumer's mind. An offhanded response due to insufficient training, attitude problems or inadequate systems can cause frustration, dissatisfaction and customer loss. Corporate image, the corporate brand, how the company is seen by the stakeholder, is built and maintained by a combination of both employees and product brands. The product brands must live up to the benefit promises made through advertising and similarly the employees must act and behave in an expected and acceptable manner if there is to be consistency in the overall corporate offering. Research has shown that, increasingly, consumers will be loath to purchase products from companies that they feel are not living up to demanded standards.

The internal customer

The implementation of the concept of the internal customer has grown apace over the last twenty years as companies fight to gain and maintain competitive advantage. It takes the basic concept of marketing and creating customer satisfaction and applies it to the way that employees interact with one another in their work activities. Each employee becomes the 'customer' of all others that they come into contact with adding value to the product or service until it reaches the end consumer.

Employee development and training

Having identified how important the employee is to the well-being of both the corporate and product/service brands it should be self-evident that development and training must be an integral part of corporate strategy, building a workforce, at all levels from customer interface though to senior manager, that is focused on creating quality products and brands effectively and efficiently that clearly meet the researched needs of the organisation's targeted segments. Training and development might be the responsibility of either the personnel, human resources or marketing department depending on company structure and the level and type of training that is needed.

Internal marketing

Marketing is about integrating the internal resources of the organisation and creating products and services that will match and satisfy the identified needs of the customer. In simple terms this means developing a valued brand, pricing at an agreed level, making it available in the right distribution channel and then using the correct method to communicate benefits and place of purchase. If this is to come together in an optimum way the integrating process has to be understood and happen within the organisation, otherwise the end offering will be flawed. If salespeople are disdainful to the finance department, production ignored by marketing people, and distribution unable to work with administration then the marketing mix will suffer and the end result will be customer service that will under-perform the competition. 'Internal marketing' is just another way of arguing that for customer company synergy to happen in the marketplace it must first happen within the organisation (see Fig. 3.1).

Developing internal communications

Effective internal communications are intrinsic to creating an internal harmonious culture, one driven by an obsessive concern for ultimate and continuous customer satisfaction by all employees. As with most activities the internal communications system can be out-sourced to a communication agency if this is considered to be a

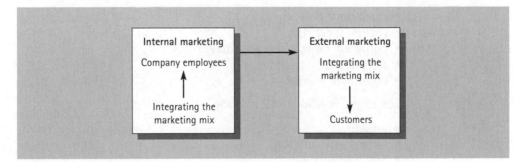

Fig. 3.1 Internal and external marketing

more productive way of achieving objectives. It is important that internal communications and culture formation are approached from a strategic perspective and built into the corporate and marketing plan as part of the long-term thinking of the company. Having said that, there are companies that seem to have been able to cultivate a free-thinking, free-talking, blame-free, open atmosphere that encourages interaction between employees, no matter the management level, almost on an intuitive level. Inevitably this will have generated from the top downward, usually emanating from the personality of the original owner (Richard Branson of Virgin and Bill Gates of Microsoft are examples that come to mind). Experience has shown, however, that as the company grows, bureaucracy spreads, layers of management grow and meaningful communication between members becomes much more difficult. It is at this stage that internal communications should be placed squarely on a formalised strategic foundation.

Barriers to internal communications include

- unawareness at the highest management level of its importance;
- lack of a formal (or informal) strategic approach;
- lack of realistic communication systems;
- bureaucratic, multi-layer structure;
- corporate functions, such as marketing, administration and production, not talking to one another;
- inward-looking, blame-fearing culture.

Internal communication methods

Internal communication systems and internal marketing will utilise similar communication techniques to those used in external communication. The simplest method must be to talk to one another, in person if possible, but other methods are identified below. This will probably mean stripping out layers of restrictive management so that senior and middle management do not lose contact with the employee who is at the sharp end talking to the customer. It also means building and working on an open, sympathetic culture where all are encouraged to talk and discuss how present practices can be continuously improved to meet ever changing, ever more demanding customer needs and wants. A knowledgeable, helpful, enthusiastic and friendly culture will shape the corporate identity and determine how the company is seen by all important stakeholders.

Conventional methods will include:

- open door policies;
- regular meetings;
- company newsletters and magazines;
- telephone;
- comment 'boxes'.

Electronic methods will include

- e-mail;
- video-conferencing;
- video-telephone;
- the intranet – the use of the internet internally with built-in security fire-walls.

Advertising and internal communications

There will be times when an organisation might want to advertise to its internal stakeholders. In the introduction above a wide view was taken on what constitutes an internal stakeholder and this includes shareholders in the case of a publicly quoted company, the ruling body (governors, trustees etc.) in the case of not-for-profit organisations, employees' families and trade unions as well as the more easily identified employee. The shareholders, as the owners of the organisation, will need to be kept informed about corporate and marketing developments. By law, company financial reports must be published once a year and companies will do this both by sending out the company annual financial statement in magazine form and by advertising in the quality press. Over the last decade the financial statement 'magazine' has taken on a more professional and glamorous image as the positive advertising opportunities are recognised. Large organisations will occasionally talk to other stakeholders by advertising in the local and national press or using direct mail. This might be to reassure employees during times of upheaval (possible takeover, fear of redundancies etc.) and aid negotiations during a trade union dispute.

Advertising on the Intranet

Several companies with large intranets are cautiously experimenting with selling space on their internal networks to outside advertisers. Houston Lighting and Power continuously displays 30-second animated spots on its intranet and is now considering offering them to outsiders in order to obtain a revenue stream. A Forrester Research survey of 50 IS managers found that 80 per cent of employees at their organizations will have access to third-party content within two years. Third-party information posted on intranets typically includes news services and industry data; managers are more cautious about adding ads to the mixture because it raises both technical and organisational issues. Many employees feel bombarded by advertising everywhere they go, and user firms will need to establish policies on which advertisers they allow.

Source: PC Week, 6 April 1998. Used with permission.

External communications

There is no such thing as a Mass Mind. The Mass Audience is made up of individuals, and good advertising is written always from one person to another. When it is aimed at millions it rarely moves anyone.

(Fairfax Cone, of Foote, Cone & Belding)

All organisations will have very many stakeholders, groups of people that have varying levels of interest in how the company is run and in the products and services produced. Whatever the industry, whether not-for-profit, government or commercial, communication channels will have to be forged at times to keep the various interested parties informed about corporate and market developments. External stakeholder groups can be many in number and be situated at both a national and multinational level depending on the sphere of market activity. Stakeholders in the immediate environment will probably need to be reached on a continuous base whilst others, in the wider environment, will need to be addressed as and when the need arises.

Stakeholders in the immediate environment include

- customers, consumers and all involved in the buying decision-making process;
- value/distribution chain members: suppliers, producers and intermediaries;
- pressure groups: environmentalists, vegetarians, moral campaigners, local communities etc;
- independent legal and regulatory bodies: media overseeing bodies, government;
- the competition.

Stakeholders in the wider environment include

- national government bodies and MPs;
- city and financial journalists;
- trade and professional associations;
- the general public.

Corporate communication

The organisation should be aware that it will send out corporate messages unintentionally as well as intentionally so that some element of control can be planned.

Unintentional corporate messages may be generated in the following ways:

- where the company is situated, the town or region from which the company operates;
- the manner and way the company operates;
- the products, services and brands the company manufactures, the prices charged, the channels of distribution used and the methods of promotion adopted.

Intentional corporate messages will be generated by the corporate and marketing communication functions. Many companies have a dedicated corporate communications department with objectives to make certain that all messages emanating from the company reinforce the image of a good company acting in a responsible and caring way whilst marketing excellent products. Much of this work will be PR using all communication methods available. The company will also use the marketing and promotional departments to send out messages that will protect and enhance the corporate brand.

A corporate communications model is shown in Fig. 3.2.

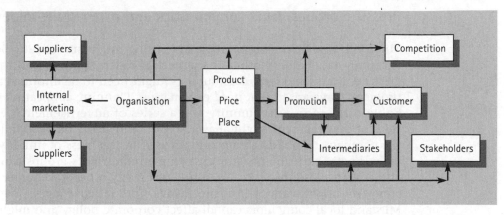

Fig. 3.2 Corporate communications model, talking to many stakeholders

Advertising and external targeting

All external stakeholders, at some time or other, will need to be generally or specifically targeted and informed in some way about different company activities.
Many stakeholders' groups in the immediate, day-to-day working environment
will need to be sent continuous benefit messages and listened to ceaselessly. Of
these the customers (the 'Decision Making Unit' (DMU)) are the most important
and their promotional and advertising needs are discussed throughout the book.
Care should be taken, however, that all other stakeholders have appropriate attention when circumstances demand. The need to keep fellow value-chain members,
suppliers and intermediaries, up-to-date with developments has taken on added
urgency with the recognition that enormous competitive savings can be made by
all talking and working very closely with one another. This will involve the use of
advertisements in both the trade and non-trade media as well as personal contact
through visits and exhibitions.

Efficient Consumer Response (www.ecr-europe.com) is a joint European trade industry
body dedicated to making the grocery sector more responsive to consumer demand and
removing unnecessary cost from the supply chain. It is open to small, medium and large
organisations including retailers, wholesalers, manufacturers, suppliers, brokers and third-
party service providers such as logistics suppliers. Members include some of the biggest
names in the industry: Tesco, Procter & Gamble, Unilever, Sara Lee and Walmart. Areas of
performance examined along the supply chain include the management process involved
in the response to changing demand, measuring performance, handling human resources
and information technology. Through discussing and evaluating category management,
effectiveness of product range assortment, shelf and display layout as well as promotional
and merchandising activity productivity, savings have averaged over 10 per cent. The key
to the process is the ability for members to talk with one another, recognising the
enormous saving to be made through mutual co-operation.

Pressure groups, local communities and other stakeholders

There will also be occasions when advertising might successfully be used to reach external stakeholders other than the customer, suppliers and intermediaries. Pressure groups and local communities might need to be informed and reassured if problems have arisen that need explanation. Planning application can cause justifiable concern in a community and a series of advertisements setting out both sides of the argument might allay suspicion and swing public opinion in favour of the company. Similarly a company accused in the press of unfairly using animals for cosmetic experiments and upsetting animal rights groups can sue but might also advertise its innocence. There are very many other stakeholder bodies that the company might want to influence. Government departments, regulatory bodies, MPs and local councillors can all affect corporate policy and might need positive influencing through the use of advertising. This might be exercised directly by aiming the messages at the relevant stakeholder body or indirectly by attempting to manipulate public backing to whatever the cause might be and relying on this to sway official opinion.

The importance of audience targeting

It is imperative that the target audience is clearly identified and profiled in detail if relevant messages are to be constructed in the correct manner and a medium used that will reach and be understood. We will examine in more detail later in the book the importance of segmentation and targeting but it should be self-evident that the wrong messages sent in the wrong way will be lost in the ether and be money down the drain. Stakeholders will often want different benefits from a company and its products (see Fig. 3.3) and this must be taken into consideration when building a communications and advertising campaign. Pressure groups will want to hear that the launch of a new product will not harm the environment, local government that it will create jobs, intermediaries that some amount of profit will be made and the customer that it will offer more value for money than existing products.

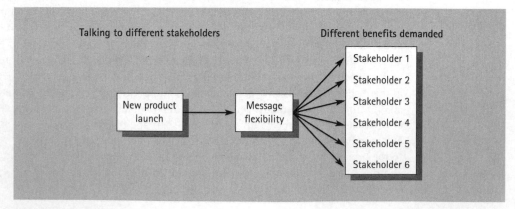

Fig. 3.3 Message flexibility

Messages and stages in the communication process

The advertising message will change at different stages in its life and simple examples are given below using the concept of the product life cycle and Rogers' innovation adoption curve.

The product life cycle

As the product moves through the product life cycle of introduction, growth, maturity and decline, the message to be communicated and the task to be achieved will change.

Introduction: mass advertising: create awareness and gain market share.
Growth: more selective advertising: sell brand and benefits, combat competition.
Maturity: selective advertising: remind and reinforce, maintain market share.
Decline: little or no advertising: sell on price, prepare to leave the market (could repackage and reposition the product; advertise as in Growth).

Rogers' innovation adoption curve

Rogers' innovation adoption curve (see Fig. 3.4) should be familiar to most readers as it is a classical part of marketing. The model plots the movement of a new concept, and its customer adoption, as it first enters the market then grows in consumer numbers until finally most have purchased and purchase moves into repurchase.

All the different groups identified above will purchase for different reasons and so advertising has a subtly different task at the various stages. Below are a few suggestions, but reasons for purchase will be different depending on the product and so should be researched.

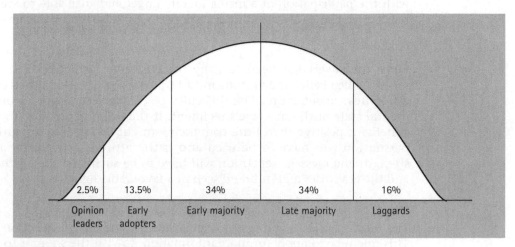

| 2.5% | 13.5% | 34% | 34% | 16% |
| Opinion leaders | Early adopters | Early majority | Late majority | Laggards |

Fig. 3.4 Rogers' innovation adoption curve

Opinion leaders: must have first ownership status; risk-takers; want others to look up to them.

Early adopters: status; slight risk-takers; wait for opinion leaders.

Early majority: Reassurance; benefits tried and tested; herd instinct.

Late majority: Reassurance; feelings of social exclusion encourage purchase.

Laggards: Price; bargain-hunters.

The communication hierarchical process

Advertisers are interested in the way that messages are seen and acted upon by the target audiences. This has led to the development of many different models all attempting to understand methods of message perception, selection, retention, analysis, decision making and eventual purchase. This interest reflects the need on the part of the advertiser to understand how the communication process works so that they are able to influence it at every stage and so make the advert that much more effective. Many models are simple whilst other can become exceedingly complex. A very basic, linear model is the three As.

Awareness, Attitude, Action: the three As

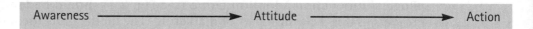

This simple model (at the heart of most other linear models) works on the concept that there are three basic tasks that communication needs to undertake.

Awareness

The first task of advertising is to get noticed. The best advert in the world is a waste if it isn't seen. This task must be achieved both in competition with others and with the participation of a media-literate target audience able to see selectively or reject advertising messages at both a conscious and subconscious level.

Attitude

Once the advert has been seen by the customer, attention gained, awareness focused, then belief and attitude must be affected in a way that will create an interest to hear or see more. The difficulty of the task will depend on the existing mental state of the message's recipient. If the existing attitude to the message's benefits is positive then little convincing might be needed, if neutral then more persuasion will have to be used and if the attitude is negative then message strength and message repetition will have to be such that the attitude is changed and the advertiser and/or brand seen in a favourable light.

Action

The third stage in the process is to persuade the audience into action of some kind. This might be to apply for more information, to visit the shop or to buy the product and to keep buying the product.

The AIDA model

There are many variations of the 3A model, perhaps the best known being the AIDA model. Here the process is stretched into

(Unawareness) ⟶ Awareness ⟶ Interest ⟶ Desire ⟶ Action

AIDA is very similar to the three As but the complexity of attitude change is recognised by the splitting of it into Interest and Desire. Other models add more (Awareness, Attention, Interest, Desire, Intention, Action and so on) in an attempt to understand the process more. It is this basic model that will be used later in the book.

Advertising cannot act alone to move the customer from unawareness through to purchasing the product. Other elements of the promotional mix – sales promotion, PR, publicity, personal selling etc. – will have to come into play. These are discussed in detail in the next chapter.

Many people argue that linear models such as the three As and AIDA are too simplistic and the dynamics of the process should be more accounted for. They argue that humans think in a more elaborate, disordered and confusing way. We see, we forget, we are reminded; we are interested for the moment, then we lose interest when more pressing thoughts come to mind; we weigh up concepts, we measure levels of importance, and we move onto other things; we talk to others; we are persuaded by a multitude of benefits and so on and so forth. Of course the more complex the model the less likely it is to be used by advertisers as it becomes too unmanageable. Unfortunately the process of advertising is not an exact science and cannot ultimately be treated in the same way as physics or chemistry.

Basic communications

It will be worth while to spend some time examining the basic concept of communications as this is at the very heart of all the many different forms of promotion used by thousands of organisations to bombard us with messages 24 hours a day, 7 days a week, 52 weeks a year through media as diverse as TV, billboards, newspapers, magazines, packaging and shop windows.

The average UK consumer is exposed to hundreds of brand messages a day all demanding that they be read. Finding ways to make yourself heard above the cacophony has lead to advertisers and agencies coming up with all kinds of ingenious tricks and ploys. 'Ambient' and 'interactive' advertising work on the concept of surprise. 'Ambient' advertising works by creeping up on the unsuspecting consumer by placing adverts in unexpected places where one would not expect to find them: petrol pump handles, inside a golf hole, on toilet seats, on parking tickets, on underground steps, on the tops of buses, on bus wheels and so on. 'Interactive' advertising draws the subject into the adverts, to participate in the process, with, for example, 'scratch and sniff' after-shave, Mars ads that dispense chocolate, bus tickets impregnated with the smell of Daz, or posters for dog food that

▶

bark; as technology develops so innovative methods proliferate. It is hoped that the consumer might, for one moment, be entertained and in return notice the ad. Advertisers are continually looking for ever more creative ways to gain attention and break through consumer indifference and apathy.

The changing role of communications

In the past the communication task confronting the advertiser would not have been as daunting as it is now. The seller and the purchaser would probably have lived in the same hamlet, village or town and so information about the product/service availability or benefit development could have been communicated to potential customers by the town crier or the sandwich-board man, or by word of mouth by both the seller and existing customers. Feedback on acceptability, price, value and complaints could be obtained immediately and action taken wherever necessary. With most product advertising this directness in the communication process is not now possible (although it must be said that the development in interactive media forms, TV, e-mail etc. is perhaps beginning to reverse the process) in the modern complex and widespread global marketplace.

The seller and the buyer may live hundreds, if not thousands of miles apart, never actually see one another, and so be reliant on some form of communications other than those described above. But these problems, though difficult enough, are not the only major factors to be considered when attempting to communicate messages to selected customer segments. Thousands of other organisations, including both competitors and non-competitors, will also be attempting to talk to the customer at the same time and the successful organisation must ensure that it is its message that is heard and remembered rather than the message of another. This problem is at the very heart of advertising and many billions of pounds have been wasted on messages that either have never got through to the intended audience or were ignored or forgotten if they did.

Understanding basic communications

I do not regard advertising as entertainment or an art form, but as a medium of information.

(David Ogilvy, advertising guru)

It is worth repeating, as it should never be forgotten (but unfortunately often is), that good advertising is all about communications, that is sending specific, benefit messages to clearly researched and defined targeted audiences, obtaining and listening to the feedback, readjusting the message if damaging confusion or ambiguity are apparent and finally being certain that the truth and core of the message is fully understood (and hopefully acted upon) by the intended recipient. Communications is something that one does *with* other people, not something one does *to* another person. So before looking at the way that advertising interacts with all the elements of the promotional mix it will be worthwhile to identify clearly and establish in simple detail the role that basic communication plays in the advertising process.

All communication activities involve the following eight elements:

- message sender;
- message encoding;
- a message;
- a message channel or medium;
- a receiver;
- message decoding;
- noise;
- feedback potential.

Message sender

The sender of the message will be a person or a group of people who wish to send some form of benefit messages to a particular audience. This might be an advertiser wanting to sell the benefits of a new chocolate bar, a motor car or a pyramid-shaped tea bag. Some form of market research (either formal or informal) should be used both to identify the selected target audience and to describe clearly the benefits needed. The sender and the receiver might be face-to-face or be on different sides of the world and this has the possibility of distorting messages. However the development of ever more sophisticated forms of information technology make distance much less of a problem. It is crucial that the sender is aware of the receiver's level of intellect and understanding and this leads us on to the process of message encoding.

Encoding

Encoding is the process of translating thought into symbolic form. Using some form of language – words, sentence structures, symbols and signs – as well as non-verbal elements such as colour, mood and music, the advertiser should encode a message that will effectively communicate the benefits to the target audience in a manner considered acceptable by the receiver.

Message

The message may be in a simple or more complex form depending on the amount of information the sender wants to put across; it may have to travel a few feet or thousands of miles, and it may need either instant or delayed feedback. It may be delivered in a visual, print, auditory, or even olfactory way (coffee grinding, bread cooking, perfume smells are now used in some retail outlets to tempt customers into purchase).

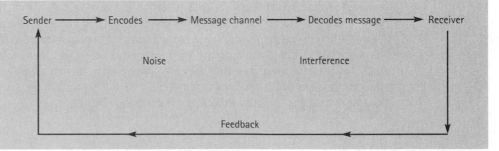

Fig. 3.5 The basic communication model

Message channel

The message channel or medium is the pathway through which the message travels from sender to receiver and this can take many forms depending on the resources of the sender and the needs of the receiver. Person-to-person methods include both verbal and non-verbal forms. Different forms will include spoken and written language, body language, and facial expressions, and use all the senses: sound, vision, taste, touch and smell. Non-human media include TV, IT, radio, cinema, theatre, all forms of print such as newspapers, magazines, leaflets, product packaging, and outdoor forms such as billboards, buses and taxis, shop windows and so on.

Message channel suitability

Communication media have certain characteristics that make them better at one form of message carrying than another. For example while TV might be good at introducing simple visual product benefits a magazine will be better at introducing benefits that need more complex description. Radio is good for products that can be described in story form whilst the cinema can be used for longer dramatic 'mini film' type description. Personal selling has advantages for product benefits that need detailed question and answer explanation and packaging for content description on the supermarket shelf.

The receiver

The receiver might be any one of the various stakeholders that the organisation wants to influence but it predominately tends to be either the existing or potential customer. The advertiser must consider in detail all the factors that might influence the way that the message will eventually be understood by the targeted audience. This will include, amongst other things, understanding how social, cultural, psychological, educational and emotional factors might influence the customer's decision-making process. Even the situation, geographical location, time of day, month and season of the year can all affect message lucidity. Whether the target market has been correctly identified has to be a basic concern because if it has not the message could very well end up in the wrong medium.

Know the audience

If the product is a child's toy and the mother is considered to be the decision purchase arbiter then the advertiser might well advertise in a woman's magazine. But if it is the child that is able to persuade its mother which product to purchase (known as 'pester power') then the message will have been wasted as it should have been placed in some form of children's media. Similarly if the target audience is seen as middle class when in fact they are of a lower class or if they are considered as having a high education when the reality is low education then again there is every chance that the advertisement will appear in an inappropriate medium and the message be lost.

Barriers and interference to communication

A message travelling through the channel will be subjected to the influences of many different factors that could all work against achieving good communications. Such interference and distortion is often referred to as *noise* or *clutter.* Some of these distorting factors have been identified above but there are many others that will need to be considered. Noise may occur at any time in the communication process: for example, the receiver may be distracted in some way whilst the advert is showing on the TV – they might leave the room to go to the toilet or to get a drink, somebody might start talking, a baby might cry, the telephone might ring. The message itself may be ambiguous and confusing and so be misunderstood or misinterpreted; a million and one things can happen to cause loss of meaning. Probably the biggest problem of all is the presence of thousands of competitor messages full of pictures, action, colour, sounds, all vying for customer attention, all attempting to gain that one moment during which product information can be imparted.

Feedback

Feedback is crucial to any process where objectives need to be achieved and this is never more so than in the communication process. The sender must check in some way to see if the message has been received and understood in the manner intended. If this is not the case monitoring, feedback and control mechanisms should allow misinterpretations to be corrected. In a face-to-face situation this is not too much of a problem for the skilled salesperson as linguistic, body and facial cues can be continuously read during the benefit presentation so as to identify any misunderstanding or concerns on the part of the receiver that can then be rectified as they happen. With other media such as TV, radio or press advertising monitoring and feedback in this way is more difficult, but many research-based methods have been developed and these will be examined later in the book.

CONCLUSION

Good communications are at the heart of successful advertising campaigns. The advertising business is replete with costly examples of programmes that have failed, some quite spectacularly, because the advertiser or its agency has forgotten this basic truism. It is too easy to become carried away with creative complex design whilst marginalising the real reason behind advertisement. Intentional and unintentional messages will emanate from the corporate body and the marketing mix. It is incumbent on the communication managers to make certain that messages are controlled and favourable from wherever they might arise. All organisations will have many stakeholders, as well as the customer (usually the most important), that it might want to talk to at various times during the year. These can be classified under internal and external audiences. Internal audiences will need to have information that will help them perform their job more effectively and efficiently in meeting customer needs whilst external audiences will need messages tailored to meet individual and group needs. The basic concepts underpinning the communication process should be remembered whenever an advertising programme is being constructed.

CASE STUDY

FT

Advertisers eyeball the net

How exactly do you make money on the Internet? Few are asking this question more anxiously than publishers. Many Net users expect the new medium – its traditions framed by its history as a network for academics – to remain free. Electronic transactions are taking off slowly. Charging people subscriptions, for all but a few publications such as Playboy's online product, just seems to drive readers away. Slate, the highbrow electronic magazine published by software company Microsoft and the US journalist Michael Kinsey, is one of several publications to delay charges.

Enter advertising. Mary Meeker, technology analyst at Morgan Stanley, the US investment bank, sees hope for Net publishing in the history of other new media. 'There was turmoil at the beginning of every medium', she says. '"How are we going to make this work?" people asked themselves. Advertising always came in as a saviour.' That is now happening. The online advertising market, which barely existed in 1994 and was worth $55m (£35m) in 1995, exceeded $340m in 1996, according to Jupiter Communications, the market research company. On the back of this advertising growth, Yahoo!, the leading search engine (or navigation service) for the Net, moved into the black in its most recent quarter, much earlier than Wall Street had expected.

'Keep all this in perspective: this is all fledgling,' cautions Peter Storck, head of Jupiter's online advertising research. But it expects Net ad revenue to reach $5bn by 2000: faster growth than that for radio, television or cable television in those industries' early years. These forecasts are spurring the advertising industry on. Softbank Interactive Marketing, the largest Net ad sales company, has recently opened in Europe, for instance, while mainstream agencies such as Young & Rubican – prompted by competition from new media boutiques – have set up departments. Audits, crucial to the confidence of advertisers, are provided by companies such as I/PRO, an associate of Softbank. This rapid expansion is due to the 'eyeballs' – the attention of consumers which advertisers covet – moving to the Net. Radio took 38 years to accumulate an audience of 50m in the US, television 13 years, and cable 10 years, according to Morgan Stanley. But World Wide Web usage in the US should reach that level by 1998, five years after it took off.

There is also the increasing sophistication of advertising on the Net, and the realisation by advertisers that the medium may be ideal for direct communication with consumers. Advertising in that arena is not an immediately obvious notion. Images, audio and video from the Net – transmitted across ordinary telephone lines at a typical rate of 28.8 kilobits per second – still do not match the quality of glossy magazines, radio and television. The frustration of waiting for an excessively large advert to download on to a web page can drive a reader to another publisher's site.

However, a standard advertising banner is emerging which, at 468 pixels (screen dots) across and 60 deep running across the top of the page – much like a newspaper masthead – takes up less than 20 per cent of a typical computer screen window into the Net. To accelerate downloading, the Net advertising industry has also set a voluntary limit on the complexity of the image.

Creative departments of advertising agencies are also making better use of the interactivity of the medium. Most banners, when clicked upon by a computer mouse, take the user to the advertiser's web site. However, many of these are an awkward hybrid of product and corporate information, inflicting the annual report and chairman's letter on unsuspecting consumers. Mark Dickinson, one of the founders of Net advertising agency Index finger, says many company web sites are the product of golf-course panic. 'Senior management just doesn't get it.' One solution is the 'microsite', whereby a banner is linked not to the advertiser's main site, but to specially designed content which expands on the banner's message. And some advertisers are reducing their own web efforts in favour of sponsoring content from independent publishers.

The inter-activity of Net adverts also helps creative departments refine designs. Publishers monitor the number of readers who, on viewing a banner, 'click through' to the linked site. That shows, unsurprisingly, that adding animation and a call to action such as 'Click here!' typically increases the response rate by 150 per cent. Giveaways are particularly powerful. While a flat banner might generate one 'click through' for every 100 views (i.e., typically only one person in 100 explores the ad), and an animated banner one in 40, a recent offer of a free trip to Iceland on Yahoo! drew one surfer in every five that viewed it.

Advertisers and publishers are doing more than cope with the limitations of the medium. In at least three ways, the Net promises progress.

First, Net marketers can design their campaigns as they go. A traditional direct mail campaign is virtually set in stone from the point at which the millions of envelopes and their contents are ordered from the printers. A Net advertiser could begin with two variants of the same offer, monitor the response day by day, and shift at no extra cost to the more successful version. 'Direct marketeers, eat your heart out,' says Tom Bowman, commercial director of ZD Net UK, a unit of the leading computer magazine publisher.

Second, online adverts can be tailored in quite specialised ways. On Yahoo!, for instance, advertisers such as Miller Brewing can now have some confidence that they are preaching to potential converts. A banner ad for Miller Genuine Draft pops up if the user searches for sites about beer.

Third, and most important, advertisers can ensure they only pay for what they get. 'Everything that is happening [during a Net session] is being recorded in a log file somewhere,' says Tim Reed, I/PRO's director of business development. Advertisers, as well as knowing exactly how many people have viewed their message, know how many were interested enough to click the ad. Companies such as Procter & Gamble, the US producer of shampoo and other consumer goods, have started to ask why they should not pay for each 'click through', rather than per 'impression', as with old media. Andrew Batkin, chief executive of Softbank Interactive Marketing, says poor creative work by advertisers is often to blame for low response rates. '[Paying by "click through"] would be like paying for photos, but only for those which came out well.' Yahoo! says it is working with 2–3 per cent of clients on 'performance programmes' under the terms of which it charges $1.00–$1.50 for every qualified lead it passes through to a company, which is much the same thing as a 'click through'. From this to a cut of any sale made as a result is but a short step. Mary Meeker believes publishers will start thinking they should be getting a royalty.

Source: Nick Denton, *Financial Times*, 17 March 1997. Used with permission.

Case study questions

1. What special difficulties might there be when using the web to communicate benefit messages to customers? How successful might it be for (a) corporate awareness and (b) brand sales?
2. Discuss the potential of advertising on the web. Would it be better for some types of industries rather than others?

CHAPTER QUESTIONS

1. Identify major internal and external stakeholders. What information might a company want to send to each group?
2. Identify barriers to communications. Will corporate communication barriers be different to product and brand communications?
3. Discuss the importance of internal communications to the whole process of advertising. How might effective internal systems be implemented?
4. Discuss why some adverts seem to work and others do not. Look particularly at the communications process.
5. How valuable is the use of communication models? How are they used and what might be their shortcomings?

REFERENCES

William Bernbach, quoted in *Bill Bernbach said...* (1989), DDB Needham Worldwide.

Cone, F. (1981), quoted in J. O'Toole. *The Trouble with Advertising,* Chelsea House, New York.

Efficient Consumer Response (www.ecr-europe.com)

Ogilvy, D. (1985) *Ogilvy on Advertising,* Vintage Books, New York.

PC Week, 6 April 1998, p.73. (www.pcweek.co.uk)

FURTHER READING

Ehrenberg, A. South Bank Business School, London Road, London SE1 OAA.

Fill, C. (1995) *Marketing Communications,* Prentice Hall, London.

The Marketing Council (www.marketingcouncil.org.uk)

McEwan, T. (1992) 'Communications in Organisations', in Mullins, L., *Hospitality Management,* Pitman Publishing, London.

Morley, K. (1995) *Integrated Marketing Communications,* Butterworth-Heinemann, Oxford.

Olins, W. (1990) *The Wolff Olins Guide to Corporate Identity,* The Design Council, Haymarket, London. (www.wolff-olins.com)

Rogers, E.M. (1983) *Diffusion of Innovations,* Free Press, New York.

4 Advertising and marketing

OBJECTIVES

By the end of this chapter the reader should be able to:

1. Evaluate the relationship between marketing concepts and advertising.

2. Identify where advertising sits within the marketing mix.

3. Identify where advertising sits within the promotional mix.

4. Evaluate the role of advertising and all other areas of the promotional mix including sales promotions, point of purchase, public relations, publicity, personal selling, sponsorship and exhibitions.

INTRODUCTION

80% of video recorders in the US permanently flash '12:00' because their owners haven't worked out how to change the time.

(www. zenithmedia.com)

Advertising is only one part in the process of matching the resources of the organisation to the needs and demands of the marketplace. All internal resources, staff, skill development, systems, structures, strategies and the culture need to be geared toward meeting the clearly identified customer needs. Many business disciplines are involved and the relevant areas are discussed throughout this chapter.

Marketing

Advertising is an integral component of the company's promotional mix, the tools and techniques that are available to communicate messages to target markets. Similarly the promotional (or communication) mix is an indispensable part of marketing and can be seen as one of the elements of the marketing mix. In this chapter we discuss the role of marketing and communications and where advertising fits within the overall process.

Marketing, as a corporate activity has many definitions but it is basically about having an overriding concern for customer satisfaction and it can be viewed both as a corporate philosophy and a management function. Marketing seen as a corporate philosophy places the wants, needs and concerns of the customer at the very centre of every activity the company undertakes and should permeate every corporate function and every department from administration, secretarial and reception through to distribution, production, finance, research and development and of course sales and marketing. It should become part of the company culture understood and believed by all from the managing director down to the car park attendant and it should find expression in the corporate mission statement, corporate statements and corporate actions.

> **DEFINITION** Marketing is 'Identifying, anticipating, satisfying (delighting? exceeding?) customers' needs and wants at a profit (or cost effectively if applied to not-for-profit organisations).' (Chartered Institute of Marketing)

Marketing can also be seen as a function within the company in common with finance, production, human resource management, purchasing, administration etc. (depending on how the firm is organised). Marketing as a company function is concerned with integrating the whole of the company marketing effort and matching it to the needs of the market. My own definition is given below.

> **DEFINITION** Marketing is a matching process; matching the resources of the organisation to the needs and demands of the market environment.

The marketing mix and communications

The 'marketing mix' is a way of describing the marketing internal resources that must be strategically integrated within the marketing plan to meet clearly identified customer needs. These are often identified under the simple (if not simplistic) acronym of the four ps: the product, price, place, and promotion. As well as deliberate messages emanating from the company through the use of planned promotional and advertising techniques, other messages, not so well able to be planned, will also be transmitted to the customer. These other messages will be sent, more haphazardly, via the products and brands a company sells as well as the channel of distribution it uses to get its products and services to the market.

For example, if the product, service or brand promises more customer benefits than actually exist (or are perceived to exist) then negative messages will emanate: the customer will be disappointed after trying the product and no matter how intensive and seductive the advertising will feel aggrieved and even cheated and will not purchase again. Similarly, wrong signals will be emitted if a product is not available in the shops after extensive TV advertising. Similarly, if the price is too high (or too low) in relation to the product value, or if the chosen channel of distribution is not at the level or quality expected (e.g. department store or market stall) although good advertising and selling might create interest and initial purchase, customer disappointment will not only militate against repeat purchase but might also cause long-term corporate damage.

The promotional mix and advertising

Promotion is the communicative element in the marketing mix and it comes into use when the other elements of the marketing mix, product, price, place, have been developed and co-ordinated and are ready to meet the needs of the identified target market. Companies should not promote their corporate image or their products and brands if in some way they are inadequately prepared to meet customers' expectations and requirements. The tasks that the elements of the promotion mix need to perform are manifold and at times exceedingly subtle, and these will be discussed as we move through the following chapters; but the basic objective of all advertising, to send transparent, unambiguous messages to, and receive feedback messages back from clearly identified target audiences, should never be forgotten. All these various techniques can be identified under the collective term of the 'promotional mix' or 'communication mix'.

It is important to understand that the promotional mix is called a 'mix' because it consists of a 'mix' of various promotional methods available to the marketing manager to communicate and persuade the customer to look favourably on the organisation and hopefully purchase its products and services. A selection of different promotional 'tools' and 'techniques' are needed because there are different communication and promotional objectives that the advertising manager must achieve, from initiating company or product awareness to creating genuine interest and generating product purchase. Different methods are needed because the tasks involved demand a tailored approach and any one method on its own would probably not suffice. Not only are more options available but existing options are getting better and offering much better value for money in terms of customer reach, segmentation, and audience measurement. It is highly probable that in any one promotional campaign a selection of promotional mix techniques will be used to complement advertising and help achieve the end objectives. In the following section we will look at the various options available to the advertising manager in seeking to achieve marketing and communication objectives within an agreed budget, beginning with the use of sales promotions.

Sales promotions

Sales promotions (known as 'below the line media' as opposed to media advertising known as 'above the line') can take many forms and refer to the use of any short-term incentive to encourage and persuade various customers along the distribution chain to purchase products. This might be the manufacturer taking in raw material supplies, the retailer taking in for resale or the end customer buying for own consumption. Sales promotions are also used to encourage and motivate the company sales force to sell more or particular products. It is important to realise that the incentive is additional to the basic benefits provided by the brand and it is used to encourage purchase over a designated period of time. In this way products are pushed through the distribution chain from supplier through to end user.

- *Employee sales promotions* are used to motivate the sales force to sell (push) more products to the wholesaler or retailer.
- *Trade sales promotions* are incentives used to encourage wholesalers and retailers to take in stock or to shift existing stock. Many large, powerful retailers now insist on so-called 'promotion' money from manufacturers purely to stock the product.
- *Consumer sales promotions* can be seen as short-term incentives used to encourage the customer to purchase and try the product, and then hopefully still repurchase when the promotion is finished.

Consumer sales promotions are used by every conceivable type of organisation and we only have to walk down the high street or visit the local retail park to see a multitude of examples. A trip around Tesco, Sainsbury's, Asda or Safeway will show in each store a choice of over 25 000 products with, at any one time, some form of incentive on 10 to 15 per cent of them. These can include price reductions, extra value, three for the price of two, buy one get one free, competitions to win prizes such as cars and holidays, sweepstakes, free trial sample size, and self-liquidating offers (e.g. buy a carton of tea bags and buy a branded mug at a very low price). Other incentives include the 'buy now pay later' option favoured by the electrical and furniture retailers and the extended free or low-price repair warranty. Price can also be used to encourage people to use the service at less busy times, for special groups of people (such as pensioners) or for larger numbers. The options seem endless with creative practitioners always looking for the innovative option to gain competitive advantage. Many consumers will now only purchase when a sales promotion is on offer.

The relationship between advertising and sales promotions

Consumer promotions

Sales promotions and advertising tend to be used together in most major promotional campaigns but each has a distinct role to play in the process. In consumer markets media advertising, TV, the press, radio etc. are used to generate long-term corporate and brand loyalty, introducing the company and the product and then continuously communicating benefits, hopefully building brand loyalty over the long term. Sales promotions are then used to create short-term excitement and added value, seducing the customer into action and actually trying the product. It is hoped that the customer will continue to purchase (not always the case) when the promotion has ended. Very rarely will a sales promotion be used on its own to create both awareness and encouragement to buy as experience has shown that customers will be reluctant to purchase brands from unknown companies even where a sales promotion exists. Sales promotions are attractive, however, to promotion managers because, unlike media advertising, the results are transparent (in terms of sales) and easily measurable and the results accruing from advertising will be much more long term and more opaque. So in times of economic difficulty it becomes safer (for job security) to take budget money from advertising and put it into sales promotions. Many argue, however, that to do this is a danger to long-term consumer brand recognition.

Trade promotions

Advertising is used far less in retail and business to business marketing compared to trade promotions. Trade press advertising is sometimes used to create the awareness but personal selling tends to take on this task because buying points are less and this is supplemented by trade promotion incentive encouraging the business to purchase. Trade promotion spend has increased over the last twenty years, taking share from media advertising, as retailers become more powerful and demand 'promotional money' on top of manufacturer's discount (even just to stock the product).

The growth in sales promotions spending over advertising

This is because of the following:

- pressure for extra incentives from retailers;
- fear of losing 'shelf space' by producers;
- decrease in brand loyalty;
- competitive activity;
- short-term sales uplift;
- consumer fondness for sales promotions;
- results more readily measured, especially in the short term, than advertising;
- media fragmentation working against mass advertising;
- increase in advertising media costs and clutter.

Push and pull, sales promotions and advertising

Sales promotions (see Fig. 4.1) are used to 'push' products through the distribution chain. The sales force is motivated to push particular products into the retailer through the use of sales force incentives. The retailer is induced to take in stock and the customer is encouraged to buy now rather than later when the value will be less.

A pull strategy (see Fig. 4.2), on the other hand, is a communication strategy specifically aimed at the consumer rather than other members of the distribution

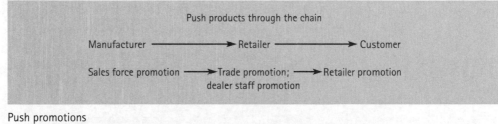

Fig. 4.1 Push promotions

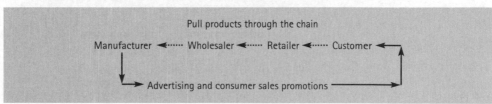

Fig. 4.2 Pull strategy

channel. So a producer might concentrate on above the line advertising and sales promotions aimed at the end consumer, rather than on wholesalers and retailers, thus creating a demand for their brand and so pulling the product down through the distribution chain.

It should be clear that push and pull strategies are not mutually exclusive. In a typical promotional campaign a manufacturer will use a push strategy, sales promotions, to get the dealer to take its product and put it on display and at the same time it will use a pull strategy, media advertising, to generate market demand. Both strategies should be harmonised and integrated so that the products are in the retail outlet to meet the demand created by the advertising and consumer sales promotion. However what should be emphasised is the changing relationship between the two. In the branded goods market the emphasis might be on the pull whilst with the marketing of more commodity type products, maybe own label, the emphasis will be on a push strategy.

Advertising and sales promotion working together

In the same way that mass advertising cannot complete the whole promotional process on its own, moving the customer from unawareness all the way through to actually buying the product, sales promotions need media advertising to create and maintain corporate and product awareness and interest. Generally people will not buy from companies they do not know and sales promotions will not encourage trial of unheard-of brands. Because of this symbiotic relationship it is common to see in most large-scale promotional campaigns both 'above the line' advertising and 'below the line' sales promotions used taking the consumer (using AIDA) from unawareness, to awareness, interest, desire and finally action, purchasing the product (and hopefully repurchasing time and time again if the product is an FMCG). The relationship is shown in Fig. 4.3.

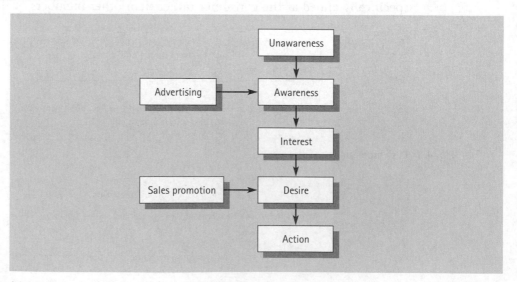

Fig. 4.3 Advertising and sales promotions working together

Advantages and disadvantages of sales promotions

Advantages

- Complement media advertising by building on interest and persuading immediate trial and purchase.
- A short-term, added value incentive.
- Can be measured easily in terms of sales (unlike advertising).

Disadvantages

- Can encourage 'cherry picking', purchasing only whilst on promotion.
- Too many promotions will propagate a 'cut' price image and devalue brand franchise.
- Sales rise when a sales promotion is on but often fall when it finishes.

Merchandising and point of purchase

Advertising moves people towards goods; merchandising moves goods towards people.

(Morris Hite)

Merchandising includes all the activity that surrounds the product at the point of purchase, or POP (much of which might be classified as 'below the line advertising'). Its importance cannot be overestimated as research indicated that as much as 70 per cent of all FMCG purchase decisions are made at the point of purchase. Merchandising covers all manner of advertising material including window banners, wall and shelf posters, displays, dispensers, dump bins and other containers to display products. New technology development has given an enormous boost to POP potential and imaginative and innovative approaches can now be seen in many retail outlets.

Packaging is an important element in merchandising 'below the line' advertising activity and will incorporate both advertising and sales promotions. New technology has opened up many new possibilities in terms of innovative customer benefits in terms of design, colour and copywriting. Packaging is crucial in the FMCG self-service market where it is seen as the 'silent salesman' because of its ability to persuade consumers to purchase.

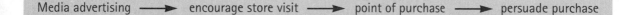

Media advertising ⟶ encourage store visit ⟶ point of purchase ⟶ persuade purchase

POP and advertising

POP is an important, and often underestimated, part of the promotional and advertising process. The importance of impulse buying means that many buying decisions are actually made in the retail outlet so along with other sales promotions and packaging it has to be seen as absolutely crucial in ultimately making the sale. If media advertising is working efficiently it will get the customer along to the store. But if the product is poorly merchandised or, as so often happens, the display material is languishing in the warehouse and has not even been put on display, the opportunity will be lost and the competitor will be the winner. More and more we are seeing retail activity for the consumer classed as an emotional 'shopping experience', something to be savoured, enjoyed and looked forward to with anticipation. In fact 'Lakeside' in Essex, an enormous retail village on the side of the M25, advertises itself in exactly these terms talking about 'enjoying a wonderful day out with the family' and busing people in from as far afield as Cornwall and Devon. This underscores the importance of creative and imaginative POP and explains why it has grown and developed in the way it has.

Advantages of POP

- Advertisements persuade at the actual point of purchase.
- Adds excitement and colour to the store and brand.
- Offers a consistent, recognisable identity for the retail outlet.
- Technological developments offer flexible innovative, advertising opportunities.

Disadvantages

- Retail corporate image can restrict advertisers' use of POP.
- Competitive advertising 'clutter' can cause confusion.

Public relations and publicity

The role of public relations in an organisation is to create and maintain a favourable image of the company on a continuous basis with regard to both internal and external stakeholders. It is the process of strategically communicating with the people who are important to the business. In many cases this involves working with the many different media forms as it is here that reputations can be both built up and destroyed. To support the process the larger organisation will probably have a dedicated PR or corporate communications department within the organisation as well as working with one of the many outside PR agencies. The smaller company, because of costs involved, might choose to work solely with a PR firm. To achieve its objectives the PR department or agency will work with employees, employees' families and trade unions, the local community, pressure groups, local and national governments, city financiers, shareholders, journalists and all media personnel and of course customers, suppliers and intermediaries, seeking to maintain good and harmonious relationships. Some PR work will be seen to be the responsibility of the marketing and promotion department whilst other PR work will be the responsibility of corporate communications, a public relations dedicated department or a human resource or personnel department.

The only bad publicity is one's own obituary.

(Anon)

Some PR activity the company will want to trumpet to the world, while other activity such as employee disputes, customer complaints, product difficulties and product tampering it will want to keep quiet. PR, used as an integral part of the promotional mix, will involve the use of planned publicity to gain free exposure in the media. The practice of PR should not be confused with the role of publicity. PR is what you 'do' and publicity is what you 'get' (or try not to get if the story could be considered harmful to the company).

Gaining publicity

To gain publicity the promotions department will cultivate relationships with media owners, editors and journalists, talking to them about what information, presented in what particular way, would best suit their readership, viewers or listeners. Hopefully favourable news stories concocted by the issuing organisation would then appear on TV, in the press or on the radio showing the company in a worthy light. Because the process is so competitive between organisations (all wanting media mentions) necessary PR media skills must be developed if the publicity campaign is to be successful and the press release should be given as much attention as the writing of an advertisement. Requirements include:

- the ability to write a press release and to hold a news conference;
- story content reflecting the needs of the journalist (and the audience) rather than those of the issuing company;
- news and not just propaganda;
- being in the necessary format demanded by the particular media.

Publicity tools and techniques

There are many different tools and techniques that can be used to elicit free publicity when undertaking a promotional campaign. What is important is that the whole publicity-seeking process is planned in exactly the same way as any other part of the campaign and planned in such a way that it both complements and builds on the all other parts. As with the advertising clear measurable objectives should be set, a budget given and measurement and control mechanisms set up. Techniques include:

- events and activities;
- sponsorship;
- news conferences;
- press releases;
- lobbying.

Publicity as a complement to advertising

An advertising campaign itself can be seen as a newsworthy event and in many cases the media coverage generated by the free publicity has by far outweighed the original paid-for advertising. The most commonly used way to obtain publicity is through the print media and to a lesser extent the TV. A magazine or newspaper needs to unremittingly fill its pages with interesting and lively news stories day after day and week after week and so a publicity campaign planned and well executed, run in conjunction with advertising, will be welcomed with open arms by the news-hungry media and so reap valuable media exposure at little or no extra cost. There is a skill, however, in presenting the story to the media and this must be learnt if advantage is to be gained.

The ASA is investigating complaints that many advertising agencies use shock tactics when creating an advertising campaign to gain free publicity from media exposure with stories about the amount of public complaint. The Benetton advertising campaign provoked international uproar and disapproval for its use of images such as a dying AIDS victim and his family, a new-born baby still attached to its umbilical cord, a priest kissing a nun and a dead Mafioso in a pool of blood but the free publicity it engendered (an intended part of the exercise) was worth millions. Similarly, the Lee Jeans 'put the boot in' advert showing a woman wearing a stiletto boot resting on the buttocks of a naked man, a Wallis advert, 'dressed to kill', showing a man about to have his throat cut because the barber was staring at a young woman dressed in their clothes, and the Nissan 'ask before you borrow it' advert showing a man holding his crotch as if in pain from a kick provoked a tremendous amount of free publicity about 'girl power' and female dominance for both the agencies and their clients. The consequence, however, of too many agencies jumping on the bandwagon could be public apathy and less publicity. It means that advertisers will have to be continually more innovative if they are to continue to marry advertising and publicity to the same extent.

Uncontrolled publicity and advertising

Much publicity generated is uncontrollable and so cannot be used in the formation of planned advertising campaigns. Unexpected events can cause stories and news items to appear that are beyond the influence of the organisation. This is not a problem if the items are favourable but it can be disastrous if the opposite is the case. Unforeseen events can happen to the most well prepared organisation and the difficulty with even the well designed, expertly written press release is that the newspaper, TV, or radio journalist ultimately has control over what appears in the media the following day. A company may well now employ a PR (or corporate communications) spokesperson, often referred to as a 'spin doctor', to attempt either to quash an unfavourable item or to turn the item around and re-present it in a more complimentary light. Advertising will often be used to achieve this.

Publicity and word of mouth

There is no doubt that the images of organisations and their products are disseminated by consumers passing on their experiences and talking to one another and the advertiser will want to build this in to the campaign if at all possible. This is wonderful for sales if the experience is rewarding and everybody is talking about the advertisements ('hello boys' by Wonderbra) but potentially threatening if it is not. The intrinsic difficulty for the promotion's manager is the inability to control the process. Many word of mouth successes have been more through luck than judgement but if 'word of mouth' is to be built into the promotion plan in a meaningful way then, as with all techniques and as difficult as it may be, objectives should be set and the results researched, monitored and controlled.

Advertorials and advertising

In the UK and most industrialised countries around the world adverts purporting to be news stories are illegal. Despite this restriction some advertisers will still attempt to disguise this fact by presenting it in a news style although it is obligatory to make it plain in some way that this is not the case (usually stating 'this is an advertisement' somewhere on the copy). There is little evidence on how successful this ploy is. More common, especially in the local press, is free publicity given in the form of editorial comment in return for paid-for advertising space. 'Advertorials', as they are known, give the impression that the newspaper is writing an unsolicited account about a company or its products when it is in fact the payoff for taking advertising space. The news story usually appears adjacent to the advertisement and can be built in as an integral part of the advertising campaign.

Crisis management, publicity and advertising

In an attempt to pre-empt and control the effects of bad publicity a relatively new management responsibility, 'crisis management' has grown up with the objective of clearly setting out general strategic guidelines on the action to take if a 'crisis' occurs. Product tampering and the blackmail of a supermarket (Sainsbury), unacceptable ingredients in a soft drink (Perrier), accusations of environmental pollution (Shell), and allegations about using child labour in third-world countries (Nike) are all examples of damaging publicity stories that companies now attempt to foresee and react to in a consistent and consumer acceptable manner. Explanatory and product recall advertising will often be used as a strategic part of the process.

Advantages and disadvantages of publicity

Advantages of publicity

- It can be effectively utilised as a complement to advertising.
- It is free of charge.
- It tends to be seen by the customer as a legitimate, third-party, independent endorsement.
- An advertisement will never really have the same impact, no matter how good, as the customer is sophisticated enough to know that the information is propaganda.
- It is more likely to be read as a news story rather than an advertisement.
- It can be very dramatic set in picture and news form.

Disadvantages

- It is uncontrollable.
- Content decisions ultimately rest with the media owner.
- It is difficult to plan as part of the advertising campaign.

Personal selling

Advertising is salesmanship mass produced. No one would bother to use advertising if he could talk to his prospects face-to-face. But he can't.

(Morris Hite)

Any form of communication or promotion that involves direct interaction between a company salesperson and the customer can be seen as personal selling. The customer might be an intermediary (i.e. the retailer or wholesaler), the end consumer, a combination of both, or another business (for own use, rather than for resale) depending on the channel relationship. It is a truism that no profit can be made until the products are sold so the importance that personal selling plays in the communication process cannot be overestimated. The salesperson is usually the last link in the promotional chain and ultimately it is his or her task is to persuade the customer, either trade or consumer, to actually buy the products. In performing this role the salesperson will hopefully capitalise on the vast amount of work put in by others in developing a customer-centred marketing mix offering. If the company gets this part wrong then all the effort that has been expended on shaping the product/service offered, selecting the right channel of distribution, advertising and integrating all the elements of the promotional mix, will have been fruitless and wasted.

Personal selling and advertising

It is possible for the salesperson to work in isolation in selling the company's products, unaided by any other elements of the promotional mix, taking the customer all the way through the decision-making process from unawareness through to desire and the purchase of the product. However this would tend to be the exception rather than the rule as customers will tend to be wary about buying from a salesperson when they are unaware of either the company or the brand name. The aphorism that 'people don't buy products from companies they have never heard of' tends to be true. Other elements of the promotional mix, notably advertising, would generally be used in some form to create initial organisation and brand awareness and so support the selling process. Advertising creates the awareness and gains entry; selling persuades people to purchase.

The role of personal selling in any industry compared with media advertising will depend on many factors including the type of industry and market, company objectives, the product and the type of customer.

Selling and advertising in business to business and consumer markets

The relationship between selling and advertising will change when marketing into different sectors. In business to business personal selling will use relatively more of the promotional budget than advertising, while in consumer markets the opposite will be true (see Fig. 4.4). The major reasons involve the differences in the two markets. In business to business there are many less buying points, the DMU can be more complex, the product/service being marketed will probably demand more explanation and the overall buying price on each call will be high. This all points towards the use of personal selling. Conversely, with consumer markets, the opposite tends to be true. The buying points are many, products less complex, buying amounts on each sale relatively small. Advertising becomes the best method.

Sales promotions are used copiously in both markets.

Sales as the end of the advertising process

There is no doubt that in most cases the salesperson is a crucial, strategic part of the marketing and promotional effort of the organisation and needs to be selected and trained with this in mind. As with bad and inconsistent advertising a poorly motivated and trained salesperson can ruin the whole marketing thrust of the company. In many cases they are at the sharp end dealing with the retail or end consumer face-to-face. Lack of knowledge, lack of motivation, inadequate communication skills can all lead to loss of sales and unhappy customers. For a company to spend a fortune on advertising to get the sales representative in to see the buyer or to get the customer into the retail outlet and for them to be greeted by deficient and often insufficient staff seems to be the height of foolishness.

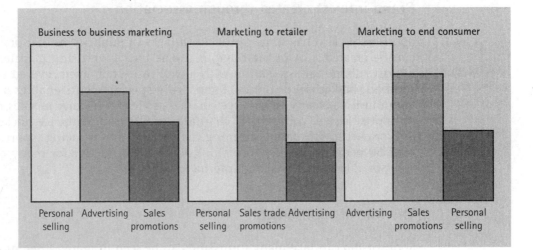

Fig. 4.4 The relative importance of personal selling, advertising and sales promotions in different markets

Advantages and disadvantages of personal selling

Advantages

- Although advertising can help by building brand awareness, with many products the salesperson will close the sale.
- High-priced, high-tech, complex products can be discussed and explained.
- Salespeople can interact with customers, communicating and obtaining feedback so that misunderstandings can be immediately rectified.
- A two-way, exclusive, intimate relationship can be built excluding immediate competition.

Disadvantages

- It is too expensive and time consuming to be used in mass markets and low-tech, low-priced industries.
- Aggressive selling can create consumer wariness.

Sponsorship

As TV and the print media fragment into ever more units it becomes increasingly expensive to reach mass markets and parade the corporate name and brands in front of them, so that sponsorship of national and global events appears for many to be the most cost-effective answer. This is especially apt when wanting to advertise and market products in world markets. Formula One motor racing is on the TV for a total of at least three hours, is on 17 times a year, and is seen by over 100 million people. The Olympics, although only on every four years, is on for two solid weeks and reaches an audience of over three billion. No other media form can give this comprehensive coverage.

Brand interest created through association

Sponsorship also has some of the advantages of publicity in that brand awareness can be created, not in the obvious in-the-face advertising manner, but by the almost subliminal association with a well respected, even revered event such as football, basketball or tennis. Sponsoring special events enables a company to communicate clearly to its target market as clear consumer profiles now exist for all sports, leisure, cultural and charitable events from darts, ice hockey, basketball and cricket to football, swimming, tennis and motor racing (sport accounts for over 60 per cent of all sponsorship) making it attractive for many companies to sponsor at local, national and international level.

The role of sponsorship

Sponsorship can take many forms and can be seen in many different public activities. In fact anything and anybody can be sponsored if there seem to be consciousness-raising advantages. For sponsorship to work the following factors should be taken into consideration:

- clear, relevant target market coverage;
- coverage in the numbers required;
- synergy between corporate brands or product and the sponsored event;
- cost/benefit measurement opportunities;
- capability to integrate into overall advertising and promotional campaign.

Sponsorship and advertising

Sponsorship is predominantly concerned with creating corporate awareness and a 'feel good' factor amongst the company target market. To achieve this, sponsorship should allow the sponsoring company to be deeply associated with its partner and in this way some of the glamour, the value, the image, the very personality of the sponsored organisation should hopefully rub off on to their own corporate image. There is an old saying (slightly altered) that companies are known by the company that they keep and this concept is at the heart of sponsorship. Much sponsorship is advertising or will include advertising and in many cases there seems to be very little difference between the two.

Sponsoring the weather forecast by having the company name at the end seems to be little different from advertising on a billboard or poster. In the same way having the corporate name in the introduction and end of a drama series telling the audience that the company is the sponsor is advertising and its value for money should be judged in the same way. Football sponsorship often consists of adverts around the ground, on the tickets, on the shirts and on the pitch, and much of this is little different from conventional 'below the line' advertising.

For the sponsorship to work in a more substantial manner than conventional advertising there needs to be added value in the way that the sponsor and the sponsee come together so that the corporate name becomes seen as an integral part of the sponsoring company image. Media advertising and publicity will often be used to inform and reinforce the facts of the sponsorship. Sales promotions will also be used to persuade product purchase and build on the goodwill hopefully developed.

Nike, the global sportswear company, is one of the biggest users of sponsorship in the world and in 1997 it signed up to sponsor the Brazilian football team for a colossal $400 million over a period of ten years – the world's biggest sponsorship deal. This gives Nike the right to manufacture and supply sportswear for the 1997 world cup holders, and feature this fact in its adverts, and to put on five friendly games per season (televised of course) in America, Europe, and Asia. In the same year it also concluded a seven-year sponsorship deal with the Arsenal football club worth £40 million. Included in the deal will be the sponsorship of Arsenal's youth development programme and promotion of the club worldwide. They will also sponsor Arsenal in pre-season and end-of-season friendly games with internationally recognised opposition. In the same year, Nike's deadly global rivals Adidas completed a record-breaking sponsorship deal with the New Zealand All Blacks worth £30 million over five years following a bidding war with Nike. At the same time Nike signed up the English Rugby Union for £20 million.

Ambush marketing and advertising

Intense rivalry has lead to the development of so-called 'ambush' or 'guerrilla' marketing, A non-sponsor will attempt to capitalise on the benefits of an event by creating a false impression of sponsorship. In the Atlanta Olympic Games Nike, a non-sponsor, managed to virtually ruin the games for the official sponsors by its ferocious and unremitting outdoor poster advertising in the city and around the stadium and use of the major athletic stars it had signed up. Research afterwards showed that many thought Nike had been an official sponsor, whilst some official sponsors were not named. The strategy was so effective that the International Olympic Committee has ordered all the poster sites in Athens for the 2004 games and will distribute them fairly so as to protect the official sponsors.

Not-for-profit sponsorship

By sponsoring in the not-for-profit area there will be the added hope that there will be some public relations spin-off and that publicity will ensue showing the company to be a good and caring corporate citizen. So companies have sponsored and had their names associated with such diverse organisations as the fire brigade, the police force and the ambulance service (by advertising on the side of the vehicle). Companies can sponsor parks and park benches, playgrounds (again by having their names on the seats, the equipment or the park gates) and road signs. The underground railway is getting in on the act with companies sponsoring different stations and having their names or products associated with each separate station. A story about the relationship can be developed and media publicity used.

Cause-related sponsorship

Cause-related sponsorship is the commercial sponsorship relationship between organisations, and charities (or quasi-charities) that can be exploited by both parties to enhance their profiles and so achieve corporate objectives. In many cases there could be an overlap between not-for-profit sponsorship and cause-related sponsorship; the distinction probably depends on the stated objectives of the relationship. It is a strategy that links a company's marketing and sales activities directly to a not-for-profit organisation by offering some form of donation to the cause with the purchase of its products or services. Cause-related sponsorship will be of interest to an organisation that wants to be seen to care about a particular cause whilst hoping to attract consumers who also have the same concern. Publicity will be sought and occasionally conventional advertising used to make known the relationship.

Cause-related sponsorship should not be confused with philanthropy. Philanthropy is support in cash, products or services to a not-for-profit organisation involving no commercial exploitation. Nevertheless, favourable publicity that might accrue would not be unwelcome. If the not-for profit sponsee is a registered charity then usually tax relief can be obtained by the sponsor depending on the particular country.

Hospitality or client/VIP entertainment

Sponsorship as a package will often include some form of hospitality. This is the hosting of key customers, donors, sponsors, or employees with such amenities as free tickets, parking facilities, food, drinks, and many forms of entertainment such as backstage tours, meeting stars, pro-am activities (depending on the form of sponsorship) or use of the sponsored amenities. It can also include a whole host of other entertainment activity including go-kart racing, horse riding, shooting, war games and so on.

Advantages and disadvantages of sponsorship

Advantages

- corporate and brand awareness in association with a respected and well-known activity;
- audience more receptive than with conventional advertising;
- opportunity for either widespread or more focused coverage;
- target markets can be clearly defined.

Disadvantages

- message dilution amongst competing sponsorship clutter;
- the strength of the event or personality sponsored overshadows and negates the sponsoring brand;
- ambush marketing causes confusion about the official sponsors.

Exhibitions

An exhibition will take many forms and can be seen as a marketplace for both the showing and advertising of products and services and as a way of facilitating the coming together of buyers and sellers. For many industries this is the most cost-effective way of meeting others in the same industry especially in international markets where other communication methods might be difficult. Exhibitions can take the following forms:

- regional, national, or international;
- trade, consumer, or a combination of both;
- indoor or outdoor.

Exhibitions, advertising and other promotional methods

Exhibitions can be used strategically as the main media method or they can be used in a secondary manner supporting the other elements of the promotional mix but it is important that objectives for being at the exhibition are unambiguous as it can be an expensive and time consuming exercise. The mounting of an exhibition may well include many other elements of the promotional mix in varying degrees of importance:

- 'above the line' advertising in the press to announce the forthcoming event; 'below the line' advertising activity such as banners and posters;
- some form of sales promotion to encourage visitors both to attend the exhibition and to visit the stand (e.g. the visitor will leave the visiting card and at the end of each day a draw is made with a magnum of champagne as the prize);
- publicity might be used to obtain a story about the exhibition on TV or in a newspaper or magazine;
- personal selling with a salesperson on the stand disseminating product knowledge and/or persuading the customer to either purchase the product or accept an appointment for a later visit;
- related companies involved in sponsorship agreements.

Advantages and disadvantages of exhibitions

Advantages

- Traditionally seen as the best method to meet industry participants.
- Opportunity to develop relationships in face-to-face encounter.
- Opportunity to display all products and observe those of the competition.

Disadvantages

- Uncertain objectives.
- Can be time consuming.
- Opportunity cost of using sales staff at the exhibition.

Integrating the promotional campaign

There should be no doubt in the minds of all involved in the process what it is that the company wants to achieve from the communication campaign. Whether it is to create long-term corporate awareness, to remind consumers about particular products, to rekindle the flagging fortunes of a particular brand or to get dealers and/or consumers to try a new product, the campaign will only function properly if there is an overall, agreed objective which must ultimately be quantified in some way or another. There will then need to be agreed strategies to achieve this promotional objective and this will include one, two, three or more of the techniques discussed throughout this chapter.

All the communication methods discussed – advertising, sales promotions, publicity, personal selling – are selectively effective at different tasks. This must be recognised when putting the campaign together. Each of the chosen techniques must have its own promotional strategic objective, quantified in the same way, building to meet the overall promotional objective. No technique should used without solid justification based on clear cost/benefit evaluation. Each communication objective must link in with all others purposefully moving the audience from unawareness through to corporate recognition, corporate acclamation and then brand acceptance and finally purchase, repurchase and recommendation.

Understanding target markets

At the very heart of good integrated communications is a clear understanding about the target markets served, the customer profiles within these markets and the best method to communicate benefit messages. Market demographics such as size, make-up, dispersal, growth and movement will all influence choice of media as will the needs and wants of every customer within the designated market segments at both a national and international level. Only if the customer is understood, really understood, can the right promotional method and the right media be chosen and transparent, empathetic messages created, positioned and transmitted. To advertise in the *Reader's Digest* when the target market is working-class males between the ages of 20 and 30 or to sponsor World Darts when the target market is middle-class women over 50 is the height of foolishness because the target market will not hear and the expenditure will have been wasted.

Media owners are critically aware of this potential for wastage (even if some companies aren't) and spend a fortune on researching the market for detailed information on their viewers, readers and listeners so that they are able to talk, advise and persuade media buyers about the aptness of their particular newspaper, magazine or broadcast channel over the competitors.

Budgets, feedback, monitoring and control

An integrated communications plan is dependent upon the necessary money being allocated to cover the costs demanded from the programme. If the budget is based, as many budgets seem to be, on what the company can afford, rather than on task and objective, there is every chance that part of the campaign will suffer. Monitoring, feedback and control mechanisms should always be put in place to make certain that all communication components remain interlocked and on course. These will oversee the different communication objectives set for the different communication forms, that is, advertising, sponsorship, PR, sales promotions, etc., discussed earlier. This should happen before, during and after the campaign so that adjustments can be made as and when needed. Contingency plans are often developed to allow for any drastic realignment demands. We will return to this later in the book when we look at the planning and control process in more detail.

CONCLUSION

Advertising is an intrinsic and crucial element in the concept of marketing and it can be seen as the part that is concerned with communicating benefit messages to the target market once the marketing mix, the product, price and channel of distribution, have been integrated, shaped and honed to meet the researched needs of the identified customer. It should not be forgotten, however, that all elements of the marketing mix – product, price, channel of distribution – have the capability of communicating messages in both an intended and unintended manner. To have a brand that falls below value promised, to price too high, or to make the product available in a down-market outlet will undo all the good work achieved by the advertising. Advertising can never be examined in isolation because all elements of the promotion mix – sales promotion, point of purchase, packaging, PR, publicity, personal selling, sponsorship and exhibitions – might have a part to play in an integrated communications campaign.

CASE STUDY

FT

In search of integration

One of the hottest issues in adland is how to co-ordinate and integrate all the marketing options available. Loyalty schemes, sponsorship, public relations, database marketing, event marketing, sales promotion, web sites and interactive media – not to mention good old-fashioned advertising – offer clients a bewildering variety of options. These demand decision. What is the right way to carve up a total marketing appropriation between, say, advertising, sponsorship and public relations – and how can they all be made to work together?

Several new agencies promise to answer these questions with a gamut of 'integrated marketing' skills in-house. In the past few years new shops have combined traditional media advertising with database marketing. But the latest agencies have combined advertising with public relations, consultancy, corporate design and, most frequently, a promise of 'the right marketing solution, whatever that may be'.

No longer do new agencies just offer the best creativity in the world, because everyone believes integrated marketing is the name of today's game. Clients have always required their communications to be coherent and complementary. But there appears to have been a radical shift of emphasis for several reasons.

First, during the recession clients sought marketing inputs that might be cheaper than traditional advertising. In those gloomy days of plummeting advertising budgets, clients experimented with different marketing approaches. That impetus continues.

Second, when the consolidation and profitability of advertising agencies peaked in the late 1980s, they began to hunt for other sources of income. Because they are restricted from taking on competitive accounts, once they reach a certain size agencies find it almost impossible to outperform the advertising market. But they can develop other marketing skills, and then sell total packages to clients. The trend towards integration has emanated as much from the needs of agencies as from clients.

Third, some of the options available, such as loyalty cards and the Internet, are genuinely new and use innovative technology. Clients have been feeling their way forward gingerly so it has been important for them to be integrated with well-established methods.

But fourth, and most important, like every other aspect of business, marketing techniques grow more specialist every year. It is difficult for anybody to be competent in all of them. But pulling together all the options is only the first stage. What criteria should be used in apportioning the total marketing budget between them? Can their relative cost efficiencies be compared? Whose is the responsibility? Should it be somebody in the client company or the agency? Or will another kind of specialist have to be invented? Finding the right answers will not be easy. Marshall McLuhan's famous aphorism, 'the medium is the message', is coming home to roost.

Source: Winston Fletcher, *Financial Times*, 23 February 1998. Used with permission.

▶

Case study questions

1. Discuss the concept that 'clients sought cheaper remedies during a recession'. What might be the results of taking this approach?
2. Discuss the fourth point made in the case study.

CHAPTER QUESTIONS

1. Discuss how all elements of the marketing mix have the potential to communicate messages to the target market. Are there other ways that the organisation might send out messages to its markets, either deliberately or inadvertently?
2. Using the 'push' and 'pull' communication model identified earlier in the chapter, discuss how advertising and sales promotions might work together in the launch of a new FMCG product.
3. It is argued that personal selling is the only communications technique that can take the customer from unawareness through to the purchase of the product. How true do you think this is? What part, if any, might advertising play in the process?
4. What do you understand integrated communications to be?
5. It is argued that publicity cannot be used as a meaningful part of a promotional campaign because of the difficulty in measurement and control. Discuss and evaluate this criticism.

REFERENCES

Chartered Institute of Marketing (www.cim.co.uk)

Hite, Morris (1988) 'Morris Hite's methods for winning the ad game', Adman, Dallas TX: E. Heart Press, p. 203.

Zenith Media (www.zenithmedia.com)

FURTHER READING

Adcock, D. *et al.*, (1997) *Marketing Principles and Practice*, 2nd edn, Pitman Publishing, London.

Blattberg, R. and Neslin, S. (1990) *Sales Promotions, Concepts, Methods and Strategies*, Prentice Hall, London.

Institute of Public Relations (UK) (www.ipr.press.net)

Institute of Sales Promotions (UK) (www.isp.co.uk)

Jefkins, F. (1994) *Public Relations Techniques*, Butterworth-Heinemann, Oxford.

Jefkins, F. (1997) *Advertising*, Pitman Publishing, London.

Jobber, D. and Lancaster, J. (1997) *Selling and Sales Management*, Pitman Publishing, London.

Kotler, P. (1998) *Principles of Marketing*, Prentice Hall, London.

Meenaghan, T. (1991) 'The role of sponsorship in the marketing mix', *International Journal of Advertising*, Vol. 10, pp. 35–47.

Meenaghan, T. (1996) 'Ambush Marketing, a threat to corporate sponsorship?' *Sloan Management Review*, Fall, Vol. 38, No.1, pp. 103–13.

Public Relations Society of America (US) (www.prsa.org)

Sales Doctor Magazine (www.salesdoctor.com)

Turner, S. (1987) *Practical Sponsorship*, Kogan Page Ltd; London.

Part 2 How the advertising industry is organised

The major players in the advertising industry consist of the advertisers, the advertising agencies and the media owners working together to offer the end customer brand information. Making an advert is usually a partnership between two key players: the advertiser and the advertising agency. In this part of the book we will be looking at the advertising chain and the relationship between the advertiser, the advertising agency, the media owners and the target audience; looking at how customer value is added (or not added) as the communication process moves from client through to the end receiver.

advertiser ⟶ advertising agency ⟶ media owners ⟶ audience

The advertising value chain, building and communicating brand and product value

5 The advertisers

OBJECTIVES

By the end of this chapter the reader should be able to:

1. Identify the role of the various industries and advertisers in the advertising process.

2. Identify why organisations advertise.

3. Analyse and evaluate the relationship between advertisers and the media owners.

4. Identify and evaluate the in-house advertising function.

INTRODUCTION

Advertisers are the interpreters of our dreams. Like the movies they infect the routine futility of our days with purposeful adventure. Their weapons are our weaknesses: fear, ambition, illness, pride, selfishness, desire, ignorance. And these weapons must be kept as bright as a sword.

(E.G. White)

Although many may have heard of one or two of the big global advertising agencies such as Saatchi & Saatchi, J. Walter Thompson or Ogilvy & Mather, it is the very many thousands of companies that advertise every day that have the greatest public recognition. This is no great surprise as this is the very purpose of the whole exercise. We only have to switch on the radio, read the newspaper in the morning, pass poster sites as we drive to work or come home in the evening and switch on the TV to be assailed with requests to buy this car or that dog food, this insurance or that holiday. It is argued that we have the opportunity to see or hear on average as many as 2000 adverts every day emanating from hundreds of different organisations.

Advertisers — the major players

The advertiser's desire to talk to customers, put over benefit messages to target markets, persuade existing and potential customers to buy more products or services, is what drives the whole advertising process. Experience has amply demonstrated time and time again that unless people are aware of your product, understand its benefits over the competition, and are convinced about its superior value they will not 'beat a path to your door' clamouring to be able to purchase. Almost every organisation, small, medium or large, will advertise in some way or another on a regular basis talking to different stakeholders about different benefits available, informing and educating, reassuring and reinforcing or persuading and cajoling. Advertising methods might be formal or informal, they might be by word of mouth, by shop window banner, on the TV or in the local press. Large companies will spend more than small companies; some industries will spend more than others; some will use advertising agencies while some will do it themselves. Whatever the situation, companies will expect the media owners to supply them with information relating to market coverage and message comprehension and they will expect them to be efficient and effective at achieving the communication task they have paid for.

Many types of advertisers

Advertisers may be local, regional, national or international; they may be global players like Procter & Gamble, Coca-Cola, IBM, Mercedes or McDonald's, small businesses like the Chinese restaurant in the high street, government agencies such as the Central Information Office, charities like the Red Cross or NSPCC, or non-profitmaking organisations such as trade unions, professional associations and mutual societies. They may want to advertise locally, regionally, nationally, internationally or globally depending on company size and market scope. They will want to choose the best method – for example, newspapers, magazines, posters, TV or cinema – suited to both their product and the market they are selling in. In any one local area at any one time there will companies such as solicitors and plumbers advertising in the yellow pages, Sainsbury advertising on billboards, Cadbury on bus shelters, Persil on the television, Whirlpool electrical appliances in the *Sun,* perhaps B&Q DIY in the local paper and Bacardi in the cinema. Ultimately the method chosen will reflect the advertisers' faith and knowledge that the medium will fulfil the allotted communication task better than an alternative; if it does not, it will not be chosen again.

Big spenders

The really big spenders are commercial companies marketing branded products in the consumer goods and car markets and in the not-for-profit sector only government spending (US government, $670 million, UK Central Office of Information, £44 million), comes anywhere near to the amount spent by such companies as Ford, Procter & Gamble, Unilever and Kelloggs. Although business to business activity accounts for over half of the gross domestic product in the UK, considerably less (£3 billion) is spent on advertising in this sector than in the consumer market (£9 billion) as they tend to use personal selling, finding this method more productive. Looking at the top ten advertising spenders for 1997 (see Table 5.1) we find, unsurprisingly, some of the biggest names in the corporate dictionary. The industries that dominate are the car industry, package branded products, retailers, communications and leisure.

Table 5.1 Top advertisers (UK and US, 1996/7)

Top ten advertisers (UK) 1996/97	£ millions	Top ten advertisers (US) 1996/97	$ millions
1. BT	126.6	1. Procter & Gamble	2,623
2. Ford Motor Company	84.2	2. General Motors	2,373
3. Procter & Gamble G.B.	77.1	3. Phillip Morris	2,279
4. Kellogg G.B.	64.2	4. Chrysler Corp.	1,420
5. Vauxhall Motors	62.5	5. Time Warner	1,410
6. Renault G.B.	58.4	6. Sears Roebuck	1,317
7. Nissan Motors G.B.	50.9	7. Walt Disney Co.	1,289
8. Van Den Bergh Foods	48.0	8. Pepsico	1,269
9. Procter & Gamble H&B	47.3	9. Grand Metropolitan	1,257
10. Central Office of Information	44.0	10. Ford Motor Co.	1,179

Reprinted with permission from AdAge.com Dataplace. Copyright, Crain Communications Inc. 1999. (www.adage.com)

Worldwide advertising spend

UK advertising spending pales into perspective when compared with the amount of money spent by US companies with Procter & Gamble, the largest advertiser in the world, spending a massive $2.6 billion in the US and a total of $5 billion worldwide. Again it can be seen that it is the packaged branded goods industry (over 50 per cent of all media advertising) and the car industry that dominate the advertising spend charts. If we look on a world scale (see Table 5.2) we find the same pattern with three packaged branded goods manufacturers, Procter & Gamble (US, www.pg.com), Unilever (UK/Netherlands, www.unilever.com) and Nestlé (Switzerland, www.nestle.com) at the top followed by car manufacturers, Toyota (Japan, www.toyota.co.uk) and Peugeot-Citroën (France, www.peugeot.co.uk).

Table 5.2 Top advertisers worldwide (estimated 1998 spend)

	$ billion
1. Procter & Gamble (US)	5.0
2. Unilever (UK, NL)	4.9
3. Nestlé (Switzerland)	3.0
4. Philip Morris	3.1
5. General Motors	3.0

Source: Advertising Age

Small and medium spenders

Although minnows when compared with the giants identified above, the spending of the many small and medium sized companies that advertise collectively amounts to a lot of money. In the past, because of the cost, coverage and wastage problems involved, they have tended not to advertise in the main media and have concentrated their advertising in more localised media such as local newspapers, specialist magazines, local radio and specific outdoor sites. In 1997 total UK spend on this type of advertising amounted to over £2 billion. With changes in technology and the onset of digital opportunities, this is all about to change making more targeted and localised use of all the main media more of a realistic possibility.

Why industries advertise

All industries will advertise to a lesser or greater extent. The high and mighty will spend billions whilst the small and lowly might spend but a few thousand pounds. This might be spent collectively, to advertise the industry as a whole, or individually, with organisations within the industry advertising their own corporate presence or product brand portfolio.

Collective advertising

Industries will advertise collectively to promote the industry as a whole (e.g. the milk industry, Danish bacon, new house building) if and when this is considered necessary. This might be to raise the level of awareness of the industry as a whole, to combat competition from another industry, to educate the buying public about the launch of a new concept, or to ameliorate a problem that might have arisen causing bad publicity amongst consumers. Examples of this happening are the electrical industry informing and educating customers about the workings and the benefits of digital TV and/or the Internet and the UK beef industry exhorting the safety of its product after the pounding it took from the bad publicity associated with 'mad cow disease'. Collective advertising will tend to be organised through the various trade associations with all members contributing a percentage towards the advertising spend.

Individual advertising

The major commercial industries are more likely, however, to use advertising to bring both the individual corporate name and a range of brands to the notice of the general public. This will be on both a national and international level as companies become more global and expansive in their market dealings. Research and empirical experience has shown that seldom will people buy products from companies they do not know or products they have never heard of. So companies advertise to inform existing and potential customers about the benefits in buying from them rather than the competitor. At the heart of the process is the need to inculcate the corporate or brand name into the public consciousness so that its very mention will unleash feelings of well-being, trust and confidence causing customers to purchase and repurchase as if buying from a well-liked trusted friend. Research shows that even the largest companies with major brands will lose sales if they cease to advertise.

Brands and advertising

Without a strong recognisable brand name a product is no more than a commodity, without advertising there is no recognisable brand name.

(Britvic brand manager)

Awareness and recognition are the most important factors in customer purchase. It is axiomatic that if people are unaware of a company, its products and product benefits then comparisons with the competition cannot happen and purchases will not be made. The development of both the corporate and product brand has become an essential part of the process. The brand name, mark, logo becomes the repository, a shorthand way of communicating all those benefits considered to be important and necessary by the organisation's various target markets. Experience has shown that over a sustained period continuous advertising of the corporate name and/or product name in association with clearly defined and targeted benefits will eventually cause the brand name itself to become identified with those benefits so that the mere mention of the name, as with Coca-Cola, Mercedes, Marlboro or McDonald's, will engender recognition and pleasant feelings amongst customers at both the national and global level. Of course the benefits offered must match up to (or even exceed) customer expectations, otherwise mention of the brand name will have the adverse effect of triggering unpleasant thoughts leading to eventual product and company rejection.

Companies buying brands and other intangible assets will in future be able to put the value on their balance sheets and will be charged against profits gradually instead of making an immediate write-off of goodwill. The Accounting Standards Board has recently published rules to allow companies to regard items such as franchises, licences, newspaper titles and brands as assets if they are bought. If the company and its auditors agree that the asset has indefinite life, it need not be depreciated. It will mean directors having to decide whether brands such as Gordon's Gin, Marmite, Oxo or the Spice Girls have lasting value and can thus be identified as a fixed asset.

The corporate brand

The power of the brand in advertising has been universally accepted at the product/service level for decades but its use and importance at the corporate level has taken longer to reach meaningful fruition in some industries. It is now increasingly recognised that the corporate name, for example Nestlé, can offer the same overarching sense of trust, stability, and consistency anywhere in the world its products are sold. Individual product brands such as KitKat, Shreddies or Nescafé can then be more closely focused to the needs of the individual markets (see Fig. 5.1).

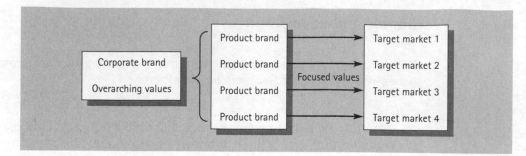

Fig. 5.1 Global corporate brand benefits working with focused product brand benefits

Product brands

Product brands, if advertised in the right manner, can offer functional and symbolic benefits to both intermediaries and end consumer. These 'benefits' will often be at both the conscious and subconscious level of human thinking.

Brand benefits for the retailer

- Adds value to the store image.
- Promotional activity undertaken by brand owner.
- Attracts customers to the store.
- Can offer guaranteed level of sales and profits.
- Aids stock-control and re-ordering.

Brand benefits for the consumer

- Offers consistency and quality of product.
- Minimises risk and guarantees the purchase.
- Speeds up and aids decision-making process.
- Offers emotional as well as functional benefits.

Branding and packaged goods manufacturers: the giants of the advertising industry

It is no wonder then that we find the giants of the packaged branded product companies such as Procter & Gamble, Unilever, Nestlé, Mars, Colgate Palmolive, Coca-Cola, Sara Lee and Johnson & Johnson to be the highest national and global spenders. Research has shown that the number one brand in the packaged goods market makes the highest profit, numbers two and below increasingly less (Profit Impact of Marketing Strategy or PIMS; www.pims-europe.com). Many major supermarkets will now only stock number one and two brands in the market so to be below this will lead to de-listing and loss of sales. To reach and remain at the top of any market demands continuous advertising first to introduce the product, in the case of a new brand, and then to maintain and reinforce the brand name and benefits in the mind of the general consumer.

Packaged goods companies and the importance of brands

Nestlé states that it is the number one brand in 35 different packaged/fast moving goods markets. Sara Lee is now outsourcing most activities, even manufacturing, and concentrating on marketing and advertising committed to its mission 'to build leadership brands in consumer packaged goods markets around the world'. Unilever states that it will 'respond creatively and competitively with branded products and services which raise the quality of life'. Few of us can be unaware of an example list of brands, advertised by the world's leading manufacturers, identified below. These are leaders in their field (some have existed since the turn of the century) and have millions spent on them every year:

- *Procter & Gamble*: Bold, Tide, Dreft, Bounce, Pampers, Tampax, Camay, Max Factor, Head and Shoulders to name but a very few.
- *Unilever*: Persil, Radion, Domestos, PG Tips, Liptons, Flora, Birds Eye, Oxo, Brut, Calvin Klein, Fabergé.
- *Nestlé*: Nescafé, Gold Blend, Perrier, Buitoni, Aero, KitKat, Coffee-mate, Shreddies, Friskies, Smarties, Nesquik, Carnation, Findus and so on.

The growth of own label branded products

Driving the spend on manufacturers' packaged branded goods advertising is the competition inherent in the power relationship along the value chain between the large manufacturers such as Procter & Gamble, Unilever and Nestlé and the large retailers such as Tesco and Sainsbury in the UK and Walmart and Sears in the US. Retailers have utilised the power of advertising so successfully that many 'own label' branded products have now achieved a status, in the minds of the consumer, once only accorded to manufacturers' brands. Over 35 per cent of all packaged goods sold in the UK are retailer own label brands and the producers know that they must spend and advertise if they are to maintain brand attraction with the consumer and so demand shelf space from the retailer.

Levels of industry spend

There is more money wasted in advertising by under-spending than by overspending. Years ago someone said that under-spending is like buying a ticket half-way to Europe. You've spent your money but you never get there.

(Morris Hite)

The industries that spend the most on advertising are retail, motoring, financial services, food and general office services. Table 5.3 shows a comparison between the US and UK dollar spend in 1997. It can be seen, as would be expected, that the US dwarfs the UK spend across all industries. Problems arise, however, when trying to compare one country with another in that different statistical methods for collection and categorisation are often used and care should be taken in assuming that that the comparisons are legitimate. This is especially problematic when looking at statistics from emerging countries.

Table 5.3 UK and US levels of advertising spending

Top ten industries UK (1997)	$m	Top ten industries USA (1997)	$m
Retail	1.998	Motoring	12.873
Motoring	1.502	Retail	10.860
Financial	1.198	Business and customer services	9.038
Office automation	.973	Entertainment and amusements	5.889
Food	.916	Food	4.194
Cosmetics and toiletries	.673	Drugs and remedies	3.981
Leisure equipment	.646	Cosmetics and toiletries	3.694
Travel, holiday and transport	.604	Travel, hotels and resorts	2.836
Mail order	.602	Computers and office equipment	2.332
Publishing	.518	Direct response companies	1.880

Source: Advertising Age

Retail

Retail, motoring, financial services, business services, leisure, food, cosmetics and toiletries account for the lion's share of advertising in both the UK and the USA reflecting their importance to the respective economies. Selling directly to millions of customers, in competition with hundreds of other retailers, demands a heavy communication spend in the main media. Retail advertising will include both the advertising spend of the large retailers (Sainsbury, Tesco, Dixons, Kingfisher etc. in the UK and Wal-Mart, Sears, McDonald's, Staples etc. in the US) and a large amount contributed by the manufacturers in joint promotion.

Motoring

The mighty car manufacturers such as Toyota, Peugeot-Citroën, Volkswagen, General Motors, Ford Motor Co., Renault, Fiat, and BMW, are heavy spenders in an oversupplied and highly competitive global market. With the development and sharing of technology and the relatively level playing field with regard to cost and efficiency comparisons between one car giant and another, it can be argued that very little functional difference now really exits between one make and another. This leads us to the supposition that it is advertising and the benefits thought to be inherent in the brand name that leads to the choice to purchase one model rather than another. This argument can be reinforced by research that shows that in many cases customers buy automobiles for emotional and symbolic reasons such as feeling good, sexual and snob attraction, rather than for functional reasons such as the need to get from 'a' to 'b', petrol consumption or the thickness of the steel used in construction.

Financial services

There has been a big growth in advertising spend in the financial services sector in the UK, as deregulation and privatisation have opened up the markets to many more companies, banks, building societies, insurance companies, leading to many more, complex, product offerings including private pensions, personal savings schemes and insurance. Customer contact methods are also changing, moving from indirect to direct channels. More competition, complex products that need explaining and direct selling explain this growth in advertising.

Other areas

Other large spending areas such as cosmetics and toiletries, leisure, travel and mail order, all reflect the changing pattern of consumer demand in affluent and market-led societies.

Big spending governments

Governments will be big advertising spenders when information needs to be imparted to the mass of the population over a relatively short period. The privatisation, in the UK, of erstwhile public companies such as British Airways, British Telecom, British Steel and the utility companies, as well as public service campaigns for such concerns as AIDS awareness, road safety and cigarette dangers, have led to enormous amounts of government spending on advertising in the 1980s and 1990s.

Factors influencing levels of advertising spending in different sectors

There will be more advertising in some sectors than others because of the following factors:

- Consumer markets demand a wider and deeper communications strategy than business to business.
- Market growth will induce major players to seek to gain the lion's share.
- Competition; those not advertising will risk losing market share to others.
- Over-supply, leading to the need to fight competition and encourage customers to buy more.
- Importance of branding; premium products must maintain brand values.
- New, high-tech, complex products need explaining to the customer.
- Changing distribution channels demand heavier advertising spend.
- Changing demands in modern market economies moving from manufacture to service industries.

Industry spending on a global scale

Research in China, Malaysia, Indonesia and Korea has shown that (despite the downturn in economic activity at the time of writing) widely advertised, well-known globally branded products are wanted often in preference to local products whether branded or non-branded. This knowledge has led to a scramble by the major players to spend a fortune on advertising on corporate and product brands that will reach billions of consumers around the world. Critical to global advertising is the availability of global media and the use of television, with its all-pervasive reach, is in the highest demand especially when coverage includes world events such as the football World Cup, the Olympics and Grand Prix motor racing.

The 1998 football World Cup was broadcast to 195 countries, a possible audience of over 3.5 billion. It is estimated that on average each match was watched by as many 500 million viewers. Twelve official sponsors took part, paying up to £20 million for the privilege of advertising corporate brands and products on TV around the world. Olympic sponsorship for Sydney 2000 will be even higher with advertisers offering up to £40 million for the rights to be associated with the event. This is almost double the amount that was paid by a large sponsor in the last Olympic Games at Atlanta and dwarfs the £3 million paid at the Los Angeles games. A spokesperson for the organising committee said that he expected the eventual revenue to reach $1.5 billion. Companies and brands involved are giant advertisers such as Adidas, Snickers, Coca-Cola, McDonald's, Fuji Films and Gillette. It could be argued that the resultant exposure must surely be cost-effective – otherwise many of the most successful companies in the world would have to be regarded as having unsound advertising strategies.

Companies will undertake global advertising for the following reasons:

- establishing and maintaining consistent corporate and product brand image with customers wherever they might be;
- using the brand image to stretch across countries, industries, companies and product categories;
- combating intense global vertical and horizontal competition between major players;
- reinforcing market share in a fiercely competitive market;
- fighting oversupply, especially in a mature market;
- the opening up of new global markets driving companies to gain market share and competitive advantage before others move in.

Problems with global advertising

The following factors must be considered when advertising globally:

- markets and audiences differ culturally from country to country;
- media ownership and usage differ from country to country;
- fluctuating exchange rates can play havoc with budgets;
- laws and regulations will vary;
- research, measurement and control mechanisms can be suspect.

Advertising is big business

Overall, advertising is big business of staggering dimensions. Every year, hundreds of billions of pounds, dollars, Yen, Marks, etc. are spent worldwide by advertisers with media owners wanting to communicate some form of benefit message to target stakeholders. In the UK this is estimated to have been nearly $19 billion in 1998; in the US, a phenomenal $112.4 billion (see Table 5.4) – and these figures are increasing in real terms every year.

Table 5.4 Ad spend (estimates for 1998) by country (TV, newspapers, magazines, radio, outdoor, cinema)

		Billions	Population (millions)
1.	US	$112.4	(268.0)
2.	Japan	$37.9	(125.8)
3.	Germany	$22.3	(82.0)
4.	UK	$18.9	(59.1)
5.	France	$10.6	(58.4)
6.	Brazil	$10.1	(165.0)
7.	Italy	$7.2	(57.3)
8.	Spain	$5.2	(39.3)
9.	Australia	$5.1	(18.7)
10.	Canada	$4.9	(30.6)
11.	China	$4.8	(1220.0)
12.	Mexico	$4.0	(97.5)

Source: Advertising Age

Value for money

With this amount of money involved the overriding concern on the part of the advertisers is overall value for money. This concern must drive the whole process and marketing and advertising managers will want to know if the amount of money being spent on a series of adverts in a particular medium are cost-effective in reaching and communicating benefit messages to the company's target customers and eventually selling more products or services. Advertising managers' jobs can stand or fall on the results of a particular campaign and they will be desperate to know what methods are the most effective and which are the least effective – preferably having access to this information before, rather than after, spending millions of pounds on a campaign.

Organisations' reasons for advertising

Although industries and organisations might have different needs and priorities in spending vast amounts of money on advertising the basic concepts driving individual advertisers are simple. They are:

- to inform and convince customers about unique benefits (both functional and symbolic) inherent in corporate and product brands.
- to persuade customers to purchase and repurchase;
- to build, reinforce and maintain customer loyalty;
- to fight competition and the growing strength of own label brands.

The relationship between advertisers and media owners

There are some companies that undertake very little advertising and are reliant on widespread reputation and word of mouth for continuous sales. With small companies this may be because they cannot afford advertising budgets; larger companies may feel it is not cost-effective and/or such is their image that there is not the need to spend large amounts of money keeping the corporate name and brands in the forefront of advertising. Marks & Spencer, often seen as the number one retailer in the UK, has been seen as an example of a leading company that has little or no need to advertise in a major way to keep its name in front of the public. This example, however, tended to be the exception rather than the rule and most organisations must advertise in some form or other to continually sell products and survive. Even M&S is now advertising through newspapers, magazines and direct marketing as it enters new markets, competition increases and the economy begins to falter.

Owners and buyers in conflict

In some respects advertisers can be seen to be in conflict with media owners. The media owners control the conduit from advertisers through to end customer and would like to dictate terms of access to their audience/readership. There is also the temptation to want to exaggerate the size and quality of their putative readership because in doing this they hope to create greater value for the potential advertiser and so be able to charge a higher price whilst the advertiser wants to communicate to his or her customer in the most effective and cost-effective manner. Discontented with the service they were obtaining from media owners, advertising companies around the world have instituted their own member organisations, getting together in the hope of bringing more objectivity to advertising.

An example of an organisation set up to promote the interests of the advertisers is the Incorporated Society of British Advertisers (ISBA; www.isba.org.uk) in the UK. It is a non-profitmaking organisation, originally founded in 1900 by a group of advertisers getting together to protect themselves from exploitation by unscrupulous media owners who had developed a tendency to exaggerate the circulation of their newspapers with the obvious intention of charging more for what, in many cases, turned out to be a smaller than declared readership. It took the ISBA until 1931 to resolve the problem and put some semblance of order into the figures with the establishment of the now world respected Audit Bureau of Circulation (www.abc.org.uk). The ABC acts as an independent auditing body measuring and confirming the circulation and readership figures of over 3000 magazines and newspaper publications worldwide. Similar auditing bodies now exist for all media forms (the ABC has recently started to officially audit media Internet web sites, the Electronic Telegraph www.Telegraph.co.uk being the first site in the UK) and no self-respecting advertiser will consider a medium unless it has some independent measure of reach and customer involvement.

Certainty of results

In response to ever growing media competition and advertiser concern, media owners seek to offer ever greater certainty and degrees of audience and readership measurement, clearly attempting to spell out how many people buy/watch/listen to/read their media offering. They will also detail when and where this happens, as well as providing intricate demographic, economic and social detail about possible audiences. For example, Postar (Poster Audience Research), set up by the outdoor poster industry, offers prospective media buyers as much evidence as possible about the certainty of their advert being seen by their target market over the period of the advertising campaign. Every poster site has as many as 50 audience variables that have been identified and measured to prove to the potential advertiser that the site will work for them in a more effective way than other available media.

What advertisers want from the media

What advertisers want from the main media will vary depending on the industry, type and size of the organisation and the products and services it offers. The following will apply to a lesser or greater extent depending on these factors.

- A cost-effective way to send benefit messages that will reach clearly defined target audiences.
- Independently audited readership and viewer figures.
- A flexible medium that can be adapted to meet the listening, viewing or reading needs of different customer types.
- A medium beloved by its audience so that association will enhance and add value to the product or service.
- A choice of media that will move the customer from unawareness, through awareness, to interest and to actual purchase.
- A choice of options covering a range of markets from extensive through to concentrated and from local through to national, international and even global.
- A medium where research can be undertaken and proof of effectiveness unequivocally obtained, preferably judged by a trusted, independent body.
- Competitive and realistic pricing.
- Above all they want good advice and assistance based on long-term mutual needs.

What the media owners want from the advertisers

- Consistent advertising business.
- Clear product positioning statements and customer profiles.
- Flexibility in terms of advert timing and placement.
- Early payment.

In-house or out-of-house advertising

Many manufacturers secretly question whether advertising really sells their product, but are vaguely afraid that their competitors might steal a march on them if they stopped.

(David Ogilvy)

Most advertisers do not have to be convinced about the efficacy of the advertising process but they do have to be convinced about the best method to use and whether to undertake it themselves or to bring in outside advertising experts. Whilst many large advertisers opt to buy expertise in and hire independent advertising agencies some organisations might decide to take on the task themselves.

The smaller company

A smaller business, for example an independent electrical retailer, might do this on an *ad hoc* basis, putting an advert in the local paper running over three weeks, constructed with the help and advice of the medium owner staff, whilst another company, if large enough and if advertising on a frequent and continuous basis, might consider installing its own internal in-house agency. In the case of the smaller company the meagre amount of advertising needed and the cost of using an agency might make any method other than using media owner staff appear prohibitive. Of course this means that the smaller company must rely on the integrity of the media owner not to sell the wrong product or to oversell the right one. It could be argued, as with any relationship, that it would not be in the long-term interest of the media owner to do this as dissatisfaction would soon spread amongst other small businesses and its reputation would suffer.

The larger company

Many larger companies prefer to develop an in-house agency capability, and take on the advertising task themselves. This might be on both a national and international scale. There are many reasons why a company might want to develop its own advertising capability, including the following:

- To maintain control over all advertising functions.
- To focus completely on its own needs and objectives.
- To enable the staff to develop a more thorough understanding of products and service benefits and the demands of the industry it operates in.
- An intimate feel for company market strengths historically developed over the years can enable in-house staff to create benefit messages finely honed to meet the particular needs of its customers. This intimate oneness with company and brands is especially important where the products and services offered are technical or unique in nature and so demand particular and specialised knowledge.
- Costs may also be contained as an in-house agency will not have to make a profit on any of its activities.

Advertising agencies will want to argue that a company's best interest will be achieved by using the services of the professional. These arguments are discussed in more detail in the next chapter.

The role of the purchasing manager

It is becoming increasingly common for purchasing managers to get involved in the process of buying advertising especially if the company is not large enough to have its own marketing or advertising department. Negotiations might be with either the advertising agency or with the media owners direct. As most purchasing managers will probably have limited knowledge of the advertising industry care must be taken with projects undertaken and contracts signed. In the UK the advertisers (ISBA), the advertising agencies (IPA) and the purchasers (Chartered Institute of Purchase and Supply, CIPS) have been examining and negotiating fair and equitable ways of working together.

The in-house advertising department

An in-house advertising department can take many different forms depending on the size and type of organisation, its markets and the importance it attaches to corporate and brand communications. It might play a minor tactical role, producing leaflets, posters, a company magazine, and small advertisements for the local paper or it might play a more strategic role with directorship level responsibilities for all media planning.

Centralised versus decentralised advertising departments

The global organisation will have the option of setting up an advertising department with a structure that is centralised, decentralised, or a combination of the two. Size will be a consideration in deciding between these options, but in general the advantages and disadvantages of the two approaches mirror one another.

With a centralised department, costs are controlled through one central point, standards can be more easily maintained, a standardised approach can allow savings through economies of scale, and advertising campaigns can be bigger and grander.

A decentralised department allows for local audience preferences to be taken into account: local resources, people, media, finance, can more readily be optimised. Decentralisation encourages divisional advertising managers to use their own initiative in creating meaningful campaigns.

Some large companies will use a combination of the two approaches, attempting to obtain the best from both. Strategic concerns such as budgets, corporate and product value advertising can be controlled centrally, whilst individual advertising managers are allowed the freedom to exploit local partialities and predilections.

The advertising manager

The head of the in-house advertising department is the advertising manager (or advertising director) who reports to the marketing manager (or marketing director) but the situation will vary depending on the size of the company, the type of industry and the predisposition of senior management. In a small company the marketing person might cover all advertising activity whilst in a larger one the marketing and advertising functions will be separate. Advertising managers in larger departments will need to discuss, co-ordinate activity and work with others within the marketing department, including brand managers and category managers as well as research and other marketing personnel. The in-house advertising manager will undertake the tasks of auditing, planning and forecasting, creating and producing advertisements, organising and co-ordinating, directing, administrating, controlling and evaluating.

Auditing involves discussing and analysing the current situation with others including marketing, brand and brand category managers, research and finance colleagues, outside media personnel etc.

Planning and forecasting involve setting objectives, evaluating and developing alternative strategies, agreeing budgets with both senior and junior management, agreeing responsibilities and putting in monitoring and control mechanisms.

Overall strategy having been agreed, advertisements are created and produced. Working with others within the advertising department (creative, art, photography, producer etc.) relevant benefit messages are constructed (all discussed later in more detail) to match the identified target market and selected media chosen.

The advertising manager will organise and co-ordinate the whole process working both within and without the company. This will entail talking with all members in the advertising department, colleagues in the marketing, production, finance, admin. department as well as outside media organisations. Campaigns will only work if all members work together as a team and the advertising manager will need to have good people management and leadership skills in communicating, motivating, decision making, delegating and empowering if effective and efficient synergy is to be created.

Last but not least the advertising manager must oversee and manage the advertising campaign making certain that what he or she wants to happen will happen. This will include a vast array of tasks including obtaining both management and legal approval, checking bills and seeing that they are paid, and monitoring, controlling and ensuring that ads run as planned, and then evaluating and presenting the end results.

CONCLUSION

Advertising is big business, contributing billions of pounds to the gross domestic product of countries around the world. Most industries will advertise at some time or another both at the collective and individual organisational level. By far the biggest amount of spend is at the individual level as companies spend to promote both corporate and product/brand portfolio benefits to gain competitive advantage. More money is spent in consumer markets than in business to business because of the different nature of each market. Some organisations will spend more than others, reflecting a multitude of needs including competition, market growth, product type and audience needs. Developments in information and media technology now enable advertisers to reach markets on an international scale and giant corporations now market and advertise brands around the world contributing to the interdependence and interactivity of the global economy. Because of the amount of money being spent advertisers demand more effectiveness from the media owners and are not willing to pay money for advertising campaigns that cannot be measured and controlled in a meaningful way. Because of the level of knowledge and skill now needed in setting up and implementing advertising campaigns companies must think very carefully whether to undertake the task themselves or to out-source to a professional advertising agency.

CASE STUDY

FT

Campaign hots up for more TV commercials

The campaign for more advertising on commercial television is hotting up as representatives of some of the UK's largest consumer companies prepare to lobby politicians and civil servants for a relaxation of the rules. But the organisation representing the advertisers runs the risk of losing the support of the advertising agencies' trade association as it steps up the pressure. Both organisations – the Incorporated Society of British Advertisers (www.isba.org) and the Institute of Practitioners in Advertising (www.ipa.co.uk) – say the costs of buying advertising air-time have increased too much over the past few years, but there are signs of a difference of emphasis between them on how the issue should be resolved. The ISBA has taken the more hawkish line in arguing that the restrictions on time allowed for advertising should be relaxed to increase the supply of air-time and so reduce inflationary pressures. It also seeks longer-term changes to help ITV win audiences back from the BBC, and to give advertisers a greater voice in decisions affecting TV advertising. It has written to members, asking for support in taking its argument to Westminster.

Last year the IPA backed the ISBA proposal (which was rejected) to the Independent Television Commission (www.itc.org), the broadcasting watchdog, for a phased increase up to the nine minutes of advertising an hour allowed elsewhere in the European Union. But now, in contrast to the ISBA's increasing pressure for more minutes of advertising, the IPA is focusing on encouraging ITV's efforts to increase the audiences for its programmes. Graham Hinton, president of the IPA, says: 'We start from the point of view that we want a successful commercial sector in broadcasting. We support what Richard Eyre, ITV's chief executive, is trying to do but it is going to take time to get it right.'

The IPA also wants research on whether extra minutes of advertising cut the effectiveness of the commercials shown. Some advertising executives are concerned that more 'clutter' on television will lessen the impact of advertisements. On average during a day there can be no more than seven minutes of advertising an hour. Within this total, broadcasters can transfer minutes between hours, up to a limit of twelve minutes in any one clock hour. Whatever the different approaches of the ISBA and the IPA to combating media inflation, there is no doubting the strength of feeling among some of the ISBA's highest-spending members. At the ISBA's annual policy conference last month Michael Heber, chairman of Unilever's advertising committee, said ITV should be ashamed of its airtime inflation rate of more than 40 per cent over five years. Along with BT, Procter & Gamble, Kellogg and Ford, Unilever is one of the UK's biggest advertisers: together they account for more than £450m a year of spending on television advertisements.

Source: Alison Smith, *Financial Times*, 15 April 1998. Used with permission.

Case study questions

1. How closely do you think that advertisers and media owners should work together in discussing and overcoming problems?
2. What do you think is causing advertising cost inflation through the TV medium? Do you think that the demand for more advertising time is realistic? Is it the only answer? How might the media owner justify the increase?

CHAPTER QUESTIONS

1. Discuss the reasons why one industry might use more advertising than another.
2. What problems arise when advertising on a global scale? Are some global regions more difficult than others?
3. Discuss the relationship between the advertiser and the media owners. Where are the areas for possible conflict?
4. Why might an organisation choose to take its advertising in-house? What are the possible pitfalls?
5. How might media changes benefit the smaller advertiser? Conversely, will the same changes have a detrimental affect on the larger advertiser?

REFERENCES

Advertising Age (www.adage.com)

Audit Bureau of Circulation (ABC) (www.abc.org.uk)

Chartered Institute of Purchase and Supply (CIPS) (www.CIPS.org.uk)

Hite, M. (1988) *Morris Hite's Methods for Winning the Ad Game,* E-Heart Press, Texas.

Incorporated Society of British Advertisers (ISBA) (www.isba.org.uk)

Institute of Practitioners in Advertising (www.ipa.co.uk)

Nestlé (www.nestle.com)

Ogilvy, D. (1985), *Ogilvy on Advertising,* Vintage Books, New York.

Procter & Gamble (www.pg.com)

Profit Impact of Marketing Strategy (PIMS) (www.pims-europe.com)

Unilever (www.unilever.com)

White, E.G. (1936), US author and editor, quoted in Andrews, R., *The Columbia Dictionary of Quotations* (1993), Columbia University Press, New York.

FURTHER READING

Aaker, D. (1991) *Managing Brand Equity, Capitalising on the value of a Brand Name,* Free Press, New York, pp.78–84.

Chernatony, L. de and McDonald, M. (1992) *Creating Powerful Brands,* Butterworth-Heinemann, London.

Corstjens, J. and Corstjens, M. (1996) *Store Wars,* J. Wiley, Chichester, UK.

Ind, N. (1993), *Great Advertising Campaigns,* Kogan Page, London.

6 The advertising agency

OBJECTIVES

By the end of this chapter the reader should be able to:

1. Identify the benefits for the advertiser of using an advertising agency.

2. Evaluate the role of the advertising agency in the relationship between the advertiser and the media owners.

3. Evaluate the various activities that agencies might undertake for their clients.

INTRODUCTION

The first advertising agencies were set up at the beginning of the nineteenth century and came into being by acting as intermediaries between, on the one hand, organisations such as manufacturers, retailers and government departments, wanting to sell products or services or to recruit staff or military personnel, and, on the other hand, newspaper owners and pamphlet and leaflet printers with wide readership and advertising space available to make extra money. Originally those wishing to advertise would approach these media owners directly and the media owners wishing to sell advertising space would employ sales people to tout around for business. As with any business opening it didn't take long for wise entrepreneurs (probably original newspaper 'space' salesmen) to see opportunities to set up as middlemen, collecting advertising from groups of companies, with the promise of a value-for-money service, and then approach the newspaper and pamphlet owners with tempting bulk advertising business in return for some kind of discount.

As technology developed these 'freelance' agents, to gain competitive advantage, began to widen the services offered and give help and advice to clients about new print and colour techniques and creating the advertisement itself. After the first world war agency services offered took off, particularly in the US, with the mass production and consequent spread of newspaper ownership and readership making it increasingly unrealistic for national companies to sort out their own advertising needs. More opportunities arose with the coming of radio and films demanding new and different advertising techniques and advertising skills and many of the great advertising agencies and advertising men were born and grew to prominence during this period. After the second world war and into the 1950s and 1960s TV evolved and developed into an all-pervasive medium and, again, new advertising techniques were demanded, leading to the setting up of modern agencies that still exist today. The spread of the World Wide Web and the advertising problems and questions it is throwing up provide challenges and opportunities for both existing and new advertising agencies.

Why use an agency?

Some companies will undertake all advertising and promotional activity in-house (as discussed in the preceding chapter) but this tends to be the exception rather than the rule and most organisations will prefer to use the services of an outside agency.

In the drive for ever greater efficiency all corporate functions are now under the spotlight as managers look for ways to gain strategic global competitive advantage and better ways of running the business. For many companies out-sourcing functions as disparate as distribution, production, customer complaints, database and payroll management seems to be a viable option, bringing the specialist into highly technical areas and allowing managers to concentrate on what it is the company is good at whether this be retailing, manufacturing, servicing or marketing. It can be argued that market communications falls in this category with the advertising agency offering its specialised skills.

Advertising is a highly skilled business: get it right and sales will rocket; get it wrong and millions of pounds can be lost and companies destroyed. There are so many different media forms – TV, radio, magazines, newspapers, outdoor sites, cinema, the Internet – and so many different functions to perform – audience research, media selection, media buying, media planning, advertisement design, TV production – that the task can seem much too daunting for anyone other than an expert. An agency with many clients will also be able to buy large amounts of advertising space from the media owners, obtaining bulk discounts which can then be passed on in terms of lower prices.

An agency will employ skilled staff in all relevant areas and allocate the client an account manager who will organise and co-ordinate the whole advertising campaign, moving from initial customer research through message development, media selection, advert implementation, measurement and control. The advertising agency will talk through with the client the message that they want to communicate (often harder than it may seem), translate this into clear objectives, then create and turn it into an advertisement that will be seen on TV, on the radio, in the newspaper, in a magazine or on a billboard and acted upon by the relevant target audience.

The agency staff, being detached, can look objectively and dispassionately at the client message from the customer's point of view. To be objective in this way can be difficult for the advertiser's staff because of preconceived ideas, often inaccurate, about corporate image, brand values and consumer needs.

The agency will be able to buy in the best specialised skills, if not available in-house, from known contacts built up over the years, adapting the campaign to exactly meet the needs of the client and the brand.

Overall a good agency should have the ability to put together and manage an integrated strategic programme that will achieve more value for money, more sales, more profit than could be achieved without their assistance.

To summarise, reasons for using an agency are

- information, experience, knowledge and expertise
- innovation and creativity skills
- expert contacts around the world
- objective, detached approach
- experts in all areas
- overall value for money.

The advertising agency

Advertising agencies, like advertisers, come in all shapes and sizes and can vary enormously in size from a single owner or partnership to a globe-spanning operation employing a staff of thousands. The 1980s and early 1990s brought a rash of acquisitions and mergers across the world as media companies looked strategically towards global markets, producing international media giants such as Omnicom Group (www.omnicomny.com), based in New York, with a gross income in 1997 of over $4 billion, and WPP Group (www.wpp.com), based in London and with a gross income of over $3.6 billion. The majority, however, are small agencies employing a handful of specialists and many stay small by contracting out to self-employed agents and buying in the very best suppliers in the necessary areas as and when a client project demands it. This saves them having to employ experts such as writers, artists, designers or media production or legal specialists on a permanent basis – instead they pay only for such services as and when needed. Even the bigger agencies might have difficulty in employing experts in every field because of the cost involved and will buy in the necessary skills from a well-known pool of experts when they are required.

Top advertising agencies are listed in Tables 6.1 and 6.2

Table 6.1 Top ten UK advertising agencies (1997)

Rank	Agency	£ millions
1.	Abbott Mead Vickers BBDO	355.86
2.	Ogilvy & Mather	271.08
3.	Saatchi & Saatchi	260.26
4.	J. Walter Thompson (London)	252.64
5.	BMP DDB	246.55
6.	Grey	214.86
7	Bates Dorland	203.93
8.	M&C Saatchi	194.73
9.	Publicis	192.23
10.	McCann-Erickson (London)	182.81

Source: Reproduced from an article in the 6 March 1998 issue of *Campaign*, with the permission of the copyright owner, Haymarket Business Publications Limited.

Table 6.2 Five worldwide advertising agencies (worldwide gross income 1997)

		$ millions
1. Omnicom Group	New York	4,154.3
2. WPP Group	London	3,646.6
3. Interpublic Group	New York	3,384.5
4. Dentsu	Tokyo	1,987.8
5. Young & Rubican	New York	1,497.9

Source: Advertising Age

In addition to size agencies will vary in the type of service or speciality that they will offer. Depending on the need advertisers can hire a full service, limited service, or a specialised agency.

Full service agencies

A full service agency, as the name suggests, is capable of executing the whole project for the client by providing all the services necessary to research, develop, implement and measure the result of the advertising campaign. The very many services that an all-service agency can offer has expanded over time, taking in more and more services. Many of these services may seem to be outside the boundaries of what we might understand to be the traditional role of the advertising agency and will include the following (all of which can be obtained individually from a limited service agency).

Services offered by an all-service agency

- **Marketing research** will be offered on markets, competition, consumers, media, brands, corporate communications, policy research, feedback, measurement and control before, during and after campaigns. Database and relationship marketing programmes can also be implemented and monitored.
- **Message construction and implementation:** creative messages will need to be thought through, designed, drawn, photographed, films produced, tested and developed in a form that matches the demands of the chosen medium. A traditional area for agencies.
- **Media advertising:** constructing, planning, production, buying and placing, across newspapers, magazines, directories, TV, radio, cinema, video, posters and now the Internet.
- **Public relations:** corporate image, consumer affairs, lobbying, management counselling, management training, crisis management, media, government, pressure group, staff relations.
- **Publicity:** press relations, news story bulletins.
- **Exhibitions and trade shows:** planning, managing, researching and staffing.
- **Sales promotions:** design and production, merchandising, loyalty cards, competitions, vouchers etc.
- **Direct marketing:** direct mail, direct selling, catalogues, sales brochures, leaflets.
- **Sponsorship:** selection, negotiations, planning, implementation and control.
- **Legal:** advice and insurance.
- **Management consultancy:** strategic communication planning and co-ordination; general consultancy.

Advantages and disadvantages of an all-service agency

Advantages

- The all-purpose agency will manage, plan and integrate every task facilitating overall synergy. Probably a 'must' when dealing on a global scale.
- 'One-stop shopping' saves client time, money and related resources.
- The all-service agency will have knowledge of the best specialised agencies to buy in and the most propitious terms and conditions.
- Legal pitfalls can be avoided (crucial after the Hoover sales promotion holiday fiasco).
- Will help client avoid catastrophic mistakes, especially if involving a high-value brand.

Disadvantages

- Can be expensive compared to self-management on the part of the client.
- Loss of control and flexibility.

Limited service agencies

A limited service agency will offer, as the name suggests, individual and selective advertising services. This allows the advertiser to buy the services it needs on an 'à la carte' basis, selecting some services from one agency and other services from another. This might be because of a reputation that different agencies have for certain services or because the advertiser might want to carry out some of the activities itself whilst contracting the agency to carry out other, more difficult and/or specialised activities. Almost all of the services identified above can be obtained individually through a limited services agency. Two examples of limited service agencies are the 'creative boutique' and the media-buying specialist.

Creative boutiques

The so-called 'creative boutique' is a good example of this type of limited service agency. It is an advertising agency that offers innovative, creative advertising concepts and messages without becoming involved in other areas such as research, media planning and media buying. It is often claimed that the most important factor about an advertisement is the idea behind the message. If the advert is to be seen and then acted upon it must have an impact on the target audience. This becomes exceedingly difficult as competition increases and the customer becomes ever more bored and defensive against commercial communications. To overcome this problem advertisers are always looking for original and exciting new ideas that will break through customer ennui and get their message noticed. The creative boutique is often highly valued because it can offer the 'great idea' at the heart of an advert.

Media buying and planning

The big growth in limited services agencies has been in media buying and this is not so surprising considering the growth in media complexity, media choice available and options within the individual media. A media-buying service agency will offer specialised services buying space in newspapers and magazines and air-time on TV and radio, selecting the particular medium, placing the ads and handling the media billing. They will often get involved in the whole media planning process both at the strategic and tactical level. Because they buy for many different clients, they are aware of current prices and can gain bulk buying economies. Usually all media prices are open to some form of seasonal, time, quantity and placement discounts. The skilled media buyer should be able to negotiate better terms with the media owners and so offer lower prices to the advertisers that use them.

Advantages and disadvantages of limited services agencies

Advantages

- Different agencies offer expert skills in specialised areas.
- Focused approach allows more client control.
- Client can pick and choose gaining the best agency from each discipline.
- Client can save money buying in some services and undertaking others themselves.

Disadvantages

- There is an advertisers' opportunity cost in having to manage the overall advertising campaign.
- Lack of knowledge about the marketplace can lead to expensive choice mistakes.

Specialised agencies

Some agencies have grown by identifying particular needs within the market which demand a more specialised approach. For example an agency may choose to concentrate on business to business, financial, leisure, educational services, IT and computer software, charity work or in the government and public sector. There are also agencies that specialise in particular kinds of audiences including ethnic minorities, women, over 50s, children, and so on. This will no doubt relate to the skills and past experience of the people setting up the agency, the expert consultant advice they are able to give being the USP they will use to encourage contracts. These agencies generally perform all the same services as an all-service agency but in a specialised field. Even companies that use an all-service agency may at times use a specialised agency if they want to reach a particular group of people buying in an esoteric area.

In-house facilities versus outside agencies

Why use an in-house facility?

- Maintain control of all activity.
- Staff can develop intimate knowledge of company and customer needs.
- Staff remain focused on company objectives.
- Cut out the agency costs.
- Build a personal relationship with media owners.

Why use an outside agency?

- Use specialists with a range of advertising skills and knowledge.
- Outside agency able to take an objective, detached approach to company problems.
- Take advantage of agency economies of scale.
- Costs of employing own specialist staff.

How agencies are paid

Experience has taught me that advertisers get the best results when they pay their agency a flat fee ... It is too unrealistic to expect your agency to be impartial when its vested interest lies wholly in the direction of increasing your commissionable advertising.

(David Ogilvy)

Agency payment has changed in manner since the beginning of the century when the advertising agency first came into being. They were originally set up by erstwhile newspaper and magazine employees who noticed the need for an intermediary to represent the naive advertiser in dealings with the more powerful owners of newspapers. Many worked for the newspaper on a commission-only basis, usually 15 per cent, so the more advertising space they sold the more money they earned. As part of the package they would often create, design and write the advert for the client as well as placing it in a relevant newspaper. They would charge the advertiser the normal price, but pay the media owners the discounted amount and pocket the difference.

It was this **commission system** of payment that became the traditional way that advertising agencies were reimbursed. The advantage in this was that advertisers obtained free help, consultation and advice, the media owners gained extra business with less effort (albeit at a reduced price) and the agencies grew in size with the incentive to keep costs at a minimum so as to make more profit from the commission received. With the advent of other media this method of payment spread, becoming known as 'above the line' payment and solidly associated with the mix of TV, print, radio, cinema and outdoor media.

Over the years, however, this commission system of payment has gradually been worn away as advertisers, and to a certain extent agencies, began to recognise and experience its many shortcomings. Some of the larger advertisers, seeking continuously to reduce costs and with millions to spend a year, moved their advertising in-house, dealing direct with the media owners and pocketing the extra 15 per cent rather than giving it to an intermediary. Others, aware of the amount of competition in the marketplace causing rivalry for their business, began to use their muscle and chip away at the 15 per cent. Many argued, from a position of strength it must be said, that to pay 15 per cent per cent on £250 000 and 15 per cent on £50 million was not comparable in term of the amount of agency work that this would involve. It is now often the case that 15 per cent commission will be paid up to a certain amount of billings (e.g. £1 million) and then less, for example 10 per cent, above this. The amount might then be reduced even further the higher the amount of money involved. Others, in true market competition fashion, played one agency off against another, reducing the amount of commission taken by the agency to 12.5 per cent and then 10 per cent, and in some cases even lower, pocketing the difference between this and the 15 per cent given by the media owners.

Other advertisers prefer to negotiate a one-off straightforward **contract price** for the period on the campaign, with some even wanting to use incentives to tie payment to results achieved. These performance-based incentives might be linked to the amount of extra discount obtained from the media owner, the time taken to put the campaign together, the extra exposure or sales achieved and the general quality of the overall campaign. The problem with this type of incentive-based performance indicator, however, is that it is not always possible to prove a direct link between effort and outcome. For example sales might rise, or fall, because of factors such as economic volatility, competitive activity, or lack of stock in the showroom, all of which are way beyond the compass of the agency. It should also be noted that the best advertising in the world cannot sell a product that people do not want to buy.

There are advertisers that will ask for a **fixed fee** for each service offered whilst others favour a fee system linked to time sheets and agency hours worked. Some organisations prefer to use a retainer system where a set amount of hours are booked and the agency will work within this remit negotiating more hours if it can be agreed that they are needed. Recent research has shown that less than one-third of all advertisers now pay on the traditional 15 per cent commission basis, choosing instead to opt for one of the very many different methods identified above.

Of course, the agency is bound to be unhappy with any method of payment that eats away at payments and makes it work much harder for less. They argue, with some justification, that they cannot offer the same personal and dedicated service to a client at continually lower prices and that this must eventually reflect on the type of work they are turning out. Others might argue that a reduced fee should mean greater effort and efficiency rather than a reduction in the quality given. In many respects it all boils down to what is fair and workable. Agencies and clients will never be in complete harmony on this issue; it would be surprising if they were. Research has shown that, in the main, agencies prefer commission-based methods, while clients prefer methods based upon satisfactory performance indicators. Ultimately the market law of supply and demand will come into play: the more creative and effective the agency, the better will be its reputation, the more its work will be demanded and so the more it will be able to charge.

Pricing alternatives

- Percentage commission on overall billing.
- Percentage commission reducing at stages on overall billing.
- Fixed fee on overall activity.
- Combination of fixed fee and commission.
- Time-based fee plus costs.

The agency–advertiser relationship

The relationship between a manufacturer and his advertising agency is almost as intimate as the relationship between a patient and his doctor. Make sure that you can live happily with your prospective client before you accept his account.

(David Ogilvy)

If the advertising agency is to act in the most effective way for the advertiser the relationship must be close and trusting. Agency staff can only develop successful campaigns if understanding and knowledge about corporate and brand issues are discussed openly and in a meaningful way. This is especially true when launching new products.

Most companies will stay with the same agency for years feeling safe in the knowledge that an intimate and deep understanding of both corporate and brand needs by agency staff adds synergy to the partnership and enables them to develop adverts that continuously add value to consumer beliefs and attitudes about these brands.

It has often been said that advertising is a 'people business' so it could be considered misleading to speak of clients 'staying with an agency' when in fact they stay because they enjoy a profitable relationship with the people – the boss, the accounts manager, or the creative director, to name but a few – who work within the agency. This is a major reason why when staff leave one agency and set up for themselves they will often take clients with them. When the Saatchi brothers fell out with a few major shareholders a couple of years ago they were able to leave Saatchi & Saatchi and set up another agency almost immediately, taking with them many large clients such as BA and Dixons.

> Top agency Lowe-Howard-Spinks (The Interpublic Group of Companies), with UK billings of £260 million, world billings of $3.7 billion and employing staff of 285, is justifiably proud that clients have stayed with them over the years and boast that out of 26 major clients, such as Whitbread, Vauxhall, Weetabix, Reebok, Olympus, Braun, Tesco and Smirnoff, 15 have been with the company for more than four years.

Why do agencies and clients split up?

Although most client–advertiser relationships go on for decades, we only have to look at the marketing and advertising press to see that advertisers do sometimes change and move their accounts from one agency to another. This change will often involve tens of millions of pounds' worth of business (billings) and can mean the difference between agency success and failure. Reasons for change will include the following:

- Existing agency too entrenched to come up with a new creative approach; important especially when wanting to reposition a brand.
- Need for a change and a new agency will equal new concepts and new ideas.
- Client acquisitions and mergers can bring too many agencies on to the roster and the need to consolidate means that some might have to go.
- Agency acquisitions and mergers can bring competing companies (e.g. Cadbury and Mars) under the same agency and despite the promise of confidentiality ('Chinese' or 'fire' walls) many clients are unhappy and will change agencies.
- Client dissatisfaction with the results of the latest advertising campaign.

A new agency

A new agency would need to understand quickly its new client and assimilate both tangible and intangible corporate and product values, often built over many years through expensive advertising, before developing campaigns. Badly constructed adverts could send out the wrong messages and years of carefully constructed image forming could be damaged or in some cases even destroyed. The new agency will now have the opportunity to establish itself by injecting a fresh, innovative and exciting new approach to company brands.

Selecting an advertising agency

There are many factors that need to be carefully considered when selecting a new agency as it is a strategic decision with long-term implications and mistakes made at this early stage can cause expensive problems later in the relationship. The process involved has sometimes been compared with the care needed when contemplating a marriage as the ensuing relationship, if it is going to work, will demand mutual trust, honesty and the sharing of confidential information. Factors needing to be considered include the reputation of the agency and its present clients.

All agencies will have a reputation and an image acquired through past campaigns completed. Even new agencies will have some form of reputation because of the people starting up the new enterprise. Large agencies such as Saatchi & Saatchi, Bartle Bogle Hegarty (BBH), or Ogilvy & Mather will have a higher profile than others usually because of the clients they have and the work they undertake, Saatchi & Saatchi working with the Conservative party, BBH working with Levi Jeans and Ogilvy & Mather with Nestlé. Other agencies will be smaller and less known but might nevertheless have some good work behind them. One agency might be good on one area and one in another; some agencies will have a reputation for taking a solid traditional, proven conservative approach whilst others might have a reputation for being unconventional, radical and more innovative.

All agencies will have a portfolio of clients and work, both past and present, and these will be indicative of the industries and companies it has worked with and the kinds of problems it has been asked to solve. It might also reflect in a pragmatic way how good it is in particular areas working on the assumption that successful commercial businesses would not employ an agency that could not deliver what it promised. Reinforcing this point would be the length of time they have worked with existing clients. There might also be the possibility of conflict of interest if they already work for a competitor.

It is very simple to obtain examples of existing work on TV, radio, billboards and so on. Factors to consider here would be innovation, creativity, relevance to brands, simplicity/complexity, humour and so on; it must, of course, be borne in mind that the target market must be considered because what might appeal to one audience will not appeal to another.

The process of choosing an agency

Listing agencies

A list of agencies should be compiled from various sources including friends' and colleagues' recommendations (the best method if possible), directories, the Advertising Association (www.adassoc.org.uk) and the Incorporated Society of Practitioners in Advertising (www.ispa.org.uk). It is not a bad idea to select a series of adverts, in any of the media forms, that appeal, find the agencies that created them and add these to the list of companies to be contacted. As much relevant literature (e.g. *Marketing Week, Advertising Age, Campaign, BRAD Advertiser,* and agency lists, the Advertising Agency Register etc.) as possible should be read, and notes made on appropriate points relating to agency activity, in order to get a flavour of the business and what an agency can and cannot do for its clients.

Contacting the agency and eliciting information

When a manageable number of agencies have been selected they can be contacted by phone, fax, letter or e-mail with details of the company's needs and a request that they send an outline of the benefits they might be able to offer, including a portfolio of past campaigns. The replies can then be sifted through and possible candidates identified, probably no more than five or six out of twenty or so contacted.

Personal visit to establish culture

Now the chosen agencies can be contacted again and appointments made to visit. It should be possible at this stage to get a 'feel' about future relationships with agency staff, the culture and the type of agency, and the possible costs and benefits involved.

Establishing criteria for comparisons

Eventually the advertiser will need to know whether the agency understands his or her industry and whether they have expertise and knowledge about the type of company and the particular problems involved. This will be particularly important in more complex and specialised areas such as financial services, charities and government information. Whether the budget is big or small, whether the customers are consumer, business to business or not-for-profit it is essential that the comparison between agencies is done on the same criteria and this should be established before any visits are undertaken.

The agency 'pitch'

When a shortlist of possible agencies has been constructed the client will often ask the agencies, including the one in residence, to 'pitch' for the business. The pitch is quite controversial because the agency time and money involved can run into many thousands of pounds which is irrevocably lost if it fails to secure the contract. There is also the worry that innovative ideas presented at this stage may be purloined by unscrupulous clients and passed off as their own. The prospective client will ask the selected agencies, probably no more than three or four as the process can become unmanageable, to come up with an example of an advertising campaign based around a brand and a theme selected by the advertiser (known as a 'beauty contest'). The process can last three or four weeks beginning with a client brief and ending with a full presentation by agency staff to the client.

Why a free pitch?

'How often have you worked for free?' I asked this question of you as often as I have asked it of myself. When invited to pitch, I'm sure you are aware of the substantial costs and man-hours in interpreting the brief, preparing graphics and story boards, the presentation itself, thank-you letters and follow up calls.

And then, how often have I seen our ideas refused but 'interpreted' by another, on behalf of the client? Am I alone in finding this frustrating? Does no one else consider that, as an industry (and a very 'cool Britannia' industry) we should get a little more reward for our efforts? I have a dream scenario, where every pitch is paid for. This scenario is found in other industries and in our private lives – just ask a dentist or a solicitor to 'pitch' for free! So how about a practice whereby a charge is levied for a pitch? Sufficient to cover costs, this would ensure better quality all round and would benefit clients as well as ourselves. I welcome any thoughts.'

(David Gregory, managing director, Brickwork Marketing Communications, Surrey)

Source: Marketing Business, July/August 1998

Decision

Eventually a decision will have to be made and an agency chosen. Ultimately it is a subjective choice and every agency, regardless of reputation or size, will at some time or other face rejection. There is consolation, however, in the knowledge that agencies have different skills and specialisms appropriate to some companies and products rather than others and rejection today will probably be followed by acceptance tomorrow.

The customer functions of an advertising agency

The various functions within the agency all contribute toward successful client management and are described below.

Account management

The accounts manager (or executive) is the link between the agency and the advertiser and in this role will interpret the needs and the wishes of the advertisers, reconciling them with the reality of the situation and the capabilities of the agency. It is probably the most important function and demands superlative communication and diplomatic skills. It is the accounts manager's job to keep the whole programme moving forward and on schedule. It is a highly pressurised job and there can often be conflict of interest between, on the one hand the account manager having a responsibility to his or her employer and, on the other hand, working on behalf of the client. An accounts manager may work with more than one client at any one time depending on the size of the account.

Planning and co-ordinating

The accounts manager will instigate the product and market research needed, agree the strategy, objectives and the budget with the client and then work with other agency personnel organising and co-ordinating the programme, making sure that it reaches a satisfactory conclusion. He or she will then talk through the results with all concerned, analysing and evaluating, looking for better ways, if necessary, to execute the programme in the future.

The account planner

The account planner is a relatively new position within agencies but nevertheless it is considered to be of the utmost importance. The role and the thinking behind the concept is discussed in the Case Study at the end of this chapter

The creative services department

At the heart of a good advertisement is the creative idea, the innovative concept that first gets the advert noticed, and hopefully talked about, and then motivates the customer to purchase and repurchase the product. Creative services is an umbrella term for a series of tasks linked to the development of an advert. The creative team, described below, is responsible for writing and designing the ads, based on the brief, and implementing and supervising all production activities.

The creative director

The larger company will have a creative director with the responsibility of supervising all the various creative functions, and co-ordinating these at a strategic level.

The copywriter

The copywriter writes the copy – the words that appear in an advert. There may be one or many copywriters depending on the size of the agency. Press adverts are dependent on the words and the position of the words and research has shown the striking difference in terms of recognition and sales when one method is used rather than another. Good creative copywriters are worth their weight in gold and can often be some of the most highly paid people within the agency.

The art director

The art director supervises the many art functions that go to make up an advertisement whether for press, TV or posters. This will include design work, drawing and painting, the use of colour, different materials, photography and the different forms of type that can appear in an advert. With the growth of information technology, the use of computers and the development of computer programming and design, and especially the development of web sites and Internet advertising, the employment of staff with both creative and computer skills has taken on a high priority. Detailed sketches and storyboards are also prepared within the art department to guide the filming of television and cinema adverts.

The production department

Print manager

Once the client has approved the creative ideas and concepts the production department will transform the art and the copy into the finished ads. Within this department the print production manager works with outside printers, colour experts and photographers, in making the copywriting and creative ideas come to life in a way that can be transferred into newspaper or magazine advert form.

Broadcast production manager

If TV or radio is to be used then the broadcast production manager will co-ordinate all the necessary services and suppliers needed. This might consist of bringing in one specialist film producing agency or it might mean separate suppliers depending on the size of the task in hand. The making of television commercials can cost hundreds of thousands of pounds – often more than the making of a full-length minor film. A Saatchi & Saatchi commercial for British Airways was reputed to cost over a million pounds to make. Film production will include the hiring of musicians, a director, writers and actors, camera and sound engineers as well as ancillary services such as property and effects acquirers, caterers, transport and insurance. Only the largest all-service agency would have the ability to perform this part of the campaign themselves and most would certainly out-source and buy in.

Traffic manager

Finally the so-called traffic department will co-ordinate the whole creative programme bringing together the copywriter, the art director, printing and production, film making, administration and so on. It is the job of the traffic department to move the whole process forward making certain that the finished advertisement is agreed by the agency and the client and finally reaches the selected media on time.

Customer marketing services

The marketing services department concern themselves with the marketing side of the agency business, identifying, tabulating and describing in necessary detail all aspects of the target audience and then matching this to the best media form. This will also involve co-ordinating other marketing promotional activities such as sales promotions, public relations, publicity, sponsorship and exhibitions if these are part of the overall promotional strategy.

Marketing and advertising research

The marketing research department will carry out research on markets and audiences under the guidance of the research director. Research will be carried out before, during and after the campaign. Research before the campaign begins will look at the advertiser's consumers and detail such aspects as geographical location, socio-demographic breakdown, behavioural activity and psychological description. It will also evaluate the media that will best reach the target audience in the required time period. Research (probably qualitative, perhaps using a focus group) will also be used at the beginning of a campaign to get a feel for current brand and corporate attitudes as well as testing out various different formulaic approaches to advertisements. Research (probably quantitative) will then be used during the campaign to measure and adjust reaction and finally at the end to measure and evaluate the success or otherwise when compared to the advertising set objectives.

Media selection

The media department, under the direction of the media director or media manager, is responsible for all the activity to do with the investigation, evaluation and selection of the correct media for the relevant target market. This will include

- knowing everything possible about newspapers, magazines, directories, TV, radio, cinema and outdoor posters;
- having intricate knowledge about circulation – readership figures for all manner of press publications and viewing and listening numbers for the ever increasing TV and radio channels;
- detailed knowledge of customer profiles – who reads, watches and listens to what;

- an understanding of the advantages and disadvantages of the various media and how each might integrate with the other to create a realistic and successful strategy;
- a deep understanding of pricing methods, discounts offered and the most propitious time of day and slots for particular advertisements.

Media buyers and planners and media owners

Successful agency staff will develop close relationships with the media staff to enable them to take advantage of special offers and favourable opportunities. The media buyer will book the time and negotiate the price of the ad, the media planner will decide which media to use, and the media researcher will be continuously looking for data on media, audiences and markets, gathering and developing an information base with information to support all activities within the media department. The media department will need to rely heavily on advice from the media owners (whilst still keeping their own counsel) and it involves trust on both sides about the truth behind audience numbers and audience make-up although the task is easier with audited figures offered by the independent auditing bodies such as ABC. It is still a very difficult task because the whole success of the campaign will hinge not only on the price obtained, but more importantly, whether the advert will reach and be seen and understood by the particular target market aimed at by the campaign.

Role of the client

I have learnt that trying to guess what the client wants is the most debilitating of all influences in the creation of good advertising.

(Leo Burnett, agency owner)

The client could be involved, at any stage, with the many processes that move the concept from idea and copy to the end advertisement. The level and degree of consultation and involvement will vary according to client temperament, the level of faith they put in the discretion of agency staff and the amount of money they might have invested in the campaign. Agency staff, whilst consulting with the client, would prefer to be left alone, exercise their own professional judgement, and get on with the job. For some client brand managers this is more easily said than done and they will insist on interfering at every stage, especially if they are in control of a brand with a customer franchise that has taken fifty years to develop and the campaign is costing millions of pounds.

CONCLUSION

The advertising agency is an essential element in the trinity of client, agency, and media owner. Advertising agencies have developed into a multi-billion-pound industry encompassing the world and agencies offer advice and assistance at a local, regional, national and global level. An organisation has a choice, when advertising, between taking on the task themselves or bringing in outside help. Advertising agencies would argue that, because of their experience, knowledge and skills, the most cost-effective way to advertising success is to use an agency. Three different types exist: full service, limited service and specialised, giving the advertiser a choice as to how much they want to do themselves and how much through an agency. Services offered within the various agency types also vary, covering almost every possible marketing and advertising need from strategic planning through to implementation and tactical control.

<table>
<tr><td>CASE
STUDY</td><td></td></tr>
</table>

The role of account planning

When one tries to define what an account planner does, it usually results in responses like: 'I thought researchers did that' or 'I thought account managers did that'. It is much easier to define the role of planning in an agency, and to say that the planner ensures that it takes place.

Relationships within the agency

Producing ads is essentially a team effort, and the way the planner relates to the account director on the one hand, and the creative team on the other hand, is worth explaining.

The planner works alongside the account director/manager. While each person has his own area of expertise and experience, there is a substantial area of overlap where the two, working together, can create something where the whole is greater than the sum of the parts. Leadership and co-ordination are the primary skills for account management. They still orchestrate the whole advertising development process, and have ultimate responsibility for the strategy and creative brief. But now they have skilled help from the planner, who brings greater understanding of the consumer relationship and more analytical depth to the proceedings. The relationship between planner and account director is one of equal status, with merit determined by the ability to make a useful contribution.

What about the planner's relationship with the creative team?

Creative people want a simple, single-minded directional brief, not a bland statement. The best planners are pithy. Most good creative teams want to know the consumer beyond a mere demographic definition. They want to know about the kind of attitudes held – to the product category, to the brand, to advertising in this market. They want to know what the consumer wants, rather than what the client wants. The good planner brings this sharply into focus – like an expressive photograph.

The planner can provide a better service in this context than the account director, who is less skilled at originating and interpreting research, or the independent research supplier, who lacks an intimate knowledge of the account and the kind of advertising the agency stands for. Too much objectivity in advertising research is not conducive to the early stage of creative development which requires sympathetic handling. A mechanistic approach to research can lead to ads which have impeccable relevance but no originality or impact. However, the positive and constructive use of diagnostic research in establishing a dialogue between the creative team and the consumer is one of the most valuable contributions planners can make to the process of producing ads. Their sympathy with the creative process can stimulate and discipline creative thinking; their research skill can interpret consumer response with sensitivity and foresight.

▶

Defining the job

The best way to define the job is as follows:

1) In an overall sense:

The planner will be concerned with the relevance of the advertising to the target audience, and its effectiveness in the market. This is done by bringing a consumer perspective to the advertising in order that the brand and the consumer are drawn together.

> Client says: 'My Product'.
> Account Director says: 'My Client'.
> Creative Director says: 'My Ad'.
> Planner says: 'My Consumer'.
> The planner implements a disciplined and systematic approach to the creation of ads.

2) In the strategy development stage:

The planner will collect and synthesise data to guide strategic development. This is done by understanding attitudes and behaviour of people; and gaining insight into the consumer relationship with the brand and the advertising. Then the planner will define the positioning and relevant proposition that encapsulates the rational and emotional appeals of the brand.

3) In the creative development stage:

The planner will commission diagnostic research on rough ads to check whether the advertising is achieving the desired responses. Feedback will be gained on how the ad is working and what effect it is having. Ad responses will be interpreted with sensitivity in order to stimulate the creative process further.

4) In the approval stage:

Bold or original work, that goes against conventions, sometimes has a rough ride. Objective justification can help to win the case. The planner will help to provide reassurance on how and why the particular piece of advertising will work for the brand.

5) In the post-campaign stage:

The planner will commission and use research to track the progress of the brand. Questions that need to be answered are:

- Is the strategy working?
- Are the objectives being met?
- Do the ads need developing?
- How should they be developed?

What makes a good planner?

- Having a passion for advertising and a sensitivity to the creative process.
- Having an intuitive curiosity about consumers, and an understanding of human relationships.
- Being an able and inspiring communicator.
- Being skilled at using marketing and research data.
- Being numerate and imaginative in order to translate research results into advertising action.
- Having credibility and authority in the context of research and advertising judgements.
- Having a strategic and visionary mind to create openings after brilliant detective work.

- Having a desire to be continuously involved as an integrated member of the account team.
- Maintaining a balance between theory and pragmatism concerning how ads work.

In conclusion

Account planning is not an end in itself. Outstanding ads were and are done without it! Hopefully account planning adds context, perspective, guidance and opinion to advertising development. Consequently the chances of getting the advertising right first time are increased. However in the advertising world no one has a monopoly over wisdom or ideas; an agency consists of a group of people with different skills, abilities, experience and personalities trying very hard to get the best possible advertising for their clients.

Account planning is central to long-term brand building and business success. If the goal is to produce better, more effective advertising, then the combination of imaginative planning and creative excellence is the means of achieving this. The planner ensures that the advertising works in a relevant and distinctive way.

The author would like to thank the Account Planning Group for permission to reprint this case study.

Case study questions

1. Do you think that there is a role for the account planner? If so, how different is it to the roles of the account manager and the creative director?
2. Do you think that there is the possibility of conflict when so many different people are involved in the process? How will this affect the client?

CHAPTER QUESTIONS

All the following questions are from the CAM Foundation certificate in Communication Studies examination in Advertising 1997. (The CAM Foundation is the Communication Advertising and Marketing Education Foundation Limited.)

1. Explain what you think are the most important considerations for an advertiser when
   (a) selecting an advertising agency
   (b) setting the advertising appropriation.
2. Describe the role and responsibilities of an advertising manager in a company which expects to achieve both value for money and a high standard of creative advertising.
3. Describe the role of each of the following:
   (a) Creative Director
   (b) Designer
   (c) Copywriter
   (d) Director of TV commercials
   (e) Sound recording engineer of radio commercials
   (f) Accounts manager
   and in each case give an example to show how you think the role may have added value to an advertisement.
4. Describe briefly an advertising campaign you consider effective and one you think ineffective. Discuss what you think are the campaign and creative

objectives and strategies of each of your examples and give your assessment of the advertising you have described.

5. Describe how the Advertising Standards Authority investigates complaints and on what grounds advertising can be recommended for withdrawal or amendment.

REFERENCES

Advertising Age (www.adage.com)

Advertising Association (www.adassoc.org.uk)

Ogilvy, D. (1971) *Confessions of an Advertising Man,* Ballantine Books, New York.

Ogilvy, D. (1985) *Ogilvy on Advertising,* Vintage Books, New York.

Omnicom (US) (www.omnicomny.com); agencies include BBDO Worldwide, TBWA International Network, and Diversified Agency Services (DAS).

WPP group (UK) (www.wpp.com); J.Walter Thompson, Ogilvy & Mather, Millward Brown, BMRD, Kantar Media Research.

FURTHER READING

Bovée, C. L. et al. (1995) *Advertising Excellence,* McGraw-Hill, London.

Dentsu (Japan) (www.dentsu.co.jp)

The Institute of Practitioners in Advertising (IPA) (www.ipa.co.uk). The IPA is the industry body and institute for UK advertising agencies.

International Advertising Association (www.iaaglobal.org)

Interpublic Group (US) (www.interpublic.com); includes McCann-Erickson World-group; Ammirati Puris Lintas; The Lowe Group; Western International Media.

Joslin, J. (1995) 'The advertising agency', in Hart, N. (ed.) *The Practice of Advertising,* Butterworth-Heinemann, Oxford.

The Marketing Creative Handbook, UK advertising agencies (www.mch.co.uk)

Quelch, J. and Farris, P. (1994) *Cases in Advertising and Promotion Management,* 4th edn, McGraw-Hill, London.

Ring, J. (1993), *Advertising on Trial,* Pitman Publishing, London.

Russell, J.T and Lane, W.R. (1996) *Kleppner's Advertising Procedure,* (13th edn), Prentice Hall, London.

Young & Rubican (UK) owns Burson-Marsteller (www.yr.com)

7 The media owners

OBJECTIVES

By the end of this chapter the reader should be able to:

1. Describe the main (above the line) media used by advertisers to reach target markets.

2. Identify and evaluate the importance and market share of each.

3. Identify the variety of services offered by each and be aware of future developments.

INTRODUCTION

The media owners operate in an extremely competitive market environment and they will want to sell the benefits of their medium over others in the business. Many media companies would not survive but for the advertising revenue and this concentrates the mind in always looking for ways to gain competitive advantage in an ever-changing world. Competition may be 'intra-competition' – that is, between owners in the same business, for example BSB against ITV – or 'inter-competition' between different media owners, for example Maiden outdoor poster sites against the *Daily Mirror*, a national newspaper. The media vehicles available to the advertiser are diverse and many more are being made available. In this chapter we will look at the major 'above the line' options whilst all other methods will be discussed in the chapter that follows.

Although going through a period of change the media mix known as 'above the line' still dominates the advertising marketplace. It includes television, print media, outdoor media, radio, and cinema.

Primary and support media

The advertiser will need to choose between the various competing media vehicles, sometimes using one major method only as the primary medium complemented by the use of a sales promotion and merchandising or one major method, e.g. TV advertising as the primary method with another major method, e.g. newspapers, as a secondary, support media, back-up.

- TV advertising ⟶ primary media ⟶ 75% advertising spend
- Newspaper advertising ⟶ secondary, support media ⟶ 25% advertising spend

Communications is a highly competitive sales and marketing operation and every media owner is continually looking to gain advantage by offering greater benefits than the competitor. By far the largest media for advertising are the use of TV and the print media accounting for over 90 per cent of all advertising spend (see Table 7.1).

Table 7.1 Main media advertising share, UK and US

Total advertising spend in the main media (1998, estimated)					
	UK $ million		US $ million		
Commercial TV	6.000	(31.8%)	44.000	(39%)	
The national press	3.000	(15.9%)	40.500	(36%)	all the press
Magazine and directory	4.350	(23.0%)	14.500	(12.9%)	magazines only
Regional and local press	3.780	(20.0%)			
Outdoor	.830	(4.4%)	1.900	(1.7%)	
Radio	.699	(3.7%)	11.500	(10.3)	
Cinema	.132	(0.7%)	not available		

Total UK spend: $18.9 billion; consumer $14.7 billion; business to business $4.20 billion.
Total US spend: $112.4 billion.

Source: Advertising Age

Television

Television consists of transmission channels that exist either by public funding or by attracting companies to pay for space to advertise their products at the beginning, during or after selected programmes. There is a history of public broadcasting in most developed countries and it started in the UK in the 1930s with the advent of the British Broadcasting Company (BBC).

Public broadcasting

Public broadcasting companies such as the BBC in the UK came into being with a mission to provide information, to educate and to entertain the general public. In the case of the BBC this remit still remains more or less the same after sixty years of broadcasting. The money to buy and make programmes and run the operation comes from the payment by viewers of a licence fee (£100 in 1999) once a year. Most countries have some form of public broadcasting facility dedicated to the 'public good' funded by public subscription or government funding and not by commercial advertising.

The BBC market share

The BBC is responsible for BBC 1 (estimated market share in 1998 30.5 per cent) and BBC 2 (estimated market share 10.7 per cent) as well as radio 1, 2, 3, 4, and 5. Although no overt advertising is allowed this could well change as we move into the new millennium when its new digital channels open up and it may well accept advertising or sponsorship on selected minority channels. Its programmes are often taken as a benchmark and it is accepted as a serious competitor by all commercial channels.

Commercial television

The vast majority of the UK media and the media in the US and around the world is commercial and exists and makes a profit by selling advertising space to organisations (and individuals) that wish to communicate with others, usually to sell products or services. Commercial TV makes its money by monthly subscription, by individual programme purchase ('pay-by-view'), and by selling advertising space.

At the present time, selling advertising space contributes the most amount in media owner revenue but this may well change if pay-by-view continues to grow at the current rate.

Technological development has affected all transmission channels in some way or another but no more so than with TV which is still in a state of revolutionary change in what benefits can be, and will be, offered to both audiences and advertisers. Three methods are available to TV advertisers – conventional terrestrial broadcasting, satellite and cable.

Conventional terrestrial broadcasting

Terrestrial TV uses radio signals via land-based transmitters to send analogue signals from the recording studios to its audience. Analogue will disappear to be replaced by digital by 2007. In the UK, at the time of writing, three commercial and two non-commercial stations are available. The commercial stations are ITV, Channel 4 and Channel 5. Channel 4 is a publicly owned channel but is allowed to take advertising to fund its activity. Channel 5 is a relatively new channel, commercially owned and again funded by the sale of advertising space. The largest commercial station is Independent Television (ITV) (www.itv.co.uk), which, as the Independent Television Asscociation, represents a consortium of 15 regional companies within the UK (ownership of the 15 regional companies changes as acquisitions and mergers take place and the current situation can be discovered on www.vbs.bt.co). Although its audiences have fallen over the last ten years ITV is by far the largest of all the commercial channels with audience share in 1998 of 32.2 per cent. It can still draw in average audiences of 16 million (one-third of the adult population) for programmes such as *Coronation Street* and can still make the claim to be a mass medium. It launched 30 more digital stations in 1998.

As well as representing the 15 ITV regions, the Independent Television Association also carries out other functions, including network programming, promotions and marketing, and speaks for the commercial terrestrial TV industry. It is jointly responsible with the BBC for BARB (British Audience Research Bureau), the independent organisation that produces audience research for the industry.

Table 7.2 Top ten UK television advertisers 1996/7

	£ millions
1. BT	98.7
2. Procter & Gamble	74.0
3. Kellogg	58.2
4. Ford	56.4
5. Procter & Gamble H&B	42.0
6. Van Den Bergh Foods	41.0
7. Renault	38.7
8. Mars Confectionery	37.5
9. Nissan	37.1
10. Elida Fabergé	34.3

Source: (MMS) Media Week, 5 September 1997. Used with permission.

Cable

Cable TV now reaches 67 per cent of all homes in the US, 60 per cent in Germany, but only 10 per cent (2.37 million households) in the UK, although this figure is increasing at the rate of 45 000 a month. At the time of writing more than 40 stations can be obtained through one of the nine cable companies in the UK that have a regional franchise. This is set to explode to over 200 channels with the advent of digital TV. Some of the programme channels are free whilst others are on monthly or programme-by-programme subscription. The cable industry in the UK is represented by the Cable Communications Association (www.cable.co.uk).

Satellite

Satellite TV in the UK (and to a certain extent around the world) is dominated by News International, owners of BSkyB (www.sky.co.uk), the company that first came to the market at the end of the 1980s. Satellite offers similar services (and as many channels) as those offered by cable, the differences being that satellite TV can be accessed by almost anybody, not only in the UK but around the world, as long as they are able to afford a satellite dish (which costs about £200) and are in a position to receive the signal from space. Cable TV, on the other hand, is dependent on an underground cable passing the house, business or school. A choice of 200 digital channels are now available.

Market share

Trends in UK television audience share are shown in Table 7.3. Commercial TV is expected to erode BBC audience share over the next five years.

Spending

Total advertising revenue on UK commercial TV is estimated to reach £3.8 billion in 1998 (31.8 per cent of all media advertising spending). The US equivalent is approx. £27 billion (44%).

Table 7.3 Trends in UK television audience share

Share of total audience

	ITV	Channel 4	Channel 5	Cable and Satellite	BBC1	BBC2
1994	39.5	10.3	–	6.6	32.7	10.8
1998	32.2	10.4	3.5	12.8	30.5	10.7

Share of commercial TV

	ITV	Channel 4	Channel 5	Cable and Satellite
1994	69.0	19.5	–	11.5
1998	54.7	17.6	6.0	21.7

The press

National newspapers

By far the biggest amount of advertising spend is through the regional and national press, magazines and directories. Individual national newspaper circulation is bigger in the UK than in any other country in the world offering advertisers a range of daily and Sunday newspapers covering the popular and quality ends of the market. The biggest selling daily in the UK, in May 1998, the *Sun* achieved sales of 3.65 million and readership of just under 10 million. Overall the 13 major national titles covering the UK achieved sales of 13.6 million in the period from June 97 to May 98 and estimated readership of over 35 million. In comparison, in the US, as with most other industrialised countries, newspapers tend to be more regionalised around big cities. The largest-selling national in the US is The *Wall Street Journal* with a circulation of 1.75 million.

Table 7.4 Circulation figures and characteristics of some UK national newspapers

	Circulation (thousands)	Characteristics
National morning popular		
Daily Mirror	2298	High circulation, tabloid, low cover price, down-
Sun	3709	market readership, high picture, feature, gossip content.
National morning mid-market		
Express	1168	Medium circulation, mid-readership, tabloid,
Daily Mail	2274	balance of news and feature material.
National morning quality		
Daily Telegraph	1076	
Financial Times	350	Low circulation, up-market readership, broadsheet
Guardian	400	High cover price, high news content.
Independent	220	
The Times	790	

Source: Audit Bureau of Circulations (www.abc.org.uk)

Circulation figures indicate the number of newspapers purchased – they do not indicate the number of readers. This figure will always be higher as research shows that on average each newspaper sold is read by two to three people.

Prices

Table 7.5 Examples of advertising card-rates in UK national press (1996)

Newspaper	Circulation (thousands)	Readership (thousands)	Cost, full page colour
Daily Star	671	2132	£15 092
Express	1195	2784	£31 500
Express on Sunday	1177	3078	£38 623

Source: (www.expressnewspapers.co.uk)

Colour will be more expensive than black and white. Additional discounts are available for more than one insert and the total number of display ads, full page or fractional, run within one year from the date of the first insertion determines the frequency rate earned. Up-to-date newspaper advertising prices are available through BRAD (British Rate and Data) which is published every month by EMAP publishers at a cost of £240 (www.emap.com). As with all media, card-rate is the hoped for price but is negotiable according to demand, competition and seasonal factors.

Table 7.6 Top ten national newspaper advertisers (UK) 1996/97

	£ million
1. Currys	27.9
2. Dixons	19.4
3. Vauxhall	16.1
4. BT	15.9
5. Ford	12.5
6. Comet	10.9
7. Citroën	10.6
8. MFI Furniture	10.5
9. Sainsbury's Homebase	10.1
10. Central Office of Information	9.7

Source: (MMS) *Media Week*, 5 September 1997

Trade association

The Newspaper Publishers Association (NPA) (34, Southwark Bridge Road, London SE1 9EU; tel.: 0171 207 2200; Fax 0171 928 2067), founded in 1906, is the trade association for Britain's national daily and Sunday newspapers and the *Evening Standard*. In co-operation with the Newspaper Society (see below) it is responsible for the Audit Bureau of Circulation (ABC) which collects statistics on the industry.

Local and regional press

There are 1351 regional and local daily and weekly, paid-for and free newspapers in the UK and nine out of ten adults, 40 million people, read a regional or local newspaper. Every village, town and city has access to a local newspaper, examples being the *Aberdeen Press and Journal*, circulation 106864; the *Kent Messenger*, circulation 43722; the *Falkirk Herald*, circulation 33312; the *Cornish Guardian*, circulation 3079, and the *Liverpool Daily Post*, circulation 72917 (source: 1997: www.newspapersoc.org.uk). It offers advertisers both display and classified advertising space. Payment and price information is through both individual newspapers' sales offices and national sales companies acting on behalf of contributing local and regional newspapers.

Free delivery newspapers

Some newspapers are given away free, usually by personal delivery or by post. They are often seen by advertisers as having a tarnished image because of the possible differences between the circulation (i.e. copies delivered) claimed by the owners and the number that are kept and read rather than being put straight in the bin. Other newspapers, both national and regional, are given away free of charge to various organisations. Advertisers are concerned that all circulation and readership figures must be independently monitored and measured because of problems that might arise through sloppy or fraudulent counting. This takes on a heightened importance when dealing with free newspapers as it is tempting (and easy) for the media owner to exaggerate circulation and readership figures and subsequent influence so as to gain advertising revenue.

The Newspaper Society (www.newspapersoc.org.uk) was founded in 1836; its members publish nearly 1400 regional weekly paid-for and free newspapers. Together with the NPA it is responsible for the Audit Bureau of Circulation.

ABC working party clarifies the new circulation auditing criteria for national newspaper bulk sales

With regard to bulk sales, the new ABC rules for national newspapers define a number of categories – airlines, hotels, trains etc. – where bulk sales will be admissible up to an agreed limited percentage of seats or rooms involved. As well as bona fide contract, publishers will additionally be required to show proof of delivery to final points of distribution. This system has been designed to reflect the auditability of such categories and limit claims to what is reasonable. Firm-sale retail level bulks, which have been the subject of recent controversy between Mirror Group and News International, will not normally be admissible. Indeed the ABC finds it difficult to conceive of circumstances where such retail bulk sales could be admitted under the new rules.

Commenting on the subject of bulk sales, the Acting Director of the Bureau said, 'although it may be possible to provide an audit trail by distributing on a sale-or-return basis we believe publishers may find it difficult to persuade the ABC that the buyer has sufficient financial incentive to make returns on undistributed copies worth the cost. This view has been made clear to, and has been accepted by all publishers'.

The revised ABC rules for National Newspapers came into effect on 29 June 1998, and the first figures to be certified under these will be for July 1998.

Source: Audit Bureau of Circulations (www.abc.org.uk)

Spending

The regional and local press accounts for £2.4. billion (1998 estimate) in national display and classified advertising, over 20 per cent of all ad spend. The US equivalent is not available because of the different newspaper structure.

Magazines

Estimates of the total number of magazine titles published in the UK vary depending on the definition employed and the moment in time chosen as the number starting up and closing down has increased with recent changes in print technology making it reasonably easy for companies to enter and leave the business. British Rate and Data (BRAD) lists for 1997 nearly 6500 magazines which take advertising. In general magazines are listed as 'consumer, general and specific' or 'business and professional'. Over the last ten years the total number of magazines has increased by over 25 per cent.

The market is dominated by relatively few large publishing companies such as Reed-Elsevier (IPC and Reed Business Publishing), BBC Magazines, D.C. Thompson, EMAP, Condé Nast, and G&J of the UK. IPC (www.ipc.co.uk) alone publishes seven major women's weekly magazines, plus three leading TV listings titles and with aggregate weekly sales of nearly 6.2 million and readership of 13 million is the leading publisher of mass market consumer magazines. There are also many small independently published titles which tend to cater for small, specialised markets.

Business to business magazines

Although considerably smaller than the consumer magazine market, there is a healthy selection of trade magazines available for business to business advertising, ranging across most areas of business and including titles such as *Retail Week*, *Accountancy Age*, *Architect Today*, *Marketing*, *Autotrade*, *Community Care*, *Catering Update*, *PC Dealer*, *Heating and Ventilating News*, and so on. Some might have a circulation as small as 5000 but could still be attractive to advertisers if the readership is tightly segmented in a specific business area. Most are given away free although some invite a subscription. In many cases they may be the only realistic way for a business to business marketer to reach a target market, especially if some distance away and/or hard to contact.

Table 7.7 Top 10 magazine advertisers (UK) 1996/7

	£ million
1. Software Warehouse	5.6
2. Great Universal Stores	4.9
3. Boots	4.7
4. Estee Lauder	4.4
5. Granville technology	3.9
6. L'Oréal Golden	3.8
7. Gallaher Tobacco	3.8
8. Britannia Music	3.6
9. Sainsbury	3.6
10. Book Club Associates	3.5

Source: (MMS) *Media Week*, 5 September 1997

Customer magazines

The big growth in the 1990s (300 per cent since 1990) has been in the use of customer magazines, linked to the use of loyalty cards, marketing information systems and purchasing patterns, generating and reinforcing customer loyalty. Of such magazines, 70 per cent are mailed out to customers, although they are available in related retail outlets, and most are free. By circulation 15 of the top 20 magazines are customer magazines. It is difficult to separate advertising revenue but it is estimated that in 1998 £190 million will have been generated in advertising revenue, production and postage.

Table 7.8 Six of the top ten UK magazines, by circulation, are customer magazines

*AA Magazine	4,084,522
*Sky TV Guide	3,403,912
*Safeway Magazine	1,997,063
*Cable Guide	1,860,622
What's on TV	1,765,369
Radio Times	1,400,331
Reader's Digest	1,302,659
Take a Break	1,273,820
*The Somerfield Magazine	1,177,307
*Debenhams	1,109,902

* customer magazines

Source: Audit Bureau of Circulations (www.abc.org.uk)

The Periodical Publishers Association (www.ppa.co.uk), established in 1913, has member-publishers covering the full spectrum of magazine publishing from mass circulation consumer magazines to highly technical business and professional journals. Approximately 80 per cent of magazine advertising revenue is represented by the association.

Directories

Over 5000 directories and yearbooks are now published in the UK and they cater for many interests including; business, professional, industrial, technical, educational and leisure. A directory and a yearbook are very similar and advertisers tend to treat the two as interchangeable. Most media are there to provide entertainment, information and news, or as in the case of outdoor posters, purely as advertisements: directories are kept as a reference source to be used over and over again. They are used by consumers and business people alike and cover every possible area from charities to the chemical industry, communications to footwear, food and drink to libraries and tourism.

Among the different types of directories are

- consumer directories, of which the Yellow Pages (owned by BT) is probably the best known, with a distribution of over 25 million;
- special interest group directories e.g. *Macmillan Guide to Britain's Nature Reserves* (£24.95); *Bed & Breakfast 1998* (£9.95): published by Stilwell Publishing, this lists 8500 B&Bs;

- local town, county, and regional directories, such as the (free) Bury St. Edmund's Pink Local directory;
- services directories such as *Waterloo Legal Publishing Guide to the Social Services* or *The Retail Directory* (£160), a comprehensive directory of retail names and addresses;
- business directories such as *BRAD* (£245), a monthly directory of UK advertising media, and *BRAD Agencies and Advertisers* (£110), a bi-monthly directory of agencies and advertisers in the UK (both published by Emap Business Communications);
- directories of professional and trade associations such as the *Royal Institute of Chartered Surveyors Directory* (£91) or the *Fish Traders Yearbook* (£44.10), published by DMG Business Media Ltd, which covers every sector of the fish and shellfish business.

Directories are an undervalued area of advertising considering that they accounted, in 1998, for an estimated £760 million in advertising revenue.

The Directory & Database Publishers Association (www.directory-publishers.co.uk) represents the interests of more than 70 British directory publishers, who produce in excess of 600 titles.

Spending

Magazine and directory advertising is estimated to have been worth £2.8 billion in the UK in 1998, 23 per cent of all media advertising revenue. The comparable US figure is £8.72 billion, 12.9 per cent of all media advertising.

Outdoor media

All other forms of media advertising are small compared with the press and TV. Nevertheless, there is a growing use of both outdoor media and radio as alternative or complementary methods of reaching particular target groups. Outdoor, a generic term which covers all media seen in an outdoor situation, has experienced healthy growth in the UK over the last twenty years and revenue is estimated at over £.5 billion in 1998. Argued to be the only 'true' advertising medium because it is not linked to any form of distracting entertainment, it has often been seen in the past as somewhat down-market, unorganised and amateur, often being associated with images of illegal flyposting. Outdoor advertising on billboards, poster sites and transport has got its act together and come of age in the 1990s, and is now a major competitor to all other media.

The outdoor market can be broken down into the following areas:

- roadside
- off-road
- transport
- miscellaneous.

Roadside

The number of roadside and off-road panels in the UK is estimated to be 36 875 6-sheet panels, 30 368 48-sheet panels, 3323 96-sheet panels and 9107 of other sizes. Many sites now have back-lighting, 3D designs and novelty movement allowing greater all-round customer opportunity to see them. We cannot walk, drive or take most types of transport without seeing many of these poster sites. Planning laws exist that restrict their usage and these will vary from region to region and country to country. Outdoor posters come in all shapes and sizes and some are listed below.

Poster sizes

As the name suggests all roadside (and offroad) panels are divided and sold by size and position. Size traditionally is in terms of 'sheet' size, and the poster sizes offered are:

- double crown: 762 mm × 508 mm (30 in × 20 in); this is the unit for larger sizes
- quad crown: 762 mm × 1016 mm (30 in × 60 ins)
- 4-sheet: 1016 mm × 1524 mm (40 in × 60 in)
- 6-sheet: 1016 mm × 2304 mm (40 in × 90 in)
- 16-sheet: 3048 mm × 2032 mm (10 ft × 6 ft. 8 in)
- 48-sheet: 3048 mm × 6096 mm (20 ft × 10 ft), the size we might all recognise when travelling in the car
- 64-sheet: 3048 mm × 8128 mm (30 ft × 10 ft)
- 96-sheet: 3048 mm × 12 138 mm (40 ft × 10 ft), the largest that can be seen in any quantity.

Examples of prices (Maiden, 1998)

National 48-sheet campaign: 500 sites £275 000 per month
National 96-sheet campaign: 200 sites £240 000 per month
National 6-sheet campaign: 250 sites £37 500 per month
National 48-sheet campaign, prime spots, back-illuminated, PVC rather than paste and paper: 100 sites Nov/Dec. Ratecard (per half month) £450 000
Motorway junction, 64-sheet: two sites, back-illuminated, PVC, ratecard £20 000 per panel per month.

Off-road

'Off-road' covers all the outdoor posters that are situated away from the roadside and those involved with transport. It includes posters in retail outlets, super-markets, shopping centres, shopping malls, retail parks, factory villages, and regional shopping centres such as the Metro Centre and Lakeside. Other posters appear at entertainment and leisure centres, holiday parks and car parks – in fact, anywhere where people congregate, posters will be seen if permission can be obtained. Some of the sites are operated by the retail outlet or consortium and many are controlled and maintained by outdoor media companies even where not directly owned. Posters here can be used to advertise national and local products and services as well as those that relate directly to the panel location.

Flyposting

Many posters appear on walls, doors, disused shop fronts, or anywhere where there is a space. They advertise meetings, concerts, gigs, overlapping each other as they fight for publicity and punter awareness of a forthcoming event. The result is often a chaotic environmental mess akin to graffiti and it is probably this side of the industry that gave poster advertising a bad name in the past as much of it is illegal. Councils will prosecute whenever they can.

Transport

Transport is an obvious area for advertising posters because of the flow of people who will have the opportunity to see the poster. Because of the nature of travel, posters can be linked with related target audiences including commuters, tourists, holiday travellers, and shoppers.

Transport posters can be seen at railway stations, alongside the track, inside and on trains; in underground stations, booking halls, escalators, walkways, inside and on the outside of the trains; on the side, back, front and top and in the interior of buses, coaches, and taxis; in bus and coach stations and bus shelters. Adshel, now a part of the More group, developed the bus shelter with lighted adverts and sold the concept to local councils.

Advans are vehicles that have no other purpose other than being driven around (and parked) with 2 × 48-sheet posters on the back in the hope that these will be seen by a prospective target audience. There have been some complaints accusing advan owners of causing media 'clutter' and environmental 'vision' pollution.

Almost anything that moves is ripe for an ad on the side and this includes miscellaneous transport such as police cars, fire engines, ambulances and business vehicles.

Examples of transport posters and prices (1999 media costs only)

Underground, 48-sheet, 100 sites, £98 500, one month
Underground, 96-sheet, 50 sites, £125 250, one month
Fully painted train, £300 000, one year
Tube car panels, £35 000, 4000 sites, one month
Escalator panels might cost £40 600 for 700 sites, one month
Tickets, 4 million, £4.50 per 1000, printing costs £10 000
Step risers, from £45 to £82 per site per month
London bus side, from £188 to £297 per month
Whole bus, £25 000, one year; £17 000 production cost
Bus hub caps, negotiable price.

Source: TDI (www.tdimedia.com)

Spending

Outdoor accounts for 4.4 per cent of all UK media advertising spending, £528 million, of which approximately 60 per cent is roadside and 40 per cent transport. This figure is up from £267 million in 1991. USA outdoor accounts for £1.15 billion, 1.7 per cent of all media advertising.

Table 7.9 Top ten outdoor advertisers (UK) 1997

	£ millions
1. Renault	7.7
2. Honda	6.6
3. Channel 5	6.1
4. Toyota GB	5.6
5. Nissan	5.5
6. BSkyB	5.2
7. Conservative Party	5.1
8. Camelot (Lottery)	5.0
9. Barclays Bank	4.6
10. BT.	4.5

Source: (MMS) *Media Week*, 5 September 1997

Representation

The industry is represented by the Outdoor Advertising Association of Great Britain (Summit House, 27 Sale Place, London W2 1YR; tel.: 0171 0 973 0315; fax: 0171 973 0138). The OAA is the trade association representing the UK poster contractors (both outdoor and transport). It is responsible for POSTAR (Poster Audience Research) which sets performance indicators for the outdoor industry.

Radio

Radio is the oldest of the broadcast media, having begun in the 1920s. It had very little competition until TV came of age in the 1950s and 1960s. During this time it moved from being a group activity, with all members of the family sitting around and listening, to being predominantly an individual one. The development of the medium over the last decade has been quite dramatic with station choices increasing from an average of 8 ten years ago to an average of 14 (25 in London) in 1998. As with TV, as the number of stations has increased, the size of the audiences has decreased, causing problems for the mass advertiser but allowing for selective niche audience targeting.

Public broadcasting

There are five public radio broadcasting channels in the UK. Radio 1, 2, 3, 4 and 5, are all run by the BBC and are national. The BBC (www.bbc.co.uk) is also responsible for the World Service. No advertising of any kind is allowed. There are also many hospital, student, local cable and match-day only football radio stations catering for minority groups but the number is insignificant when compared with the whole of radio broadcasting.

Commercial broadcasting

There are three commercial national radio stations in the UK – Classic FM, Virgin and Talk Radio – but over 140 local and regional ones. Station ownership is varied and continually changing with some companies owning many stations. (As with TV and newspapers ownership levels are controlled by law, and this is a controversial area.) The plethora of stations allows all manner of minority groups and tastes to be catered for including classical, ABC1, 40–65; jazz, BC1C2, 25–50; pop, C1C2D, 15–25; etc.

Table 7.10 An example of quarterly radio listening figures, January to April 1998

	thousands
All BBC	27,114
BBC1	9,721
BBC2	8,954
BBC3	2,614
BBC4	8,161
BBC5	5,553
BBC local/regional	8,894
Total BBC Asian	176
	thousands
All commercial	28,739
Classic FM	5,034
Virgin Radio (AM only)	3,384
Talk radio	2,267
Atlantic 252	3,098
Commercial local/regional	17,021
Local commercial (examples)	
	thousands
Capital Radio London	3,365
Premier Christian radio	163
Kiss 100 FM	829
Total Jazz FM	774
Heart 106.2	1,352

Source: Rajar/ISPSOS–RSL Quarter 1 1998

Listening figures

As with TV, listening figures are the currency advertisers pay for. Low listening figures can mean failure in an extremely competitive business.

Prices and spending

Of course prices are dependent on both listening figures and demand. Falling listener numbers will be matched by falling revenues. The prices below are for national coverage and will reflect the numbers listening at different times of the

Table 7.11 An example of a UK national commercial radio rate-card

		Mon.-Wed.	Thurs.-Fri.	Sat.	Sun.
Breakfast	0600–1000	£2500	£3000	£500	£400
Morning	1000–1300	£1000	£1200	£800	£600
Lunchtime	1300–1600	£950	£950	£250	£250
Afternoon	1600–2000	£750	£1000	£100	£150
Evening	2000–0000	£150	£200	£75	£60
Night	0000–0600	£50	£50	£50	£50
Slots by seconds	10	20	30	40	50	60
To obtain price multiply by	0.5	0.8	1.0	1.3	1.6	1.8

day. Breakfast time is the most expensive, reflecting larger audiences. Local advertising will be considerably cheaper, again depending on the listening figures and the need to attract advertisers. As with all media, discounts will be available.

Table 7.12 Top UK radio advertisers 1997/98

By company	£ 000s	By industry	£ 000s
1. Carphone Warehouse	7661	1. Business & Industrial	64 862
2. Vodaphone	7370	2. Motors	63 381
3. COI (Central Office of Information)	6800	3. Entertainment/media	57 160
4. British Telecom	6380	4. Retail	53 329
5. Renault UK	4998	5. Household equipment	40 868
6. Dixons Group	4624	6. Finance	25 760
7. Coldseal	4578	7. Leisure equipment	25 529
8. Camelot Group	4384	8. Govt/Social/Political	24 562
9 Ford Motor Co.	4227	9. Travel & Transport	18 601
10. McDonald's	4,093	10. Drink	14 453
11. Coca-Cola UK	4,092	11. Food	11 305
12. Health Education Authority	3,940	12. Pharmaceutical	10 520

Source: (MMS) Media Week 1998

Radio sold £0.444 billion advertising space in 1998 (3.7 per cent of all media spend). The US equivalent is £2 billion (3 per cent).

Audience research

The Commercial Radio Companies Association (77 Shaftesbury Avenue, London W1V 7AD; tel. 0171 306 2603) jointly owns Radio Joint Audience Research Ltd (RAJAR) with the BBC.

Cinema

Cinema (and its baby offspring home video) is the smallest of the main media, accounting for a mere 0.7 per cent of all advertising. However, it is used regularly by particular companies because of the nature of the target market. Cinema audiences declined in the 1970s and early 1980s but with the opening of new multi-screen complexes average weekly cinema audiences have risen steadily year by year from 112 million admissions in 1993 to 160 million in 1998 (Mintel). Cinema owners have woken up to the fact that they are in the entertainment business, have adopted marketing, and now that they offer an evening's 'total experience' including seat booking, seat choice, film and screen choice, free parking, the use of a restaurant and bar combined with other leisure facilities and shopping malls, they are attracting a wider audience, both younger and older than the traditional one. Other venue opportunities include films at airports, on aeroplanes, on ships and from mobile cinema vehicles. Advertising on cinema screens is handled by two major players, Pearl and Dean (www.pearl-dean.com) and Odeon cinemas.

The entertainment giant Warner Village Cinemas is converting the Battersea Power Station site in London into a massive 32-screen, 8200-seat cinema leisure complex. The site has been derelict for over 15 years but when complete, in the year 2000, the Warner Village 'megaplex' will be one of the biggest cinemas in the world. At a cost of £35 million it will become the UK's largest entertainment and leisure centre and to mark the event a time-capsule containing artifacts from the new Batman and Robin film was sunk into the structure of the new foundations. It is expected to attract over 100 000 visitors a week.

Cinema advertising spend in 1998 is estimated to have been £84 million, 0.7 per cent of all media advertising. US figures are unavailable.

The Cinema Advertising Association provides statistics on the cinema industry annually through CAVIAR (Cinema and Video Industry Audience Research).

Prices

Any prices quoted above are 'card-rate'. This is the full price the owners of the media would like to obtain. The ability to obtain full card-rate price, however, will depend very much on supply and demand. When demand is heavy then the full price may well have to be paid but if demand is slack then discounts will always be available because the opportunity cost of a poster site or a TV or newspaper spot is nil once the sell-by date has passed. Discounts can be as much as 60 to 75 per cent of card-rate and in some cases the spot might even be given free to a regular customer offered with the knowledge that it is better to have an advertising spot full, because of appearances, rather than empty. Price discounts off the card-rate might also be offered for advertisers prepared to accept any slot, for example, over a two- or three-month period. TV slots might be offered at a discount but if other advertisers come along before the broadcast date and offer the higher price then they can claim the spot. The price discounts available probably make a sound argument for the use of media buying specialists aware of the intricacies involved.

Prices will fluctuate according to

- the level of competition, both in the amount of media available and the numbers of businesses wanting to purchase;
- economic activity and the business cycle – an economic downturn will usually create less demand for advertising, but this is not always the case as some companies will still advertise, conscious of long-term brand considerations;
- seasonal factors causing more demand at certain times of the year such as Christmas and in the spring;
- exceptional circumstances, such as an election or the football world cup, which create more demand so that prices rise;
- the amount of advertising space wanted, the time frame for the purchase and the specific slot wanted;

Ultimately buyers are after the most quality coverage for the least amount of money.

CONCLUSION

In this chapter we have discussed the main media available to the advertiser looking at TV, national and local press, magazines and directories, outdoor, radio and the cinema. The giants of the industry are the press and TV, accounting for over 90 per cent of all media advertising revenue. Commercial media owners are in the business to sell products and make money. Part of their income comes from customer price contribution and the rest comes from advertising. Advertisers are prepared to pay for advertising but must be convinced that the media they use will work and deliver benefit messages to their identified market. In return, to be successful, each owner must attempt to persuade the buyers that their medium offers better value for money in achieving the desired outcome than others, whether competitor media owners in the same line of business, for example different newspapers, or those in a different line of business, say television as against print. In many cases alternative media would be able to achieve the same outcome and the choice is straightforward in terms of price and coverage. But in other cases one medium, by its character, might be better than another and it will be up to the media owner to convince the buyer of this.

CASE STUDY

FT

Stefano Hatfield looks at the system of selling commercial TV airtime

Do you know where the money you spend on TV air-time goes? Do you know the cost of the air-time, what discount your media buying agency is obtaining and how much of that discount is passed back to you? Many finance directors and marketing departments will have given these issues little thought until recently, when the dispute between CIA, the media buying agency, and Laser, the TV sales house, blew up. Writs are flying between TV companies and the agency over discounts and shares of ITV revenue due in a row that highlights just how complicated but informal the process of trading TV air-time is in Britain. Commercial TV air-time, apart from Channel 4, which sells its own, is handled by three sales houses:

▶

- Carlton UK Sales, which sells for Carlton and Central,
- TSMS, owned by United News and Media, which sells for Meridian, Anglia, West country, HTV, UTV, Scottish, Grampian and
- S4C, which represents Granada, Yorkshire Tyne-Tees, LWT and Border.

Together they have about 600 minutes of ITV air-time to sell each week and last year they pulled in combined revenues of more than £1.6bn. They trade using a pricing system known as 'station average price'. This is best explained through a hypothetical example. If you wanted to advertise in London, you might find that in one month Big Ben TV sold perhaps 40m of advertising. Against this, research tells Big Ben that it delivered an average audience for its commercial breaks of 4.5m viewers. The station average price would be 40m divided by 4.5m, or 8.89. Media buying agencies try to get discounts off this figure to please their clients. They do this by pledging a certain share of their clients' total ITV spend to the individual sales house. For their part, a sales house representing a franchise which reaches, for example, 15 per cent of ITV viewers, wants at least 15 per cent of an agency's budget – the total of the agency's clients' TV budgets. If the agency pledges, say, 17 per cent of its budget, the sales house will give it a discount. As competition between media buyers becomes ever more fierce, the temptation to over-promise increases. So agencies may end up pledging 104 per cent of their budgets – many buyers argue they have to do so to get the discounts their clients demand.

There are other reasons why the media buying agency may fail to meet its share pledge. For example, a large client might decide halfway through the year to cut its advertising spend, or pull a campaign. Sometimes buyers fail to discover a deal has been missed until the TV company's auditors go through the books. Rather than punish the buyer, however, the sales house is more likely to incorporate the shortfall into the following year's agency deal. This means that an individual client cannot be sure that its spend with that salespoint is entirely necessary, and not being used in part to pay off debt.

It is easy to understand how sales houses can over-trade, too, largely by failing to deliver the audience ratings they have promised, and pledging ever bigger discounts in return for share. It is not unheard of for ITV sales staff to push agencies to spend more of their money outside ITV, as long as they obtain a greater share of what is spent for themselves. This is not as crazy as it sounds, for some salespeople earn bonuses based primarily on the share of ITV revenue they win for their sales house. Given these circumstances, over-trading is common, and at any one time many agencies and sales houses will be over- or under-trading with another party. What usually happens is that it all gets totted up at the end of the year and outstanding monies are rolled over. But if over-trading is so widespread, why is Laser kicking up such a fuss, calling in forensic accountants, writing to 30 CIA clients, and threatening a court showdown which will embarrass both parties, and possibly attract the attention of the Department of Trade and Industry? Some media buyers believe Laser is just being tough, making an example of CIA to extricate itself from the roll-over situation. But the money involved is unusually large. To be £100 000 or so up or down at any given time is considered part of the normal trading cycle, but 1m out of CIA's 30m annual spend with Laser?

More interesting still is the speculation over the future ownership of the Laser client, YTTV, in which Granada has a substantial stake. Of the £979 357 Laser is claiming, £785 081 is owed to YTTV, and the TV company will want its accounts cleaned up. Many agree that the system is flawed, and undermines efforts to devise effective media strategies for clients. But it is clearly in the interests of some of the bigger buyers and advertisers for the status quo to be maintained and no one seems to be able to come up with anything better. Talks have already taken place aimed at developing a more transparent trading system. While many observers feel that the system will have changed considerably within two years, few believe it will disappear.

Source: Stefano Hatfield, *Financial Times*, 21 November 1996. Used with permission.

Case study question

Discuss the problem highlighted in this article from the point of view of the three parties involved. Who do you think is correct?

CHAPTER QUESTIONS

Questions 1 to 4 are from the CAM Foundation examination paper on the media in June 1997.

1. The radio medium has been growing rapidly in terms of advertising revenue and is confident of its future. What is attracting advertisers to the medium? Explain and give your comments on the current research.
2. Write a report comparing and contrasting terrestrial television in the UK with satellite television. Within your answer cover current average audience levels and how you see the balance changing (if at all) over the next five years or so.
3. Not only have cinema audiences risen over the last ten years but the medium is no longer dominated by 18 to 24 year olds. The spread of audience has increased in the 10 to 18 year age group as well as the 24 to 35+ year old grouping. What has caused the change? Do you see it continuing and what types of advertisers do these changes attract?
4. Write detailed and concise notes on five of the following:
   (a) BRAD
   (b) Pass on Readership
   (c) ABC
   (d) The advertising use of the Internet
   (e) Cost ranking
   (f) Cost per Thousand
   (g) Acorn.
5. Discuss the relationships that might exist between the advertisers and the media. What will both partners want from one another?

REFERENCES

The Audit Bureau of Circulation, www.abc.org.uk

British Rate and Data (BRAD) (www.brad.co.uk)

Broadcasters' Audience Research Board (BARB) (www.barb.co.uk)

Cinema Advertising Association, 12 Golden Square, London W1R 3AF; tel.: 0171 534 6363.

The Commercial Radio Companies Association, 77 Shaftesbury Avenue, London W1V 7AD; tel.: 0171 306 2603. The CRCA jointly owns Radio Joint Audience Research Ltd (RAJAR) with the BBC.

Express Newspapers (www.expressnewspapers.co.uk)

Independent Television (www.itv.co.uk)

Maiden Outdoor (www.maiden.co.uk)

Media Week (www.mediaweek.co.uk)

Mintel (www.mintel.co.uk)

Newspaper Society (NS) (www.newspapersoc.org.uk)

Outdoor Advertising Association of Great Britain (OAA), Summit House, 27 Sale Place, London W2 1YR Tel 0171 973 0315

Periodical Publishers Association (PPA) (www. ppa.co.uk)

Radio Joint Audience Research (www.rajar.co.uk)

TDI; solely transport (www.tdimedia.com)

FURTHER READING

Directory & Database Publishers Association (DPA) (www.directory-publishers.co.uk)

Mills & Allen (www.millsandallen.com)

More group now merged with J.C. Decaux (www.adshel.co.uk)

Poster Publicity (www.posterpublicity.com)

Poster Research (www.postar.co.uk)

Radio Audience Bureau (www.rab.co.uk)

The Radio Magazine (www.theradiomagazine.co.uk)

www.raynetmarketing.com

RSL Media Research Co, responsible for RAJAR (www.rslmedia.co.uk)

Russell, J.T and Lane, W.R. (1996) *Kleppner's Advertising Procedure* (13th edn), Prentice Hall, London.

8 Below the line, and new media methods

OBJECTIVES

By the end of this chapter the reader should be able to:

1. Identify the role that the direct response media play in the advertising mix.

2. Describe and evaluate the worth of new 'below the line' advertising methods.

3. Describe and evaluate the contribution of the Internet to the advertising mix.

INTRODUCTION

In the last chapter we have been looking at the conventional 'above-the-line' media available to advertisers and there is no doubt that at the present time they take the bulk of all advertising. However, the scene is imperceptibly changing with 'below the line' activity beginning to increase. With the advent of relationship marketing and producers' desire to be close to the customer, direct response advertising has come to the fore. The realisation that the consumer can be influenced at the point of purchase because that is where many buying decisions are made has led to innovative developments here. Technological development has helped drive many imaginative advertising methods including the most awesome of all, the World Wide Web.

Direct marketing and direct response

I would just say vis-à-vis the retailers broadly, it is our belief that the consumer is not looking to do business one-to-one with 500 companies.

(Denis Beausejour, VP, Advertising Worldwide, Procter & Gamble)

The term direct marketing is used when producers and buyers deal direct with one another rather than through an intermediary. Direct response advertising is when messages are sent direct to the customer, business to business or end consumer, hoping to create a direct and interactive line of communication.

Direct response advertising can be undertaken by all the following methods:

- mail
- magazines
- newspapers
- telemarketing (on the telephone)
- broadcast direct (TV, radio)
- the Internet.

The growth in direct response

The enormous growth in direct response advertising has come about because of the need of advertisers for ever greater accountability, value for money and waste elimination coupled with explosive technological developments that have improved techniques for effective personalised audience contact to a level undreamed of twenty years ago. This improvement looks set to grow even further as we move into the millennium.

Direct mail

Direct mail is the most important and the most widely used of all the direct response methods and the industry is expanding at over 15 per cent a year. Over 75 per cent of all direct mail takes place through the Post Office and they offer a comprehensive service including sales letter creation, promotion, order taking and order processing, distribution, billing and payment.

Royal Mail recently commissioned a study to provide the mail order industry with insight into what sort of promotional literature home shoppers like to receive. Undertaken by the Direct Mail Information Service, the Sector Intelligence Report On Home Shopping has a lot of good news. For instance, 63 per cent of respondents said that they found out about home shopping through direct mail, while 34 per cent said that direct mail influenced their buying (compared with 29 per cent for TV). Most importantly, the report points out that direct mail makes the majority of home shoppers feel like valued customers. The first serious attempt to quantify direct response radio was undertaken by the Direct Marketing Association, for their 1996 census. The census showed that, at that time, an average of 32 per cent of radio advertisements were for direct response campaigns. At the same time it showed that telephone direct response contiued to grow at 40 per cent a year. It has estimated that direct marketing expenditure in the UK is in the region of £6 billion.

Source: The DMA Census of the Direct Marketing Industry 1996 (www.dma.co.uk)

Direct response in newspapers and magazines

Most newspapers and many magazines will offer a direct response facility, called off-the-page advertising. Organisations will use this to advertise direct to the customer to sell or to elicit a response of some kind. The big users tend to be manufacturers by-passing the retailer and companies offering financial services. Print owners will offer advertisers a receiving service and consumers a protection service.

Direct response in broadcasting

TV and radio have a growing direct response usage similar to the advertising industries identified above (one-third of all radio ads are now direct response). Response is by telephone, increasingly by e-mail and occasionally by letter. Many telephone consumer response calls are charged at a premium rate (often over £1 per minute) with the profit on the calls going to the broadcast owner. Many consumer protection organisations have condemned this as bad practice and a customer 'scam'.

Telemarketing and direct response

The use of the telephone for direct response is another growth area. It is quick, direct and inexpensive, and most people will be prepared to come to the telephone. Many advertisers will out-source their telephone marketing, sales and advertising operations and many specialised telemarketing companies now exist.

The Internet and direct response

This will be discussed in more detail further on in the chapter.

'Junk' messages

Junk mail, telephone calls, faxes and e-mails are now a growing problem because of the development of so many different methods. It is argued that so-called 'junk' messages are messages wrongly directed and if all were targeted accurately it would not be a problem. Although research has shown that nearly three-quarters of the population will open mail that still leaves a quarter unhappy. It is seen as 'junk' for the following reasons:

- it is intrusive (this is especially true of phone calls at inconvenient times);
- it causes unnecessary litter and is environmentally wasteful;
- it creates confusion between functional, needed information and advertising and sales messages.

E-mail seems particularly susceptible to junk downloading. Known as 'spamming' it consists of advertisers targeting millions of e-mail addresses and sending some type of mass communications. We will look at this in more detail later in the chapter. At the moment it seems to be a problem without a solution.

Pushing a free newspaper into a letterbox of somebody who does not want it is trespass, a court has ruled. Robert and Julie Breckman, of Radnor Walk, Chelsea, London, received £6 compensation and £10 costs at West London County Court because the *Chelsea and Knightsbridge Eye* was delivered to their home despite a plaque stating that they did not want freesheets. They went to the law after the paper kept arriving despite repeated letters to the publishers pleading for the deliveries to stop. A spokesman for the Direct Marketing Association, whose members are responsible for targeted mailshots as well as 'un-addressed' mail, expressed surprise at the judgment. 'Intrusion is one thing but I think calling it trespass is probably a bit harsh,' he said. 'If somebody doesn't want to receive this type of mail, there should be a mechanism to prevent them receiving it.'

Reprinted from a newspaper article – source unknown

Direct response, relationship marketing/database/advertising

The enhanced capability offered by database marketing also enables the advertiser, and the agency on their behalf, to develop an ever closer relationship with existing customers on a direct response, long-term basis. Research has shown that it is much more expensive to gain new customers than it is to hold on to existing ones. So manufacturers such as Heinz or Ford, service providers such as the AA or the Royal Sun Alliance and retailers such as Tesco, Somerfield and Boots are now writing and advertising personal customised messages direct to their product users with information about new and existing products, offering both paid-for and free magazines (according to the Association of Publishing Agencies (www.apa.co.uk), the Heinz magazine now has a readership of over 4 million) and offering the opportunity to be involved in some form of sales promotion. The concept underpinning relationship marketing is the hope that this form of customised communication will win and hold the customer for life. Many relationship marketing campaigns are run through advertising agencies.

Point of purchase

Point-of-purchase advertising has grown in importance with the realisation that many purchase decisions are actually made at the point of purchase. It is an enormous business involving many different producers and manufacturers. There are literally thousands of companies in the UK and hundreds of thousands around the world offering products, services, advice and consultancy in the incentives, premiums, giftware and promotional merchandising sector. As with all media methods point of purchase is taking advantage of technological developments to create ever more exciting advertising, using, for example, lights, colour and animation to make the customer's shopping experience that much more informative and exciting.

Imaginative advertising concepts

Virtual media technology proves to be the solution to advertising problems, particularly in sports coverage. The technology features images which appear to be included in the picture even if there is a movement of the camera. One of the most interesting applications of the technology in UK sports broadcasting is removing the offending advertisements such as cigarette advertisements from programs in real-time, and replacing them with the super-imposed images on the exact areas. Virtual advertisements have appeared on the walls and playing areas of sports events.

(Ed Shelton, *Marketing*, 19 June 1997)

Product placement

Product placements, encouraging film and TV programme makers to use your product in the production for all to see, both as a means of income for the media owners and as a method of advertising for the brand owners, is a relatively new concept. When the extraterrestrial in the 1983 movie *ET* was enticed from his hiding spot by a trail of chocolate-covered peanuts, sales of the small company that manufactured the sweets jumped by 65 per cent and product placement became an important part of the movie business. The amount of product placement allowed on TV will be restricted from country to country according to government regulations and industry codes of conduct.

The makers of the 1997 James Bond film *Goldeneye* negotiated product placement sponsorship deals to the tune of £20 million from a total budget of £65 million. So the fifth James Bond, Pierce Brosnan, can be seen driving a BMW car and motor cycle, drinking Smirnoff vodka, using an Ericsson mobile phone, using a Visa credit card, wearing an Omega watch, drinking Heineken beer, using computer technology provided by Gateway 2000 and smashing a tank into a Perrier lorry. Pierce Brosnan is reputed to have received over £600 000 for his personal endorsement of Omega watches. BMW is reported to have supplied 10 BMWs for the car chases, and to have put on a global advertising campaign to promote both the film and its products in an agreement costing £17 million. In return BMW has said that it received 10 000 advance orders for its cars worth some £190 million.

Source: National press 1998

Other media advertising

Anything can be used for advertising and poster and panel development is happening in increasingly innovative ways; some are more effective than others, and advertisers would be wise to take advice before spending money on some of the more esoteric ideas. These include the following (to name but a few) with an idea given on the prices that might be demanded.

Supermarket trolleys: total up for hire, 530 000 at Asda, Kwiksave, Budgens, Somerfield, Food Giant, Sainsbury's, Savacentre. £60 000, 66 000, 4 weeks.

Floor media: various retail outlets, shopping centres and stations; £375 for 4 weeks.

Take-away food tin covers: nationwide distribution 1.5 million, £37 500.

Petrol pump handles: 83 000 nozzles, 4900 sites; £55 per site, 17 nozzles.

Golf holes: 570 golf courses, £8 per hole.

Hot air balloons: custom designed and built.

Washroom posters: 500 outlets: £22 000, 4 weeks.

Street furniture including bus shelters, road signs, seats, waste bins and public toilets. In many cases the outdoor advertising companies have free advertising rights in return for maintaining the facility e.g. bus shelter.

Wall projection: advertising images projected onto the sides of buildings; price negotiable.

There seems to be nothing that an advertiser's imagination can't mould into advertising material.

Advertising and the Internet

As a means of communication the Internet and the World Wide Web are developing at a breathtaking and awe-inspiring speed. The rise in commercial use of the Internet is also accelerating. There is now fierce competition between companies in setting up innovative, informative, attractive web sites to which Internet surfers will want to return again and again. From generic web advertising, expertise has already developed in specific areas such as retail, financial services and computer sales. It is interesting to note that many organisations are setting up sites, uncertain about their objectives, but desperately afraid that they might miss out if not involved.

There should be clear reasons why a company might want to set up a web site, sponsor the web site of others or just buy advertising space. However, because this is such a new medium there is not always clarity, and reasons for use are often uncertain and confused.

Reasons given for using the web include the following:

- It is seen as a marketing and promotional opportunity not to be missed.
- It 'fits' with company brand and promotional objectives.
- Fear of being left behind in the technological revolution.
- For company manager prestige.
- Because the competition is there.
- Stakeholders might view non-participation as a sign of staid conservatism.

As with any media form, clear web advertising objectives should be established. Advertising can be used for all the following activities:

- corporate and product brand building in the same way as 'above the line media';
- to provide corporate information for all stakeholders;
- to support the main media and remind and reinforce brand values;

- to develop sales leads;
- to sell products (e-commerce);
- to provide customer services.

All elements of the promotional mix used with the Internet – TV, newspaper, magazines, direct mail – can be used to help drive traffic to the web site by:

- adverts in main media publicising the web site;
- direct mail complementing and adding value to the main media;
- offering incentives to go to the site;
- the company web domain name on all company ads, literature, vehicles etc.

As with all other media advertising, web advertising should not be seen in isolation but as another technique that must work in harmony with promotional and marketing activity. The site must offer real benefits to the viewer if they are expected to use the site on a regular basis.

US leader in the field

There is no doubt that the USA is the leader as far as the Internet is concerned, with most of the major developments taking place in this marketplace. Because of the lightning pace of change, up-to-date, reliable figures are difficult to come by but the following will give an indication of the speed of development:

People on-line 1997	1998 on-line or have access
US, 1997: 45 million	US: 61 million
UK, 1997: 5 million	UK: 8-10 million

Advertising spend, 1997	1998
US, $900 million	US, $1,600 million
UK, $5-6 million	UK, $18 million

On-line retail spend 1997	1998
US, $2.4 billion	US, $8-20 billion
UK, $20 million	UK, $400-600 million

Of course the World Wide Web can be, and is used for many different purposes both by the business and private consumer. This includes its use as an information source, an educator, as a form of entertainment, buying and selling and marketing and advertising. It is its use as a marketing and advertising tool that is our concern here.

The Internet structure

Although many existing advertising agencies and media owners have become involved with this exciting new medium, because it is so different and because it demands different technical skills, it has spawned a whole completely new breed of players.

Internet media owners

In theory anybody with a web site is a potential media owner and can offer advertising space to the advertiser. In practice, of course, the advertiser will only pay if the advert has the potential to be seen by the company's target customers in large enough numbers to make the exercise cost-effective. Media owners will consist of companies offering the following services:

- transactions
- information
- marketing
- entertainment.

Transactions and e-commerce

As with all the above, the potential for selling products (e-commerce) through a web site is largely unknown. Figures are bandied about the amount of business achieved with the US dominating the field (approximately $3 billion in 1998). It is difficult to know what products might and might not sell on the net and it would take a brave forecaster to make definitive choices. As well as advertising and selling their own products web retailers will also take on the adverts of others thus obtaining revenue from two sources.

Retailers and the Internet

Companies are selling on the net around the world at an unknown rate even as you read this book; examples of products sold on-line include the following:

Amazon Books, selling books on-line (www.amazon.com)
Tesco Supermarkets, selling groceries (www.tesco.co.uk)
Dell Computers, selling computers (www.dell.com)
Interflora, selling flowers (www.interflora.co.uk)
Dixons, selling 'brown goods' electrical products (TVs, Music Audio Systems etc)
   (www.dixons.co.uk)
Boots, selling cosmetics and variety products (www.boots.co.uk)

Interested parties can seek out many, many more examples.

Retailers become Internet service providers (ISPs)

Dixons, the UK electrical retailers, has become the second most popular ISP in the UK after offering a free service to its customers in the middle part of 1998. Figures issued by BMRB, the research company, show that Freeserve (Dixons' ISP company) has captured 13 per cent of the market (500 000 users) in just six months. AOL has 18 per cent and CompuServe, which was first in 1997, is now third with 11 per cent. In February 1999, Tesco, the largest supermarket chain in the UK, announced that it was to offer free access to all its 10 million Clubcard users, usage just costing the price of a local phone call. In this way it hopes to boost the use of its home shopping service. There are now at least six ISPs offering a free service hoping to make money through advertising and technical support services.

Information

Many publishers, directories, magazines, newspapers, encyclopedias, news-sheets and archives, from all corners of the world are now on-line. With so many information sources now available and increasing, it is a problem for media owners to know what information to put onto the web site and what to leave off. There is the fear that traditional publishing methods could suffer if too much information is made available on the web. Some sites ask viewers to log-on with personal information and in this way they hope to identify market segments. Other sites attempt to charge for information but may find that this discourages site traffic and large audiences which devalues the attraction for advertisers.

Some examples of information sources are :

Ray Wright marketing and communication directory (www.raynetmarketing.com)
Reader's Digest, worldwide consumer magazine (www.readersdigest.com)
Financial Times, UK business broadsheet newspaper (www.ft.com)
Detailed information on every country of the world
    (www.adci.gov/cia/publications)
International Advertising Association, world trade association (www.iaaglobal.org)
Indian Express, daily Indian newspaper (www.expressindia.com)
Washington Post, US newspaper (www.washingtonpost.com)
Mintel Research Organisation (to be paid for) (www.mintel.co.uk)
Yellow Pages, business directory (www.yellowpages.com)

Some companies have found many ways of utilising web benefits. Federal Express uses it to allow clients to download paperwork and then track the product being delivered from place to place anywhere in the world (www.fedex.com).

Information portals

The sites that can make the most advertising money at the moment are those sites that can attract the most people. A 'portal' is a site entrance, the point of contact for anybody when first coming onto the Internet. These sites will offer the browser an information category and directory service enabling the visitor to move comfortably around the World Wide Web. Having control of the visitor means that they can be directed deeper into web pages owned and controlled by the search engine. The potential for advertisements and sponsorship opportunities thus becomes massive (reflected in the sharply climbing search engine share prices). Both ISPs and search engines can be default portals ('default' meaning the site that comes to view when the internet is first visited).

Examples of browser portals include:

Freeserve (www.freeserve.co.uk)
CompuServe (www.compuserve.com)
Infoseek (www.infoseek.com)
Yahoo! (www.yahoo.com)
American On Line (www.aol.com)
Excite, www (excite.com)
Altavista (www.altavista.com)
Lycos (www.lycos.com)

Marketing

Marketing opportunities abound for retail, research, information dissemination, incentives, sponsorship, PR, publicity and advertising. Any web marketing activity should be seen as an integral part of the overall marketing and advertising plan and should always be tackled with this concept firmly in the forefront of company thinking.

Advertising and sponsorship on the web

There is some confusion about advertising and sponsorship on the web with banner advertising often being sold as advertising sponsorship.

Advertising, is the use of banner ads (discussed later) placed somewhere on the web page. The ad need not have a direct connection with the web site, so long as it is a product/message aimed at the web site target audience. Banner ads dominated the ads category in 1998 with approximately 58 per cent of advertising spend.

Sponsorship, on the other hand, is different from straightforward advertising. In sponsoring the site the following conditions should apply:

- The advertiser must want to be associated with the web site owner.
- Ads placed should delve deeply into the site appearing on many web site pages.
- The tie-up between the two companies should be very clear.
- The ad content should integrate in some way with the web owners product/brand offering, e.g. joint advertising or sales promotions.

Money spent on advertising sponsorship in 1998 came to approximately 37 per cent of all advertising spend.

The categories that led on-line spending in 1998 on advertising and sponsorship include computing (26 per cent), consumer-related (24 per cent), financial services (13 per cent), new media (13 per cent), and telecom (9 per cent). Most ads were for e-commerce, accounting for about 56 per cent of all transactions (www.iab.net).

Entertainment

Advertisers want viewers to linger on the web pages that contain their ads and entertainment products can provide this condition. Individual or interactive activities can keep the participant lingering on the web page for ages, making ad awareness that much more certain (this will of course be charged at a higher price.)

Interactive advertising agencies

Conventional advertising agencies are taking on web advertising activity but because the medium is so different it has spawned a whole new generation of advertising groups specialising in web and web advert design combining both technical skills and advertising experience. Which agency to use will be subject to all the conditions identified in the chapter on advertising agencies plus the recognition that the medium is young, most participants are inexperienced and so caution should be the watchword.

Banner advertising glossary

Internet Service Providers (ISPs) enable people to access the Internet supplying users with e-mail addresses, an incoming mail-box and space for a web site. Many ISPs now offer search engine facilities.

Search engines offer users a way around the web publishing and categorising information for ease of use.

Internet portals are the first browser entry into the Internet, crucial for commercial purposes because users tend to stay with the same portal once established.

A domain name is the personal name of the visitor e.g raywright @mcmail.com or web-site domain name www.raynetmarketing.com. Web-site domain names should be simple and reflect the company or its activity e.g. www.tesco.co.uk or www. painterand decorator.com.

A default search engine is the domain company (the Portal) that opens up to the viewer when first coming to the Internet. It can be altered by the browser, but tends not to be.

Auditing is the process of verifying the number of visitors to a web site or page. Auditing can also include 'hits' or page and file 'requests'.

A banner – also called an 'ad-banner' or 'in-line ad' – is a graphic image hotlinked to a sponsor's site. Usually they range in size from 400 x 40 pixels up to 468 x 60 pixels.

Click-throughs – also called 'ad clicks' or 'requests' are when a visitor clicks on a hotlinked banner ad and is transported to the site of the banner's advertiser.

The click rate – also called 'ad click-rate' or 'click through rate' – is the number of times an ad is clicked on versus the number of times it is viewed.

Impression – when an ad is viewed it is called an impression. If an ad has 100 impressions (is seen by 100 people), and 10 of them actually click on it, then we would say that it has a click rate of 10 per cent.

CPM – a term used in the traditional advertising world. Refers to the total cost of making an ad seen by 100 people. On the web, it can be thought of as the cost for 1000 impressions/adviews/exposures.

Hits – the number of machine hits required to construct a page. Example: a page with five images and text is equal to six hits, five for graphics and one for text. Essentially, each file used to build the page that is served is counted as a hit. However, most people use the term 'hit' interchangeably with 'impression'.

Page views – also known as 'page requests' or 'page transfers' – occur when a web page is presented to a web-site visitor. Home pages generally get many more page views than sub-pages. More popular pages will cost more for advertising.

Unique host impressions – exposures or adviews to visitors from unique domain names. Example: The statistics program running on the server can tell where the visitor has come from, thus representing a unique host impression. If he or she returns in just a few minutes, the program will recognise this and not count the visit as a new impression. If he or she comes back the next day, however, it will be counted as a unique host impression again. Usually to be counted as a unique impression, at least an hour must pass between visits. If the visitor logs off, re-dials in, and visits the page again in just a few minutes, it will probably be counted as a unique host impression.

Server 'push' and client 'pull'

Client 'pull' refers to the viewer actively seeking information by clicking onto web pages, articles, advertisements and so on moving around the site seeking information.

On the other hand, server 'push technology' allows sales messages and advertisements to be 'pushed' through to the viewer via e-mail, ISP or default search engine (yahoo etc.). Companies now offer an e-mail push service offering to send messages anywhere in the world to lists of potential consumers charging by the thousand, hundred thousand or million. Called 'spamming' it has become the 'junk mail' method of the Internet. If planned and used properly, with tight segmentation and willing customer participation, it can be a useful marketing and advertising tool for keeping customers abreast with current and new developments.

The law and issues of invasion of privacy

As with all marketing and media techniques there is a concern about invasion of privacy, particularly concerning children and salacious material. International policing is difficult because Internet publishers can operate anywhere in the world and are able to move their site from region to region and country to country as and when deemed necessary. Governments are addressing the problem and regulatory needs and methods of enforcement are under discussion. Large, reasonably established, participating organisations such as ISPs, publishers and e-commerce businesses can be made to conform but, unfortunately, many smaller operations may be beyond control. Many reputable companies now issue codes of conduct they intend to abide by.

Internet Service Providers Association

The newly-formed Internet Service Providers Association is to provide publishers with a means of classifying information on the Internet, to enable parents and teachers to regulate children's use of the medium. Ispa, which staged its first AGM at the Internet World International conference in May 1996, is setting up a software standard called Pics (Platform for internet content selection). Under the scheme, publishers will grade magazines and news articles according to the level of sex, violence, nudity and bad language, so parents will be able to edit out pages deemed unsuitable for children. The Pics scheme will flash a rating before users download each page. Publishers refusing to comply will have their site banned. Ispa, which comprises 51 British members, including BT and Pipex, aims to issue a code of practice. (www.ispa.org.uk)

Security on the web

Security on the web is a problem whenever information needs to be secure or money is changing hands. Web designers argue that impenetrable 'fire walls' can be created to stop information such as credit card numbers leaking into unsafe areas. At the time of writing there is little evidence that a real problem exists with evidence of fraud below conventional credit usage (Network Associates, www.nai.com). However, research has shown that nearly 50 per cent of users are still wary about using their credit card on the net.

Importance of measurement

As with all media methods measurement, or lack of measurement, is a key factor in its usefulness. The impact of an ad on the viewer is the result of several factors – hit rate, length of exposure, level of awareness created, interest generated, correct target audience and so on. The benefits of good advertising are dependent on the number of people who see the ad, and this is why unambiguous, independently audited numbers are so important. They should show clear user profiles, just who is viewing, and of course the costs involved.

Web-site owners would like to charge by the number of people visiting the site, while web advertisers would like to pay by more tangible measures such as proof of brand awareness or sales levels.

Advertisements on the web

There are many creative choices for adverts on the web with technological development bound to throw up continuous improvements. There is a problem with consistency of approach and the standardisation of size. This can cause problems with advertisers being uncertain about the product they might be getting for their money. As with all areas of the web there is an attempt to bring order to the advertising offering but it tends to be very difficult because of the worldwide usage. In Fig. 8.1 we can see an example of some suggested sizes. These are offered in terms of 'pixels' which are the number of 'dots' that go to make up the visual image on the screen.

Types of advertisements

There are different types of ads available according to costs and level of sophistication wanted. At the present time the more sophisticated the ad offering – the more movement, colour, flashing lights, noises etc. – the more bandwidth is used and the longer will the web page take to download. This should improve in the future but in the meantime this may well cause the frustrated browser to close and move elsewhere. Different ad types available are described below.

The ad banner

We're going to look back at today's banner advertising and chuckle fondly, just like we look back on the TV advertising of the 1950s.

(Paul Rapaciolii, Web Site Editor, Reed Personnel, July 1998)

An ad banner is a type of graphic advertisement on a web page usually including the logo and/or name of the advertising organisation. Ad banners can be linked to

Fig. 8.1 Internet advertising banner sizes

the advertiser's web site and/or to any other relevant page that might stimulate browser interest. Ideally, advertisers would want the viewer to click onto the ad either to open up another web page with more information or to go to the advertiser's own web site.

Standard ad style

This is the simplest and most common type of advert seen on the web at the present time. The ad is usually at the top of the page and is static with no movement. It is seldom presented in isolation and will most likely be surrounded by other images and icons all competing for attention. Some web sites change the banner on the page every ten minutes or so. This means that if you visit a site now you will see one image but if you visit in 30 minutes you will see another. It might be that the server has many ads all following one after another and you will not see the same advert unless the site is visited more than once.

Advantages include:

- easy and relatively inexpensive to implement as only a few HTML (Hypertext Markup Language) web page layout language tags are necessary;
- uses little bandwidth.

Disadvantages include:

- little to draw attention to it and runs the risk of not being seen;
- advert moves out of sight as the page is scrolled down causing it to disappear off the top of the screen.

Rotating ads

With rotating ads a number of banner ads will be displayed consecutively in the same location, one following the other, hence the term rotating. The number of adverts and the time displayed can be varied according to the wishes of the participants. Average display time might be 10 seconds but will vary according to the message as long as it is time enough to catch the attention of the viewer and deliver the requisite information. This method can be used to deliver different ads, different but connected ads or ads all of the same kind.

Advantages are that

- movement can attract attention as long as the ads are relevant, interconnected and have important benefits to offer;
- curiosity may keep the viewer waiting for each subsequent ad;
- the images are downloaded and the viewer will continue to see them even when disconnected from the Internet. Uses little bandwidth;

Disadvantages are that

- although relatively inexpensive your advert is only one of many and can easily be missed depending on how long the viewer stays on the site;
- as with the standard ad the banner will scroll upwards out of the screen as the viewer moves to the bottom of the page if the banner and text are on the same page.

Both the techniques discussed above can be placed in a separate window using an HTML technique called 'frame'. Thus, the banners will not disappear from the screen, even if the viewer scrolls a long text, staying at the top or the side of the screen. This obviously increases the potential exposure time significantly although it can cause some viewer irritation because of loss of screen text potential.

Rotating ads with effects

This type of ad is similar to the rotating ad described above in that a number of ads can be displayed for a short period of time one after the other. However, instead of straightforward scrolling, special effects are added to the changing images.

It should attract more attention than the rotating ad because the additional effects create more attention and interest. However, the more complex the advert the longer it might take to download and run the ad, causing the frustrated viewer to move on.

Attractive backgrounds can be used on all the above to both complement the ad and add extra interest for the viewer.

Interactive programs

This ad style incorporates Java applets (i.e. small application programs). Java is a programming language created by Sun Microsystems, to be used on networks, particularly the Internet. When a person visits a web page that includes a Java applet, the applet will be downloaded to the viewer's computer (provided the viewer is using a Java enabled browser and has agreed for this to happen) along with the text and images on the same page.

Advantages:

- allows for creative and innovative input;
- interactive programs allow the viewer to affect events on the screen by clicking on to areas of interest and ignoring those that are not;
- it draws the viewer into participating.

Disadvantages:

- it can use large amounts of bandwidth making it difficult to download and slow moving from page to page;
- more expensive to purchase than other types;
- some computer equipment unable to download;
- some individuals uncertain about downloading Java programs.

More complex offerings

Compared with other media like TV and the cinema, web advertising does not yet offer the bandwidth to create full-featured multimedia presentations but time and technological progress is bound to make this happen especially when the TV and the web combine.

Pricing on the web

As with all activities associated with the web, advertising pricing methods will vary from country to country and from web site to web site. Advertising advertisers would love to measure by results – for example, by levels of brand awareness and ultimately sales achieved. Web site owners would like to charge by the CPM (cost per thousand visitors to the site). Whether this would be a charge for visitors to the site, visitors who click onto the ad or visitors who reply to the advertiser by e-mail would be open to negotiation. Because of the newness of the medium there are few precedents on price and all pricing levels and methods would probably be open to discussion and negotiation, with newer sites willing to take lower prices.

Agency payment

In traditional media, an advertiser might spend 20 per cent of the budget on creating and planning with 80 per cent on media spend. With 15 per cent commission, the agency would earn 15 per cent of the 80 per cent. With web advertising this ratio is nearer 50:50 and so the agency would only earn 15 per cent of the 50 per cent of the total budget. Because of this, the agency is likely to prefer a fee-paying basis.

CONCLUSION

Although most of the money spent on advertising in the UK and around the world is spent on above the line media there has been an enormous upsurge in the use of other, below the line, advertising media, especially in direct response advertising using TV, radio, and direct mail. The fragmentation of the main media brought about by digitalisation now makes it more difficult for the advertiser to hit the mass market in the old tried and trusted ways and direct mail offers some form of solution. The exponential growth in technology has thrown up many new and exciting advertising media opportunities most notably with the development of the World Wide Web. Still in its infancy it is expanding and developing at an unbelievable rate and there is no doubt that marketing and advertising opportunities, although still not fully understood by advertisers, agencies and media owners, abound.

CASE STUDY

FT

Making the online image match the product

Web site visitors must be persuaded to stay, but too many features could put them off by wasting their time. The process of going online can be like 'getting changed in a public place,' according to one information technology expert. 'No-one wants to be seen sporting purple Y-fronts when everyone else is wearing Calvin Kleins,' says Alex Gibbons, a consultant in the new media skills division at TMS Information Solutions of the UK.

Indeed, who among even the most avid computer buffs would have thought less than five years ago that the humble web page would today be capturing large amounts of research and development spending, be scrutinised by focus groups and be declared the coolest thing in marketing since the cinema ad?

Yet companies are still in experimental mode, assessing the new medium. Some say web graphics work, others decry them. Some say the web is the new place to be, others that it is merely a fashion. 'While there is a lot to consider, establishing the right strategy for your presence is not really that frightening. The same principles can be applied to this as with any new marketing effort,' adds Mr Gibbons. Certain basic principles can be identified. Content is the key, notably in the all-important first contact, the point at which visitors enter the site. They must be persuaded to stay.

Then there is a balance to be struck between lots of eye-catching features and none at all. The site should not look dull but it also must not introduce unnecessary delay. Also, the user must be able to move around the site, although there is much discussion about how to assist navigation. But for many organisations, just finding the way to an online presence is tricky. Lucky companies might find the skills in a web enthusiast already employed on the helpdesk. But for most, the best and easiest way forward is to seek outside help. In common with other forms of corporate communication such as advertising, this means a degree of outsourcing. 'Web publishing is no different and in some respects more complex,' says Luca Menato, executive producer of Brann Interactive. 'Unless these companies have marketing skills in-house, they are best served by outsourcing the web design and building requirements with a specialist company or web intermediaries.'

However, this can be risky. 'Culture shock' can occur when established companies come into contact with zippy web design consultancies, although many of these young start-ups are rapidly becoming attuned to the sensitivities of corporate communications. AKQA, the UK-based media consultancy, is a leading example, with a number of international brands

▶

on its books. Director Ajax Ahmed works with the metaphor of DNA to unpick the strands of a good web site.

The backbone of any site is based on performance, reliability and ease of use, but more is involved than this. His first point is that the web site should not be regarded as a new medium so much as an extension of the product. 'The secret is to have on the web site what the customer will expect, which is not what traditional advertising would say,' he suggests. Enhancing brand by association is the classic ploy in the advertising world. But this approach usually does not work online. Neither does using the web site to present a collection of related but confusing information. For example, on the BMW site, AKQA constructed an approved used car directory through which customers can find second-hand BMWs. 'We didn't bother with things like road traffic information. Customers go to the AA for that,' says Mr Ahmed.

Similarly, for Orange – the UK mobile telephone company – the web is a customer services application. Users can send text messages from its site to mobile phones, for example. There is little point in companies providing what is in effect only an online brochure if they want repeat users of the site. The deeper point is that web sites must not open up a credibility gap between themselves and the product. Mr Ahmed believes that vendors of fast moving consumable goods are particularly prone to this. 'They think that they are media owners opting for teenage content, lifestyle features or acting as a gateway to music,' he says. 'But the product is the hero. I am not saying that you cannot have stuff [which is] not about the product, only that it must be credible.'

Intuitive navigation of the site is vital. Users move away if they get lost or cannot find what they want. 'Just because it is the web does not mean it has to look like a web page. It must have a purpose,' says Dharmesh Mistry, a director at another UK consultancy, Entranet. The company designed an innovative site for the Co-operative Bank on which no service is more than one click away. Further, with a number of subtle features, the interface tries to ensure that the user always feels in control. Advertising is a key component in many web sites, although Forrester Research of the US warns against too much Internet advertising. The findings of its report, *Media's Online Challenge*, suggest a failure on the part of advertisers to attract consumer attention and establish an effective advertising vehicle. 'The fact is, consumers love online content,' says Shelley Morrisette, director of quantitative research at Forrester. 'To be effective, online media companies and advertisers need to enhance and leverage this content to gain consumers' attention and trust.' Simply asking for personal details in a registration form is not subtle enough.

Source: Mark Vernon, *Financial Times*, 2 December 1998. Used with permission.

Case study questions

1. Identify the problems associated with web design discussed above. How will this affect advertising?
2. Who are the people that should be involved with web design? Discuss the prospect of out-sourcing the process.

CHAPTER QUESTIONS

1. Discuss the relationship between 'above the line' and 'below the line' media, paying particular attention to media advertising and direct response.
2. Why has there been such a growth in direct response? Which might be the most effective method?
3. Discuss the relationship between direct response and main media advertising.
   (a) How might they be used together?
   (b) Why has ad spend moved for main media advertising to direct response?
4. Discuss web site usage; what part will advertising play?
5. Discuss the differences between web advertising and web sponsorship. What other factors should be considered when advertising on the web?

REFERENCES

Amazon Books (www.amazon.com)

Association of Publishing Agencies (www.apa.co.uk)

Boots (www.boots.co.uk)

Dell Computers (www.dell.com)

Direct Marketing Association (www.dma.org.uk)

Direct Selling Association (www.dsa.org.uk)

Dixons electrical products (www.dixons.co.uk)

Dixons, Freeserve (www.freeserve.co.uk)

Electronic Telegraph (www.telegraph.co.uk)

Federal Express (www.fedex.com)

Institute of Sales Promotions (www.isp.org.uk)

Interflora (www.interflora.co.uk)

Internet Advertising Bureau (www.iab.net)

Internet Service Providers Association (www.ispa.org.uk)

Network Associates (www.nai.com)

Ray Wright (www.raynetmarketing.com)

Sun Microsystems (www.sun.com)

Tesco (www.tesco.co.uk)

FURTHER READING

Bird, D. (1994) *Common Sense Direct Marketing*, 3rd edn, NTC Business Books, London.

Brann Research (www.brann.com)

British Promotional Merchandising Association (www.martex.co.uk/bpma)

Forrester Research (www.forrester.com)

Global Ethics (www.globalethics.org)

Internet Watch Foundation (www.iwf.org.uk)

Rockwell, B. (1998) *Using the Web to Compete in the Global Market Place*, John Wiley and Sons, Chichester.

Stern, J. (1998) *Advertising on the Web*, Que, Advertising and Training, US.

Part 3 Knowing and understanding the audience

Pester power brings rich pickings

It is a cold Wednesday and a group of children are facing a man with a clipboard who is asking them what they want for Christmas. Sid wants a remote control car, Crash Bandicoot 3 for his play station, Adidas trainers, a Puma top and a Boyzone CD. He is 5 years old. Sid is one of a number of kids taking part in a focus group (yes, even at 5 years old) held by advertising agency McCann-Erikson (www.mccann.com) to discover which brands children really want. Katherine Hannah, McCann's head of planning, says that children are increasingly sophisticated. Even at 5 and 6 they can talk about different brands and they know what they want. One of the group is so advertising literate that he even has some idea on why he is at the ad agency. 'It's like a birthday party where we eat and talk about things and then we get paid,' he says. Brian Young, a psychologist at Exeter University, says that such precociousness is not unusual. 'Recent research has shown that not only do children recognise brands at an early age, but that brand loyalty is well established by the age of 2'.

Source: Laura Collins, *The Scotsman*, 9 October 1998

In this part of the book we will be looking at the need for information from clearly identified customer segments if advertising is to be successful.

Tango, the wacky drink, attacks traditional thinking to attract the attention of the rebellious young. This irreverent spoof on religion was used in a campaign during the Christmas period.
Client: Britvic Soft Drinks Ltd   Agency: HHCL and Partners

Smirnoff's 'Through the bottle' campaign (TV and posters) showed the pure thrill of Smirnoff – a world where anything can happen. The gestalt perceptual tricks demand attention.
Client: Smirnoff   Agency: Lowe Howard–Spink (<u>www.lowehoward-spink.co.uk</u>)

This TV ad uses sophisticated humour to tell a story. A man gives red shoes lovingly made for his mother to a barmaid, in exchange for a pint of Stella Artois. Those who appreciate good lager would give anything for a pint of Stella.   *Client: Whitbread Beer Company   Agency: Lowe Howard-Spink (www.lowehoward-spink.co.uk)*

In these TV ads (entitled *Barber* and *Metro*), 'girl power' is used in a controversial way.   *Client: Wallis clothing   Agency: Bartle Bogle Hegarty   Photographer: Bob Carlos Clarke*

The Levi Strauss 'Clayman' TV ad used a cartoon and sex to sell the product.
Client: Levi Strauss   Agency: Bartle Bogle Hegarty
Photography: Directed by Mike Mort for Passion Pictures.

Here, dramatic novelty images are used to put over a fun image for a TV channel considered dull and uninteresting.
Client: Discovery Channel   Agency: Bates UK   Termite (image by) Buggy. G. Riphread/Sublime photography.

Here, bright colours and instantly recognisable images in unusual and novel poses demand audience attention.
Client: Van den Bergh   Agency: Ogilvy & Mather

" LOVE AND MARRIAGE. LOVE AND MARRIAGE. GO TOGETHER LIKE A HORSE AND CARRIAGE "

CAHN & VAN HEUSEN

NOT EVERYTHING IN BLACK AND WHITE MAKES SENSE. GUINNESS

" NUCLEAR POWER IS COMPLETELY SAFE, WITH NO ENVIRONMENTAL PROBLEMS "

PROF. D. HEARDMAN

NOT EVERYTHING IN BLACK AND WHITE MAKES SENSE

When surrounded by colour, black and white stands out and attracts attention. The use of simply irony and of black and white are now associated with Guinness.   *Client: Guinness   Agency: Ogilvy & Mather*

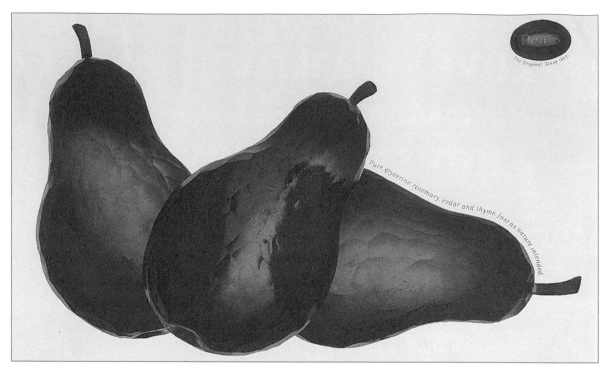

The 'pear' is used semiotically to represent both the soap and the brand.
Client: Pears   Agency: Bartle Bogle Hegarty   Photographer: Jonathan Lovekin

Semiotics imply here that the cheetah/Audi is so superior to greyhounds/lesser cars that comparison is futile.
Client: Audi   Agency: Bartle Bogle Hegarty   Photographer: Simon Mooney

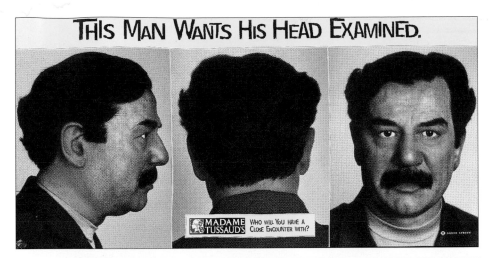

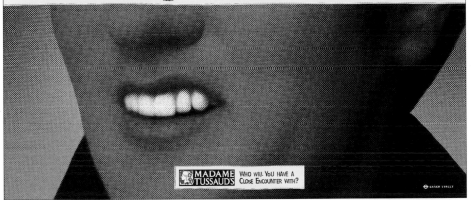

These poster images of famous and controversial figures, coupled with arresting captions, startle and demand attention.   *Client: Madame Tussaud's   Agency: J. Walter Thompson*

(*Yellow poster*) This ad illustrates the use of semiotics. Yellow and black are usually associated with vehicle breakdown (the AA), but are appropriated here to mean mental breakdown. (*Green poster*) This ad illustrates the use of gestalt grouping. The audience is drawn in, looking for order in disorder, and attempting to make sense of the poster.   *Client: The Samaritans   Agency: Ogilvy & Mather*

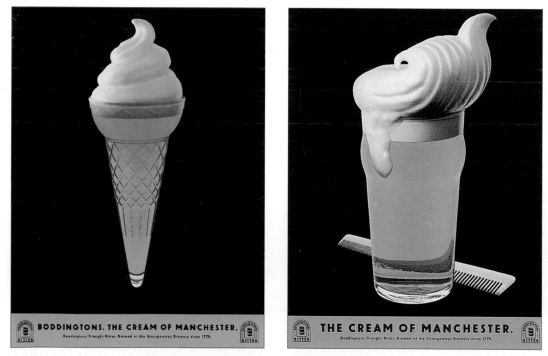

Boddington's fun and novel signature images are so well established that semiotics take over, and no product name is necessary.   *Client: Boddington   Agency: Bartle Bogle Hegarty   Photographer: Tiff Hunter*

9 The importance of information for advertising

OBJECTIVES

By the end of this chapter the reader should be able to:

1. Identify which bodies will use advertising research and why.

2. Identify and evaluate the types of research information needed.

3. Evaluate its increasing importance in the role of advertising.

INTRODUCTION

Such is the power of change we need now to take our audience's skin temperature daily.

(Anon)

The whole advertising management process has to begin with the collection of information so that sound decisions can be made about the future strategic direction of the company. Without a continuous supply of good up-to-date, relevant data on customers, target markets, competitive activity and technological media developments, any attempt to forecast and plan for the future will be confounded. It is true that some decisions have to be made without total access to all of the facts but very often action is taken based on inadequate or wrong information, leading to disastrous end results when, with a little more effort and planning, this could have been avoided. Advertising research is no different, whether undertaken by the organisation or by the advertising agency: the wrong information will lead to distorted messages sent by the wrong medium to uninterested customers and be a complete waste of time and money. In this chapter we will examine the part that information and research plays in the whole process of advertising.

The need for information

Information, the right information, is the lifeblood of any advertising activity and it has to be continuous as markets and customers change and what might be relevant and needed to successfully perform the task today might be irrelevant and redundant tomorrow. As information needs change, and becomes more demanding, so the methods and the help available to understand these changes become ever more sophisticated and numerous and the advertiser or agency that is unable

165

to keep abreast will flounder and eventually lose competitive advantage. Media owners, advertisers and advertising agencies all rely on, and instigate, copious amounts of consumer and market research, on both a national and global scale.

Media owners need information about their audiences – size, whether growing or declining; make-up; behaviour; reactions to programmes and adverts – because they have to persuade the advertisers to buy their offering in preference to others. Their need for information is in a sense reactive: the more the advertiser, the customer, demands the more they must supply or be superseded by the competition.

Advertisers and advertising agencies must have consistently reliable socio-demographic, geographic, behavioural and psychographic information about markets and audiences because they have to construct advertising messages that will have meaning, that will reach the largest possible audience, and that are seen and acted upon in a positive way by their customers.

Advertisers and advertising agencies want from the media owners reliable, verifiable information about readership, audience levels and customer reaction to adverts; they want independent, verifiable proof that the amount they spend with the newspaper, TV, outdoor or radio company works and is value for money. This can be on either a syndicated, shared cost, or customised basis.

Ineffectual advertising

Marketers of prescription drugs in the US will have spent more than $1.3 billion in 1998 on consumer advertising – a 50 per cent increase in spending over the previous year. Yet a new national study indicates consumers find most of the resulting messages more than a little hard to swallow. The national Drug Advertising Effectiveness study, completed last month by communications agency Campbell Mithun Esty (CME), polled more than 1000 men and women to determine what is remembered and liked in direct-to-consumer pharmaceutical advertising for 18 prescription drug brands. Contrary to the intent of multi-million-dollar ad spenders like Merck, Pfizer and Schering-Plough, the study revealed most pharmaceutical marketing dollars are spent on ineffective messages, with surprisingly few consumers responding favorably to the advertising for these brands.

Source: PR Newswire, 2 December 1998

The need for audience data is growing at an ever-increasing rate as result of a number of factors including the following:

- globalisation of markets; companies moving farther afield
- new technology, new media sources – must all be explored
- audience and media fragmentation – deeper exploration needed
- changing tastes and habits, causing information needs to change
- increasing industry competition – needs to be continually watched
- deregulation and the opening up of markets; opportunities to be had.

The information–gathering process

Advertising people who ignore research are as dangerous as generals who ignore decodes of enemy signals.

(David Ogilvy)

The information-gathering process can be formal or informal or a mixture of the two and it will vary in different organisations depending on size, wealth, style and the industry itself. It will also depend on the operating climate. The more turbulent the environment and the more technologically dependent the product the more will be the need for a stream of relevant up-to-date information.

Informal research

Much information gathering is done on an informal basis and tends not to be seen as advertising research, but its value cannot be overestimated. It could be argued that the successful person is the knowledgeable person who has an inquisitive inquiring mind, always asking questions about customers' viewing or reading habits, how markets are changing, competitive promotional activity and how different products are being advertised, and storing the data in their long-term memory for later use. The wise manager is the one who generates this sort of culture, encouraging employees to seek out and report back any relevant information that might have an influence on, and be beneficial to the running of the business. Sony is said to create this type of culture. Many a successful advertising campaign has been created on the back of this type of research, reinforced by more formal research.

Formal advertising research

Eventually the information-gathering process will need to be placed on a formal footing and information researched and collected, saved, built upon and used from campaign to campaign, complementing an overall professional approach. With the growth and development of information technology any advertiser, whatever its size and financial situation, can now afford to have access to information technology data storage and analysis equipment and services either by outright purchase, leasing or rental to assist in the running of an in-house research programme. Alternatively they can out-source and have the research programme run by one of the many out-of-house specialist research agencies.

International Information Service (IIS), a subsidiary of Mintel Research (www.mintel. co.uk), claims to be the world's largest product intelligence agency, operating a global product monitoring and retrieval network in 135 countries. For a fee it will initiate market and media reconnaissance, set up competitor intelligence projects and issue information on the latest relevant global product launches.

The Marketing/Advertising Information System

Advertising research is a branch of marketing research and this formal information-gathering system can be identified under the heading of a Marketing/Advertising Information System (MIS), (see Fig. 9.1). This formal gathering process will be geared to the needs of the advertiser and can be broken down into the following four areas.

Internal marketing/advertising information

A company and its advertising agency will have a whole range of internal quantitative and qualitative performance indicators within its many functions and this information is essential to the advertising manager in the accomplishment of his or her job. It can be surprising how often this source of information is not utilised as effectively as it should be. The advertisers should have salespeople's reports, customer complaints, research feedback on past promotional campaigns and a marketing/advertising information system if one exists and these should be made available to complement the agency internal information sources.

Marketing and advertising intelligence system

It was stated earlier that for a company to be successful information about audiences and media types must be collected in a systematic way. It was argued that the superior performer will know more about the markets than any other participant. An advertising intelligence system is put into place to monitor the environment on a continuous basis for any relevant information that might have some bearing on the present or future advertising activity of the company and/or its agency.

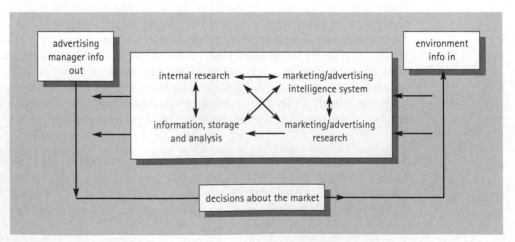

Fig. 9.1 Marketing/Advertising Information System

Obsession

The size of the intelligence unit collecting information is relatively unimportant and will depend on the size of the company. It may be a whole department or just one person working part-time. What is important is the motivating thrust. There should be an almost obsessional need to unearth and classify any snippet of information, no matter how small, that will relate to the advertiser's particular industry and can either be used immediately or stored for future use. All staff, not just those who work directly in the intelligence unit, will need to be motivated and trained in intelligence gathering so that it comes to be seen as an essential part of the company culture. In larger firms employees will spend much of their time scouring magazines, newspapers, the trade press and the Internet, pulling out any article that might supply a vital insight into the workings of advertising and so help improve performance. Working in this way a database of information can be built up and used to analyse and forecast movements in the immediate and wider environment.

Marketing and advertising research

Apart from intelligence gathering there will be a need to initiate both secondary and primary research *specifically for a new campaign* and/or a new client, covering, perhaps, a fresh problem, a new product, brand repositioning, a new client or a different medium. This aspect of the MIS will be examined in more detail shortly.

Information computer, storage, cross–fertilisation and analysis

Information from all sources identified above needs to be classified, stored, analysed, and where necessary cross-fertilised and cross-referenced ('data-mining' in the current jargon). In the distant past this task would have been undertaken manually (probably through the use of a carded classification system) but now even the smallest of companies can have access to ever more sophisticated information technology methods. Information technology and the use of computers provide the means for large amounts of information to be stored, or 'warehoused', in an information database, retrieved in moments, cross-informational comparisons made, and statistical and computer models used to examine and test the scientific validity of research undertaken or assumptions formulated.

The marketing and advertising research process

There will come a time when the advertiser or more likely its agency will want specific research to support and back up an advertising campaign. If the agency is an all-service one, the task will be performed in-house; if not, a research agency (some are identified below) will be brought in and discussion will take place about the nature of the problem. A typical advertising campaign will need detailed information about the prospective consumer, strength of feeling and reaction to the positioning of a brand, what kind of message will appeal, readership, listening and viewing habits and motivation and intention to purchase (and repurchase in the case of FMCG products).

Research objectives

The beginning of the advertising research process, and arguably the most important is to identify what information is needed. This may sound simplistic but often this first part in the process is the most difficult, often characterised by confusion and ambiguity. If the real problem is not identified at the very beginning the whole process will be distorted. So the problem holder should seek, in discussion with others, to be crystal clear about the advertising research objectives. This will probably mean knowing the answers before the research programme begins. The researcher, whether working for his or her own organisation or for an outside agency, must develop skills in getting to the heart of the problem. There might well be a series of research sub-objectives moving from exploratory concept research using small focus groups to discuss general advert ideas, perhaps using story boards or mock-up TV adverts, which then become the basis for a larger test sample.

The client agency 'brief' and research

This will involve talking to the client, going away and analysing the information, and then returning with the 'brief' that sets out the client's needs as the researcher understands them. This process will be repeated, back and forth if necessary, until nobody is in any doubt about the purpose of the advertising research. Despite the amount of professional support available in survey design, there exist advertising research reports commissioned by companies that are gathering dust in boardroom cupboards because the wrong problem has been identified and the wrong objectives set at the beginning of the process, nullifying the end result.

The budget

There is always a cost involved with this kind of project and advertising research is no different. So a budget must be set spelling out intermediate and overall costs. If an outside agency is being used, a written estimate can be obtained detailing the various options and prices. A cost/benefit analysis will reveal whether the research is worth undertaking as the cost of the research should not outweigh the value of the information collected.

The target sample

Crucial to the whole process is a clear description of the target market segment to be interviewed. It is self-evident that if the information collected is to be of value it must come from the customers who are or might be involved in the transaction and it is hoped might eventually influence the purchase, buy or use the product or service. The sample chosen must be representative in terms of sex, age, social class, lifestyle and so on of the target segment as a whole and be in large enough numbers to allow for differences of opinion. Sampling is a sophisticated process but small, medium or large numbers of respondents can be used depending on the stage of the advertising process, the kind of information needed and the statistical levels of probability demanded by the outcome. Get this wrong and the advertising research will be meaningless and money will be wasted.

Method of information collection

Many methods can be used in collecting the information and these will be discussed in more detail later on in the chapter. Factors dictating the method to be used will include

- existing level of market knowledge
- time available
- costs
- type of information to be collected
- size of the sample
- level of statistical exactitude needed.

Implementation and control

The advertiser will have to rely to a certain extent on the professional integrity and the reputation of the advertising research agency in ensuring that the research programme is scheduled and implemented in the most positive away. Monitoring and control mechanisms must be implemented to make certain that

- the correct respondents, in the right numbers, are interviewed,
- there is no interviewer bias, and
- the results are analysed in an objective, realistic fashion.

Analysis and information presentation

If the research has a progression of sub-objectives moving through the campaign these will discussed before moving on to the next stage. The client may or may not be there depending on the level of involvement demanded. The analysis should, of course, be as objective and realistic as possible avoiding any hint of subjective interpretation. This is easier with quantitative research than it is with qualitative because of the nature of methods used. Any misinterpretation at any stage will distort the final outcome and could lead to fundamental mistakes (still made) such as misidentified audience segmentation, wrongly coded benefit message or inadequate media usage. The final presentation should be simple (not simplistic) and clear, taking into consideration that the client audience may not be wholly research literate.

When to use advertising research

Can advertising foist an inferior product on the consumer? Bitter experience has taught me that it cannot. On those rare occasions when I have advertised products which consumer tests have found inferior to other products in the same field, the results have been disastrous.

(David Ogilvy)

When implementing a promotional campaign research information will be needed at the beginning, during and after the campaign.

At the beginning of the campaign

Advertising research can be very simple, take place over a few days and cost little more than the price of the phone calls. Or it could be more intensive and take place over many months and cost tens of thousands of pounds. Some form of advertising research will always be initiated at the beginning of a campaign to establish the present situation ('evaluation and diagnostic pre-testing'). Both qualitative methods (such as focus groups) and quantitative methods (such as closed-question surveys) can be used, one often complementing the other.

Establish starting point

This research will establish the base point from which to set advertising objectives and measure subsequent improvement. Research will continue as the campaign programme is developed, testing and re-testing the designated audience reaction to the brand and message concept, the advert idea and copy platform, colour and design evaluation of alternate positionings. As the media schedule is put together research will establish the optimum cost/benefit media method combination to be used.

During the campaign

Often called 'tracking studies', survey research will take place during the campaign, talking to the target audience to monitor awareness, interest, and hopefully action to see that what needs to happen is happening (see www.gallup-robinson.com for tracking study research services). If levels of audience awareness are not being reached contingency plans can swing into action to rectify the situation. Off-the-page advert reaction can be measured, coupon returns counted and retail audits used to measure daily product sales, depending on campaign objectives.

After the campaign

Research will always take place after the campaign ('evaluation and diagnostic post-testing') to check to see that objectives have been achieved. It is at this stage that evaluation will take place and questions are asked to attempt to find out if the campaign could be run more effectively next time around.

Secondary research

Secondary research is the seeking out of information that has already been collected by others and it is available from many – seemingly, infinite – sources as long as the advertiser is persistent, uses his or her imagination and knows where to look. This form of research would probably be undertaken first (perhaps as a prelude to doing some primary research) preparing the background to the advertising campaign and it can be undertaken at relatively little expense, on the phone or on the Internet, without ever leaving the office (this is why it is sometimes known as 'desk research'). It is infinitely cheaper than primary research which can be horrendously expensive if used in any significant amount.

Government and other official sources

There are too many government and official information sources that exist to be able to list here. Most governments are committed, in some way or another, to helping industry grow and sell products and services both at home and abroad. In the UK the 'open government' web site (www.open.gov.uk) lists hundreds of government departments. Other sites include:

Office of National Statistics (UK) (www.ons.gov.uk)
Department of Trade and Industry (DTI) (www.dti.gov.uk)
Office of Fair Trading (www.oft.gov.uk)

Other world sites include

United Nations (all sites) (www.unsystem.org)
World Bank (www.worldbank.org)
International Monetary Fund (www.imf.org)
World Trade Organization (www.wto.org)

Trade and professional associations

A few of the many advertising trade and professional organisations both in the UK and around the world (US especially) where information can be obtained through membership are:

Advertising Association (AA) (www.adassoc.org.uk)
International Advertising Association (IAA) (www.iaaglobal.org)
Institute of Practitioners in Advertising (IPA) (www.ipa.co.uk)
Chartered Institute of Marketing (CIM) (www.cim.co.uk)
Direct Marketing Association (USA) (www.dma.com)
Independent Television (ITV) (www.itv.co.uk)

Advertising trade and professional organisations will offer information and research services to members to a limited or greater extent depending on the strength of the membership, how representative the organisation is and the services it is felt should be offered to retain membership enthusiasm.

Commercial research organisations

Top research companies include:

AC Nielsen (www.nielsen.com)
Taylor Nelson (AGB audits) (www.agb.mediatel.co.uk)
Research International Ltd (www.research-int.com)

Millward Brown (RSMB) (www.millwardbrown.com)
BMRB International (www.bmrb.mediatel.co.uk)
Research Services Ltd (RSL) (www.rslmedia.co.uk)
Mintel (www.mintel.co.uk)
Mori (www.mori.com)
Gallup (www.gallup.com)
National Opinion Polls (NOP) (www.nopres.co.uk)

AC Neilsen was the largest research company in the world in 1997 with a turnover of nearly $1.4 billion, Millward Brown following with $190 million and Gallup with $187 million. Many of the research companies are subsidiaries of large media companies, and, as with advertising agencies, some offer a comprehensive service, some a limited service and others specialise in particular areas.

Services offered by commercial organisations

Experian (www.experian.com) is an example of a commercial research company offering very many advertising services. It had a worldwide turnover in 1997 of over $1.5 billion.

The particular services it offers advertisers and advertising agencies include the following

- target marketing research; identifying customers and markets;
- developing customer geographic, socio-demographic, behavioural and psychographic profiles;
- consumers mailing list compilation and management;
- telemarketing and call handling;
- customer data capture including advertising response, questionnaires, application forms and coupons;
- developing specific consumer communication strategies;
- media buying and management;
- working on relationship marketing strategies;
- pre-testing new concepts and strategies;
- public relations.

Experian owns MOSIAC, the geodemographic segmentation targeting system (similar commercial systems include ACORN and PINPOINT) which identifies consumers according to the type of neighbourhood. They claim to have nearly 780 million people classified in 16 countries. Software is available on CD in map form with geographic locations and areas coloured to match the different consumer profiles. Business Geographics Ltd offers a similar Geographic Information System (GIS) and an example can be seen on www.geoweb.co.uk with the history and construct behind the process.

Media research

My only concern is not programme quality but viewing figures, these are the currency we trade in, I stand or fall by this researched information.

(TV station executive)

Media research is at the very heart of advertising research and advertisers and agencies use media research to attempt to glean answers to the following critical questions:

- who watches, listens and reads which media, for how long and in what numbers;
- which strategic and tactical combination of media will be best suited;
- which particular channel, newspaper, magazine, progamme will be used, and why;
- what the price will be including discounts available off the card-rate;
- what ideas, copy and colour messages will be the most effective;
- what the opportunity to see/hear (OTS, OTH) will be;
- how often to advertise and whether in 'short bursts' or 'long drips';
- how each medium effectiveness is measured.

Measurement and accountability

At the heart of media research and media advertising is the overriding concern for measurement, accountability and value for money. Permeating almost every aspect of advertising is the question 'does it work?'. It can be very difficult to tell if a TV, outdoor, radio or Internet advert is working, whether it is reaching the target audience, what the reaction might be and if it is persuading people to take action. Media owners will lean toward the optimistic, assuring advertisers about levels of audience coverage and intensity of interest, whilst advertisers will be more circumspect (it's their money being spent!), suspicious that audience reaction figures can be stretched, exaggerated and even falsified by media owners wanting to trumpet the efficacy of their communication vehicle over others. In an attempt to overcome the problem and reconcile these differences the research bodies identified below have been inaugurated by all interested parties both to undertake advertising research and to monitor the results. Most are independent and attempt to offer an objective and detached account and this must carry greater validity than individual industry generated initiatives.

TV research resources

The Broadcasters Audience Research Board (BARB; www.barb.co.uk) is the joint industry committee set up to measure both BBC and commercial TV audiences (terrestrial, satellite and cable). It is an independent organisation funded by the television companies, advertising agencies and advertisers. It is responsible for quantitative and some qualitative television audience research in the UK. BARB achieves this by awarding contracts to independent research companies which maintain panels, collect, process and disseminate the data on behalf of BARB.

The current contracts are held by Taylor Nelson AGB (www.agb.mediatel.co.uk; data collection, processing and delivery), RSMB, a subsidiary of Millward Brown (www.millwardbrown.com; viewer panel control) and Research Services Limited (RSL) (www.rslmedia.co.uk; limited qualitative research in some TV areas only).

AGB has a 'Peoplemeter' in approximately 4700 homes which are a representative sample of the UK viewing population. Each household member will press their own designated button on a hand-held modem to signify when viewing, when leaving the room and when returning. The viewing figures are registered and sent automatically by phone line late at night to the main frame at AGB to be analysed and published. These viewing figures (Television Viewing Rates, TVRs) become the measure of the price to be paid for any one advertising slot. The peoplemeter is supplemented by both quantitative and qualitative research. This method is bound to get more difficult, and complex, with so many more digital channels opening up. A similar system for measuring TV audiences exists in most industrialised countries, the largest by far being contracted to AC Neilsen in the US.

Print media research

Audit Bureau of Circulation (ABC) (www.abc.org.uk), was founded in 1931 as a non-profitmaking organisation by the ISBA, providing international industry standard verification of circulation and attendance data. The ABC has a tripartite membership structure of media owners, advertisers, and the advertising agencies. It is an independent body, owned by its members and funded by subscription. It is committed to the setting of the highest benchmark standards used in the verification of accurate and comparable data. It audits newspapers (including free newspapers), directories, magazines, exhibitions and now web sites. It audits over 1600 newspapers and over 1400 consumer and business publications.

The National Readership Survey (NRS) (www.nrs.co.uk) is a non-profitmaking but commercial organisation which sets out to provide estimates of the number and nature of the people who read UK newspapers and consumer magazines. It is the British currency for the buying and selling of space in the print media. Currently the Survey publishes data covering some 300 different publications. The survey is carried out by Research Services Ltd. It is funded by the Institute of Practitioners in Advertising (16 per cent), the Newspaper Publishers Association (42 per cent) and the Periodical Publishers Association (42 per cent), and some 38000 adults are personally interviewed.

The Target Group Index (TGI) is conducted by the British Market Research Bureau (BRMB; www.bmrb.co.uk), a profitmaking commercial organisation providing much more detailed product information than the NRS, but for a smaller number of publications (about 180). As well as standard socio-demographic information it also covers over 4000 brands in more than 5000 product fields. Areas such as fast moving goods, banking, motor cars, airlines and holidays are comprehensively covered. The survey questions around 25 000 people using a questionnaire. TGI is published annually with a 6-monthly update.

JICREG (www.jicreg.co.uk), the *Joint Industry Committee for Regional Newspaper Research*, is an independent research organisation which provides readership and location figures for over 1300 regional newspapers. It is paid for by members' contributions.

Radio Research

Radio Association Joint Audience Research (RAJAR) (www.rajar.co.uk) is owned and funded jointly by both the BBC and commercial radio. Its aim is to independently measure the size of the radio audience in the UK. It has an annual sample of over 160 000 listeners filling in self-completion diaries. Listening figures for all radio stations are published quarterly with extensive and detailed target market definitions. It is the largest sample single-media research study in Europe.

Outdoor Media Research

Joint Industry Committee for Poster Audience Research (JICPAR), an independent industry research body, represents the Outdoor Advertising Association, the ISBA and the IPA. POSTAR (Poster Audience Research) was launched in April 1997 by the outdoor industry, replacing OSCAR (outdoor site classification audience research) as a more effective way of measuring the value of each and every poster site by visibility rather than output. It offers media buyers over 50 different factors by which to measure the value of every site they might want to purchase in terms of location, road type, traffic flows, bus routes, speed limits, traffic lights, angle and distance of OTS, obstructions, height from the ground, illumination, pedestrian or car, audience size, social class, sex, age etc. It is explained in detail on the Maiden Outdoor web site (www.maiden.co.uk).

Cinema research

Cinema Advertising Association (CAA) (127 Wardour Street, London, W1V 4AD; 0171 439 9531) is the association for the UK cinema industry. It commissions and conducts research into the cinema as an advertising medium including cinema admissions, publishing master lists on cinemas taking advertising and providing an industry umbrella for the annual CAVIAR (Cinema and Video Industry Audience Research) studies. The CAA also commissions both quantitative and qualitative cinema advertising recall studies. It is not an independent body.

General media

British Rate and Data (BRAD; www.brad.co.uk), owned by EMAP, is a monthly directory that supplies information about advertising rates for both classified and display ads as well as circulation figures and mechanical data, senior personnel etc. for all the newspapers and magazines in the UK (over 6500 separate titles). It also gives information for advertising on TV, radio, posters and cinema. Addresses and phone numbers are also given and it is updated monthly.

Meal Media Expenditure Analysis Ltd is a subsidiary of top US and global research company AC Neilsen (www.acnielsen.com) and it provides the latest information expenditure in the UK (and around the world through the parent company in the US) and is published in their Meal Quarterly Digest each month. Established in 1986, the Meal Register monitors more than 150 000 adverts across 360 product groups and provides total advertising expenditure on all brands within the top 1000 advertisers in television, radio, cinema and outdoors.

Media research and the Internet

As with any new media the concern for potential users is whether it will work or not. Web site owners are vigorously looking for ways to research and measure all the essential ingredients to convince advertisers that it is a worthwhile medium to use either in its own right or as an adjunct to other media. At the present time many are indecisive about measurements used in areas such as who uses the different sites, whether it is better to sponsor rather than use a straightforward display advert, and which size and position of adverts work and which do not. In the meantime research continues apace.

VNU Business Publications website mag.net, http://www.vnu.co.uk, made history when it became the first UK Internet site to receive an Audit Bureau of Circulations (ABC) audit for the traffic on its site. The site reviewed by ABC //electronic, set to an independent globally agreed standard of 'page impressions' and not 'hits', is the first Internet site audit of a UK based organisation by and for the UK industry. (www.abc.org.uk)

The audit will measure web site visits, but not a viewer profile, essential if advertisers are to know that it is their target audience that will have the opportunity to see a company advert. This can only be obtained by encouraging visitors to give more information or by research using conventional survey methods.

Integrated behaviour and media research

Ultimately advertisers, agencies and media owners want desperately to know, with optimum accuracy, who reads what newspaper, magazine and directory, watches what TV channel, listens to which radio station and might see which outdoor poster. This information will be linked to behavioural research to identify customer buying and consumer profiles so that the two patterns of behaviour, media seen and products bought, can be productively integrated.

Marketing Week (www.marketingweek.co.uk) has been blackballed by industry regulator, the Advertising Standards Authority. The magazine has been wooing potential advertisers with research that shows that 94% of marketing and advertising people read each weekly issue. But rivals at *Campaign* have objected because the sample used by independent research agency, Gordon Simmonds, was chosen from *Marketing Week's* own subscription list. So what the research really shows is that 6% of people who receive the magazine do not read every issue.

© Telegraph Group Limited, London 1996

Media measurement on a world scale

The problem is magnified when evaluated on a world scale. Most developed countries have sophisticated independent measuring organisations whilst media figures from most developing countries should be treated with caution until the source of the information is confirmed. The following factors are essential if industry figures are to be of use:

- standardisation of research methods and techniques so like can be compared with like;
- clear definition of what is meant by the use of terms such as 'circulation', 'readership', 'viewing', 'listening' and so on;

- respected and approved research collectors;
- clear source identification;
- all methods and figures to be independently audited by an accredited body.

Free and paid-for information

Everything has a price and the acquisition of information is no different. Some information can be obtained free of charge whilst other information must be paid for. Charges will vary from a few hundred pounds for an existing general market report to several thousands for more intricate information. Government information is both free and charged for, professional and trade associations supply information as part of the membership fee and commercial companies supply one-off reports for a fee and/or continuous information in return for a regular subscription (e.g. BRAD, £240 a month, Mintel market reports £500).

Advanced computerised delivery systems

IT development has revolutionised the collection and usage of information and advertisers and media owners can now have previously undreamed-of amounts of information literally at their fingertips. Advanced computerised delivery systems ensure that global information can be accessed by clients quickly, easily and whenever needed. Through a single desktop terminal, contributing research company customers can move seamlessly across a range of different databases, gathering specific information they require about a whole a range of problems across the world to use in making accurate and informed commercial decisions. Information can be supplied in many different ways: by fax or telephone, across the Internet, by CD ROM, on-line to a desktop PC, or direct into a client's own information management system.

The use of secondary research

I notice an increasing reluctance on the part of marketing (advertising) executives to use judgment; they are coming to rely too much on research, and they use it as a drunkard uses a lamp post – for support rather than illumination.

(David Ogilvy)

Secondary research can be seen as the first option in the marketing research process for many different reasons. It prepares the background to the research problem being undertaken as no decision should be made without first establishing the existing circumstances. Often the information is relatively inexpensive to collect costing little more than a local phone call, using e-mail or the World Wide Web. Even where the information is charged for it will be less expensive than if the company had to go out and undertake the research itself and competition and new technology is persistently holding and driving down prices. Other advantages include the speed in which the data can be obtained and the broad scope of global information now available.

Limitations

There are occasions when secondary research data cannot measure up to the research objective needs as inevitably it is going to be somewhat out-of-date by the time it is available for public release. Having proclaimed the use of the Internet even the best of the information obtained often applies to a year ago and in a fast moving industry such as IT this just might not be good enough. Many research problems are specific to particular companies, brands, customers and markets so although secondary research might satisfy some very basic needs there is every possibility that it might not be able to supply information needed in an explicit area. Secondary research should also be treated with caution and a certain amount of scepticism with regard to its authenticity. Information can be collected in many different ways and for many different purposes and not all agencies are as meticulous, painstaking and honest as they should be when collecting and disseminating information especially if there is some form of cost or benefit involved.

Advantages and disadvantages of secondary research

Advantages

- relatively inexpensive to collect;
- an almost limitless amount;
- can be collected quickly;
- can be obtained over the telephone, or on the Internet.

Disadvantages

- outdated;
- not specific;
- collection method unknown and could be flawed.

Primary research

It might be that the whole research problem can be solved by using secondary research but it is often the case that new information, not available through secondary search, has to be obtained and this would entail the use of primary research, first-hand research, which is the collecting of specialised information not already available. Existing research has been identified as secondary research but there will be many occasions when the information needed does not exist, or if it does, it is not specialised enough to fulfil the need. When this is the case the company will need to undertake first-hand research itself, either in-house or by the use of an outside, specialised agency. It should never be undertaken lightly because of the high cost involved.

Advantages and disadvantages of primary research

Advantages

- customised to meet identified need;
- control over collection and analysis;
- ownership.

Disadvantages

- expensive;
- can take time to organise, collect and analyse;
- security considerations.

Basically primary research can be broken down into three different types: experimental, observational and survey-based.

Experimental research

With experimental research, the researcher attempts to isolate the variable that needs to be tested from all other variables. Selected potential or existing consumers in the product/service target audience are then used to test out the value of a particular assumption. It is often used in direct mail advertising as this lends itself to this kind of experiment.

The split-test

A common experimental technique is the split-test, in which a magazine or newspaper splits its circulation so that an advertiser can run a separate ad in each portion and then compare effectiveness. A scientific approach is adopted with one group the 'control group', being given the standard advertisement and the other, the 'experimental group', being given the changed advertisement. Alterations in the advert given to the experimental group can be made to the artwork, size, colour, position, headline, slogan, wording, fount size etc. to try to see what has the greatest effect on recall or sales.

Observational research

Observational research is attractive because it is relatively low in cost and it can be carried out by 'human' and/or 'machine'. In simple terms it consists of observing phenomena and counting, recording or interpreting so as to observe behaviour and identify differences, similarities, usual and unusual behaviour. Increasingly videos are used to endlessly watch the movement of customers to see what catches the attention and what is ignored (this has stimulated civil rights complaints about unacceptable intrusion). Cameras are used in supermarkets to study how shoppers move around the store, which adverts are noticed and which are passed by without a second's glance. Video cameras are even used in people's homes (with their permission of course) to look at behaviour before, during and after the showing of adverts (the videos being studied and analysed later often by professional behavioural psychologists).

Individuals can also be watched to see how they read a newspaper or magazine: front page first, then back page? do they look from left to right or right to left? where do they pause and where do they skip by? And as they pass advertising display panels, billboards and poster sites they are watched, counted and notes taken, using both human observers and mechanical electronic methods. Mechanical electronic methods are used to count numbers of cars that use a particular highway (and have the chance of seeing a billboard), and more recently the number of browsers that visit ('click on') a particular web site measured and charged as 'cost per thousand' (CPT).

Database marketing

The retail trade, particularly the supermarkets, have discovered a priceless resource with the development of EPOS (electronic point of sale) and EFTPOS (electronic funds transfer at point of sale). Combined with the loyalty card this gives them access to the customer's name and address and weekly grocery spending pattern, and if you know the content of somebody's shopping basket you can work out socio-economic, behavioural, psychographic and lifestyle factors invaluable for tight segmentation and realistic customised database communication activity such as direct mail.

All this individual shopping information can be encrypted on to the customer loyalty card allowing a whole range of exciting and innovating advertising and sales promotion programmes to be developed. Some of the following ideas are in use already and others are being tested for early launch. The customer can put the card into an interactive TV modem as they enter the supermarket. Offers in the store will be displayed and the consumer can touch the screen for money-off vouchers. The card can be used with an advertising display screen on the customer's shopping trolley and relevant products then advertised on the screen when passing. Advertising and sales vouchers, linked to information on the card, can be issued at the checkout announcing suitable new product offers as well as vouchers with value added offers as the customer leaves the supermarket.

Surveys

The use of the survey is probably the method of marketing and advertising research most recognised by professionals and lay-people alike. The image of the person in the high street, holding the clipboard and stopping passers-by and asking questions about adverts, is widespread. There are different forms of survey that can be used depending on prevailing circumstances. It can be by post, telephone, TV, Internet, or face-to-face. A company might use one or a combination of methods – for example, using TV or a poster with a telephone number somewhere on the advert encouraging an audience response.

Postal surveys

Research agencies offer a total direct mail research package from content design through to a targeted postal service almost anywhere in the world. In the UK the major player is the Post Office (www.postoffice.co.uk), which processes over 75 million letters a day.

Advantages:

- relatively inexpensive;
- Mosaic and Acorn offer pinpoint target market accuracy;
- one-stop research package.

Disadvantages:

- very low (1 to 2 per cent), slow return rate;
- 'junk' mail reputation;
- only simple information can be obtained.

The telephone and telemarketing

Over the last decade there has been a major increase in the use of so-called tele-marketing, both as a means of selling and as a means of market research. Over 95 per cent of the population now own or rent a telephone so the advertiser has potential for immediate, inexpensive access. It is highly successful for gleaning simple, limited, straightforward information. Unfortunately some 'teleselling' is disguised as research so undermining this form of marketing research.

Advantages:

- quick and relatively inexpensive;
- accurate targeting can be achieved.

Disadvantages:

- often seen as intrusive ('junk phone calls');
- a reputation that it's really selling;
- only limited, and at times suspect, information can be gleaned.

Person-to-person interviewing

Personal interviewing can take place in the high street, in a shopping centre, in the home, at work etc. It is extensively used to measure advertising recall. The respondent is asked to recall adverts seen on TV, in the newspaper etc, the day before (un-prompted recall). These are then listed. Alternatively he or she is shown a series of adverts and asked to name which ones were seen the day before (prompted recall – not as strong a measure as un-prompted recall). 'Omnibus editions' are available in which interested parties can buy in two, three or more questions to be asked as a small part of a larger survey.
Advantages:

- respondents can be easily identified and persuaded to participate;
- respondents can be guided so the questionnaire can be longer and more complex;
- many techniques, such as videos and show cards, can be used in an interactive manner.

Disadvantages:

- considered to be the most expensive method;
- interviewer bias can affect outcome if training is inadequate;
- can be a very lengthy process from inception to conception.

Quantitative research methods

Most questionnaire surveys will use questions that have been rigorously tested before use, and which are structured so that the answers can be quantified into clearly defined, coded compartments. This facilitates the collection, classification and analysis of the data and allows computer and statistical techniques to be used to analyse and cross-fertilise the viewing, reading and listening habits of the customer. Most government statistics are collected and presented in this way. Questions asked tend to be of a closed or multiple choice type so that answers can be obtained in as objective a way as possible hopefully eliminating on the way researcher bias and subjectivity. The quantitative method is attractive because the process can be undertaken in a quasi-scientific manner, the results presented in a detached and objective statistical way and year on year trends compared. Most of the media information (TV, print, radio, outdoor) discussed earlier is collected and presented in this way.

Advantages of quantitative research include objectivity – it is quasi-scientific; results can be readily statistically analysed and trends compared. Its disadvantages are that it is unable to uncover opinions, attitudes, emotions, 'gut' feelings or latent or subconscious thoughts.

Motivational research and psycho-analytical techniques

Advertising research analysts have adopted many psycho-analytical techniques from the discipline of psychology to help in understanding perception and its relationship with the innermost workings of the human mind. This form of research works on the theory that people are not able to express many of their real thoughts and concerns through more overt research methods because of subconscious constraints and other more circumspect methods must be employed. Many advertising agencies employ teams of psychologists and other social scientists to carry out motivation research in order to match their advertising campaigns to human motivation.

Focus or discussion groups

The informal discussion or focus group is probably the most used, and the most successful, of all these techniques. An organiser is employed by the research agency to select and invite a representative number of individuals (usually numbering from 5 to 20) from the target market to an informal discussion session at a hotel, a specially prepared venue or the advertising research agency itself. A facilitator then presents the group with a problem to discuss. The sessions may be semi-structured or unstructured and many different techniques can be used to stimulate discussion including TV, films, magazines and sound equipment. The focus group discussion can be recorded (through a two-way mirror if at the agency) by tape, by video or by written transcript for later expert analysis.

Electronic research methods

There are many forms of electronic gadgetry that are now used in this continuous search for understanding audience reaction to advertising messages. A galvanometer measures the strength of a subject's interests or emotions aroused by an advert or picture. It picks up chemical changes, such as sweating, that accompany levels of emotional arousal (it is the same method used with the lie-detector). Using a tachistoscope, the eye is observed and movement, pupil dilation, contraction and blinking are measured to try to ascertain the level of interest from a series of adverts offered for consideration. Increased pupil dilation and increased blinking are supposed to be indicators of high levels of recognition and interest.

Advantages and disadvantages of qualitative methods

Advantages

- can get opinions and innermost, even sub-conscious, thoughts;
- can be used as a basis for more substantial quantitative research.

Disadvantages

- small unrepresentative samples;
- subjective facilitation and interpretation.

Strategic considerations for good advertising research

- **Objectives, planning and control mechanisms**
  Clear, agreed, strategically integrated research objectives monitored and controlled in implementation and feedback.
- **Target audience**
  Clearly identified, representative, target segment with detailed audience profile.
- **Budgets**
  Objectives matched by an adequate and cost-evaluated realistic budget.
- **In-house or out-of-house**
  Out-source to an outside research agency or undertake the programme internally.
- **Accuracy**
  If any part of the process is flawed information collected will be vitiated and if used could lead to unrealistic and potentially dangerous decision making.
- **Time**
  Markets and customers are in a constant state of change and could have moved on making information outdated and useless if too long in the collection.
- **Security**
  Market advantage may well be lost if the research programme is uncovered and ambushed by a major competitor.

CONCLUSION

Detailed information about markets, customers and the media is vital to the advertising manager in making strategic and operational decisions about advertising campaigns. At the heart of advertising is the concern that, first, the message is seen, then understood and finally acted upon. If any part of this process is confounded then the whole operation, possibly costing millions, will be seen to be a failure. Market and audience research is crucial at every stage and will dictate message concept, content, style and presentation, choice of medium and the intensity of the campaign. Despite the many difficulties involved meaningful research must be the concern of all participants, advertisers, agencies and media owners if they are to justify their part in the campaign. Because of ever-rising media costs and competitive pressures advertisers are insisting on evidence, preferably independent, that rigorous research is continually being undertaken before entering into any advertising campaign. This is particularly apt when addressing the problem on a global scale.

CASE STUDY

FT

Why market research is so crucial

If you went out with a clipboard and questionnaire, or asked a focus group what they associate 'globalisation' with in the marketing industry, you would probably receive answers about worldwide branding campaigns or mergers of advertising agencies. Less visibly, but no less importantly, market research is expanding and becoming more international. According to the European Society for Opinion and Marketing Research, the world market for such research rose by about 10 per cent last year. The behaviour of multinational companies is at the core of this growth. As organisations, especially those in packaged goods, seek to improve revenues and profitability, they are becoming more interested in analysing the similarities and differences between consumers in various countries. They want to develop a common language that will enable them to achieve economies of knowledge and co-ordination. For example, Niall FitzGerald, Unilever chairman, recently addressed senior managers on the issue of 'Unileverage – without it the best in Unilever will always be less than the whole of Unilever'.

A strong element of covering one's back also lies behind the expansion in market research.

Differentiating products and services is becoming harder, and product life cycles are becoming shorter. So intuitive decision-making is riskier. It is now rare even for those who rely most on intuition to make decisions without reference to research-based analysis. On the other side of the equation, market researchers have improved the service they can offer. Historically, one of the problems with the industry has been its slowness to respond. Often the time taken to devise a questionnaire, address a particular problem, obtain the answers, and analyse the data involves such a long process that the problem itself may have changed. Given developments in PC technologies and the growth of the Internet, it should be easier for companies to develop ways of analysing and responding to problems more quickly. The service is also becoming more sophisticated as the market research and direct marketing industries move closer together. The development of database marketing and data-mining mean that clients will be able to use their own databases and 'mine' information from them to analyse consumer behaviour and predict future trends. However, there is a darker side to the development of the industry. By pursuing greater efficiency, companies have also closely examined areas of their cost structures. And because the resources of internal market research departments have been cut back so much, the function has been outsourced. It is not merely in consumer goods companies that it seems unwise to reduce market research capabilities so drastically. In essence, market research is about understanding consumers and their needs – which should be a core competence at any company's heart.

Source: Martin Sorrell, chief executive of WPP Group, writing in the *Financial Times*, 20 October 1997. Used with permission.

Case study questions

1. What is the thinking behind developing a 'common language'; and how will this affect advertising?
2. What is meant by the 'darker side to the development of the industry' and, again, what will be the affect on advertising?

CHAPTER QUESTIONS

1. Discuss the comment that we now live in the 'information age'. How will this affect the role of advertising?
2. Give examples of the part that information will play in good advertising decision making. How will the advertising information system help the process?
3. What do you consider the value of secondary research to be and why is there so much more available? Evaluate the many sources, especially the Internet.
4. What audience information might be obtained by qualitative research that possibly could not be obtained through the use of quantititative research? Discuss the value of the methods that are currently in use.
5. Discuss the role of the ABC, NRS, TGI, BARB, JICREG, RAJAR and POSTAR.

REFERENCES

ABC (Auditing Bureau of Circulation) (www.abc.org.uk)

Advertising Association (AA) (www.adassoc.org.uk)

Audits Great Britain, BARB contract (www.tnagb.com)

BRAD (www.brad.co.uk)

Broadcasters' Audience Research Board (www.barb.co.uk)

Experian (www.experian.com)

Institute of Practitioners in Advertising (IPA) (www.ipa.co.uk)

JICREG (Joint Industry Committee for Regional Newspaper Research) (www.jicreg.co.uk)

McCann-Erikson (www. interpublic.com)

Maiden Outdoor (www.maiden.co.uk)

Marketing Week (www.marketingweek.co.uk)

Mintel Research (www.mintel.co.uk)

The National Readership Survey (NRS) (www.nrs.co.uk)

AC Nielsen (www.acnielsen.com)

Ogilvy, D.(1985), *Ogilvy on Advertising,* Vintage Books, New York.

The Post Office (www.postoffice.co.uk)

Poster Research (www.postar.co.uk)

Radio Joint Audience Research (RAJAR) (www.rajar.co.uk)

Research Services Limited (RSL) (www.rslmedia.co.uk)

RSMB, viewer panel control (www.millwardbrown.com)

Target Group Index (www.bmrb.co.uk)

FURTHER READING

Association of Publishing Agencies (www.apa.co.uk)

British Market Research Association (www.amso.co.uk)

Crouch, S. (1986) *Marketing Research for Managers*, Pan Books, London.

Hart, N.H. *et al.* (1995) *Advertising*, Butterworth-Heinemann, Oxford.

International Market Research Companies (www.imriresearch.com)

Kent, R. (1994) *Measuring Media Audiences*, Routledge, London.

Market Research Society (www.marketresearch.org.uk)

The Media Village (www.mediatel.co.uk)

Office of National Statistics (ONS) (www.ons.gov.uk)

Procter, T. (1997) *Essentials of Marketing Research*, Pitman Publishing, London.

Radio Audience Bureau (UK) (www.rab.co.uk)

Radio Audience Bureau (US) (www.rab.com)

10 Customer behaviour and segmentation

OBJECTIVES

By the end of this chapter the reader should be able to:

1. Identify and analyse the influences on customer needs, wants and purchase behaviour.
2. Identify and evaluate the ways that the target market and the target audience can be segmented.
3. Describe and evaluate the relationship between segmentation, targeting and brand and message positioning.

INTRODUCTION

Experience has shown that markets cannot be treated as one amorphous mass and customers increasingly demand more customised benefits. Before markets can be segmented into meaningful groups there is a need for marketers and advertisers to understand the many influences on human behaviour. Only then can groups with the same needs and wants be segregated and personalised, relevant and welcomed benefits messages be created and then successfully targeted to receptive audiences. If the advertising department is to devise messages that will grab attention and appeal to the audience the people involved, copywriter, designer, artists must have an understanding about both the product benefits demanded and the most effective method to communicate these benefits to the target audience. Unfortunately the reasons for purchase are not always the most obvious and will often need more complex and intricate investigation if mistakes are not to be made. For example customers might state that the reason they bought one brand of motor car rather than another is because of better petrol consumption or merely as a means of transportation. However extensive research might then show that this is not the case and the real reasons for purchase are much more complex than these simple functional reasons. It seems that other factors such as the need for 'status' or 'belonging' linked to deep-seated feelings of inferiority or insecurity must be considered. If this is correct then only if these more abstract reasons are understood can the real needed benefits be clearly identified and communicated in the most appropriate and successful way.

Cultural and social influences

Sixty per cent of the newspaper space may be filled with advertising, but that advertising does not command sixty per cent of the average reader's attention. We are inured to most of these advertisements and commercials; they wash over us without even dampening the skin. We often do not stop to watch or read the ads at all, and when we do they rarely penetrate or connect with our consciousness, let alone transform our identity. True we are all persuaded and seduced from time to time by these ads, encouraged to make irrational impulsive consumer choices. But that kind of persuasion and seduction is endemic to social life; we run across it constantly and develop mechanisms to filter it out and fend it off.

(Rodney A. Smolla)

Advertisers and agencies need to understand the culture and sub-culture of societies, groups and sub-groups, because of the different needs and wants demanded both in products and in message content which will often vary from region to region and will most certainly vary from country to country. For example, symbolic colour varies from culture to culture. Black in the US is a funeral colour, whereas in India white is the funeral colour. A bride may wear white in America, but red in China. Education and levels of literacy will be different as will work and leisure activities. The things people eat, the clothes they wear, the transport they use, the way that they talk, the level of status that exist between one another will all vary according to age, gender, social class and upbringing. Advertising must reflect these differences if it is to be successful in getting its messages across.

Cultural influences

The culture of a society consists of the language, common attitudes, beliefs, ways of living, thinking and acting that are passed on from one generation to another by means of social agencies and institutions such as the government, the family, peer groups, schools, religious institutions, universities, workplaces, the police and the media. With the infrastructure, buildings and artifacts handed down from generation to generation, this all contributes to an overall common perception of the world that will vary from ethnic group to ethnic group.

Sub-cultures

A sub-culture exists within the overall culture of a society and is a minority way of living and behaving adopted by groups of people that is different in some way from the accepted widespread culture of the majority of the population. A sub-culture can be a more or less permanent way of living, affect a small or a larger part of a group member's life, and is open to change as customs and practices change to meet and adapt to new circumstances.

Examples include gay and lesbian groups; black groups; vegetarian groups; freemasons; ballroom dancing, fishing or model railway enthusiasts – all these are examples of like-minded people developing their own codes and ways of living while coming together. Perhaps one of the largest (and most profitable in advertising terms) sub-groups in the UK, and in many countries around the world, spawning its vast own sub-culture, is the world of football. Sub-cultures are the source of many 'niche' market products such as black hair care products, religious icons, ethnic foods and skateboard paraphernalia.

Religion

Religious influences in people's lives will be very different depending on upbringing and country of origin. Christianity, Buddhism, Islam, Hinduism,

Judaism, as well as religious sub-sects such as Rastafarianism, Scien Hare Krishna, all influence day-to-day living, products purchased an content. In the UK and most Western countries Christianity is very minority concern whilst in many Moslem countries Islam is at the very cen social, political and economic life.

Social influences

Although becoming less of a controlling influence than it used to be social class will still have some kind of effect on the type of person we are and the sorts of products and services we like to purchase. It is argued that social class differences vary and are more important in some countries than others. Newspaper readership still identifies broad readership bands in this way and it is common to refer, for example, to 'ABC1s', the people with the greatest disposable income, or to 'C1, C2', the largest group (see Fig. 10.1)

Social institutions

Social agencies and institutions exist whatever the level and development of society and they impose ways of thinking and forms of behaviour on group 'members'. These include basic social institutions like the family, peer groups, school, college, university, government and place of work as well as voluntary institutions such as membership of the church, social club, golf club, women's institute and so on. Some groups we are born into and others we choose to join. The importance and influence of the groups will vary from society to society and country to country affecting to a lesser or greater degree the reasons for wanting one product or brand rather than another. The most important social institution is the family and many argue that early upbringing, from birth until 7, is the period when personality and attitudes are predominantly formed. Family values are expressed in many adverts such as Kellogg's, OXO, Persil, Hovis bread and Andrex toilet tissues.

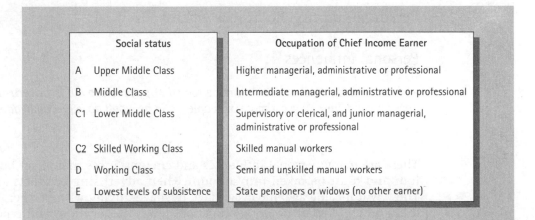

Social status		Occupation of Chief Income Earner
A	Upper Middle Class	Higher managerial, administrative or professional
B	Middle Class	Intermediate managerial, administrative or professional
C1	Lower Middle Class	Supervisory or clerical, and junior managerial, administrative or professional
C2	Skilled Working Class	Skilled manual workers
D	Working Class	Semi and unskilled manual workers
E	Lowest levels of subsistence	State pensioners or widows (no other earner)

Fig. 10.1 Socio-economic groupings

ms

'ms' are expected ways of thinking, living and behaving imposed on
f a group or sub-group by the social agencies described above. Methods
nation used range from the informal that will take place within the
ie formal that happen at school and college. Refusal to conform can
y different levels of reproach ranging from mild disapproval to terms
nent. The pressure to conform is so strong, however, that by far the
y comply. This need for social inclusion is the source of many an
...ertising campaign implying that purchase of the product will result in high
levels of social acceptance (examples include adverts for alcohol and soft drinks).

Reference groups

We also tend to develop attitudes, beliefs and ways of living from groups of people,
'reference groups', we would like to be associated with in some way or another. This
might be the groups of friends we always hang around with, the middle-class people
next door, the members of the squash club or the followers of an 'underground'
music sect. We buy products to signify association and advertisers will stress in brand
messages and images a particular brand's contribution to the process. Fashion clothing, foods, alcohol, sports equipment are all advertised at some time or other with
reference group association needs in mind, often using a well-known 'role model'
(footballer, film star, model, businessman etc.) to front the advert.

Status

The position held in relationship to others can confer elements of power, privilege
and respect. Different positions of status will develop norms and demand different
ways of behaving. So the secretary of the golf club will be expected to dress and act in
a particular way as will the sales manager, the bank manager or the boss of the company. This will manifest itself through the cars that are bought (a BMW for the
manager, a Ford Mondeo for the lowly salesperson); holidays (the Bahamas for the
bank manager, France for the staff); houses, quality of clothing; dining out, and so on.

Personal and psychological influences

Personal influences

Anyone who thinks that people can be fooled or pushed around in advertising has an in-
accurate and pretty low estimate of people – and he won't do very well in advertising.

(Leo Burnett)

There are many personal influences and circumstances that affect buying behaviour and must be taken into account when advertising products and services.
These will include age, life cycle stage (teenager, living with partner, having children, no children at home), occupation, level of education, and type of lifestyle
(socialising, home loving, sports or health fanatic etc.). We will have different
needs at 8 compared to 80; we will respond to different messages when single than

when married, and will want a whole range of different products when the children leave home than when they where first born and growing up.

Psychological influences

The purchase of products is heavily influenced by psychological influences.

Awareness, belief and attitude

We may be aware of the existence of an organisation or we may not. If we are aware then we may have developed some element of belief about the type of company it is, its image, and the value of the brands that it offers for sale in the marketplace. The strength of these beliefs is measured in terms of attitude and from attitude we develop opinions.

Belief   ×   strength of the belief   · =   attitude   →   opinions

Research has shown that customers tend to develop attitude preference mind 'sets' about companies and products from their own and others' experiences. Each 'set' contains a repertoire of corporate and product brands that they might or might not consider for purchase. This might be for FMCG products (e.g. coffee); electrical products (e.g. TVs), cars and so on. An organisation might be in the customer's positive (they like the brands), negative (they dislike the brands) or neutral (have no attitude) mind set. The task the advertiser has to achieve will vary according to the strength of the customer attitude about its products. Self-evidently the task of persuading people to purchase will be greater if the company is in their negative rather than positive set. A hypothetical example using TV manufacturers is shown in Fig. 10.2.

Advertisers go to great lengths in attempting to measure the strength of attitude towards products and many attitude tests have been developed.

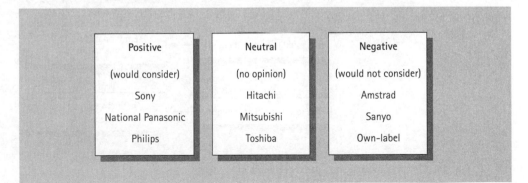

Fig. 10.2 Attitude mind 'sets'

Motivation

Motivation is the strength of feeling attached to action of some kind. In the case of producers they would like this action to include a visit to the retailer and the purchase of their product. It is the job of the producer to provide the product benefits and the job of the advertising to translate this into appropriate message incentives that generate motivation. Many theories have been propounded over the decades on the concept of motivation and it is not intended to explore this in any great depth here. However the following three will give a representative feel for

incentive ⟶ strength of feeling ⟶ motivation ⟶ action.

Plato's divided soul

This theory works on the simple concept that customers think with three basic 'brains': the rational ('the head'), the emotional ('the heart') and the instinctive ('the gut')(see Fig. 10.3). When buying products we think with an element of all three 'brains' but some individuals and groups think predominantly more with one element than with another. So some products might be purchased for instinctive reasons – impulse purchases, chocolate, alcohol, cigarettes; some for emotional reasons – perfumes, cars, fashion; and some for rational reasons – plumbing services, petrol or electricity supply. Research has indicated that 70 to 80 per cent of all consumer products purchased are for mainly emotional reasons whilst rational reasons account for 70 to 80 per cent of business to business sales.

The advertiser, recognising the existence of the three brains, will need to construct benefit messages that reflect the relevant customer need. To communicate messages about the benefits of a new car couched in rational terms such as miles per gallon, thickness of the steel used or the number of paint coverings used will be pointless if the customer wants more emotional benefits such as sex appeal, glamour or status.

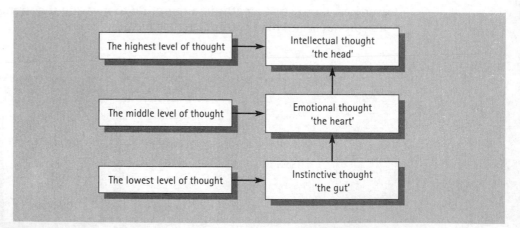

Fig. 10.3 Plato's divided soul: the three levels of thought

Maslow's hierarchy of needs

Maslow's theory on the hierarchy of needs (see Fig. 10.4) has been contorted over the years by many business commentators but part of the basic premise is still considered useful by advertising practitioners. That we are motivated by a series of different needs, some physiological and driven by genetic factors, some driven by external competitive concerns and some by deeper spiritual longings, is generally accepted by the advertising industry. As society becomes more affluent the needs and wants become more sophisticated.

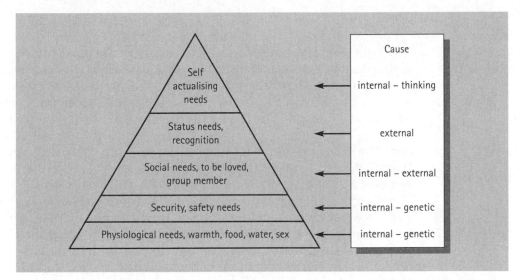

Fig. 10.4 Maslow's hierarchy of needs from *Motivation and Personality* 3rd. ed. by Abraham Maslow. Copyright 1954, 1987 by Harper & Row Publishers, Inc. Copyright 1970 by Abraham Maslow. Reprinted by permission of Addison-Wesley Educational Publishers Inc.

Safety needs may be of most concern to one group, social and 'needing to be wanted' concerns for others. For some people it may be status and recognition that matter most, while for others it may be self-actualisation and spiritual needs. The needs driving the demand might also change from product group to product group: for example, safety needs when buying financial services and status needs when buying a car. They may also change from country to country: a bicycle might be bought for sport, and so for self-actualising needs, in the UK but for transport or work, and so for security needs, in China. Advertising must reflect this veritable kaleidoscope of changing benefits demanded if it is to be recognised by the target audience.

Life roles

We adopt or are ascribed many roles in life including those of son or daughter, father or mother, sister or brother, husband or wife, lover, breadwinner, friend, student; car driver, shopper; worker, manager and so on, and we act out each role in a continually changing pattern of behaviour. There are some that argue that we have no 'core self' but 'act out' a series of roles as we move through life. Others argue that we have three selves, a 'core self' (the 'person' we think we are), a 'mirror self' (the 'person' we think others see us as) and the 'ideal self', the person we would like to be. Marketers and advertisers argue that we might buy products to satisfy the needs of any of these so-called 'life role' positions. So a woman, for example, might buy different types and qualities of product at any one time to satisfy her role as a mother (fun yoghurt for the children), her role as a 'female' (more expensive, 'self-indulgent' yoghurt) or her role as the organiser of the school Christmas party (economy yoghurt). We might buy brands that compensate for insecurity felt within the 'core self', to improve the image of the 'mirror self', or to facilitate attainment of the 'ideal self'.

Sigmund Freud

Perhaps the most controversial, and certainly the most interesting, of all the motivational theorists is Sigmund Freud. Although much of his work is now criticised and discredited there is no doubt that he had a gigantic influence on Western thinking in the earlier part of the twentieth century, not least in the advertising industry and especially in the US. To outrageously simplify an immense and detailed body of work, his great contribution to communication and advertising was to predicate the concept of the unconscious mind, an area of the mind *below* levels of thinking that could and did affect human motivation. Although, in a sense, 'stolen' from Freud's overall theory on the workings of the human mind, this basic premise had tremendous consequences for advertising and the sending of benefit messages. If true it meant that, when asked why behaviour happened in a particular way, individuals either might not know, or might articulate one conscious reason thought to be the cause when in fact a deeper reason, buried within the subconscious, is the real truth behind the motivation (see Fig. 10.5).

Personality

Personality can be defined as the sum total of individual characteristics e.g extravert, introvert, happy-go-lucky, morose etc. and will tend to manifest through ad agency lifestyle segmentation groups, discussed later in the chapter.

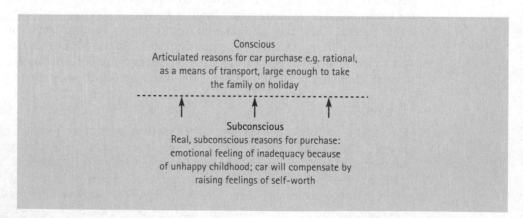

Fig. 10.5 'Freudian' conscious and subconscious activity

Advertising and psychological influences

Advertisers must use many forms of qualitative research to get at the 'real' reasons for purchase; otherwise, confusing signals will be sent to the prospective consumer. This area is probably the most difficult for advertisers as it is operating in areas of human need that are subjective and open to interpretation. Professional psychologists will often be used to aid the process of understanding and there is no doubt that promotional campaigns that have managed to reach new levels of consumer understanding have reaped the reward in terms of advertising success.

Needs, wants and demands

Advertising is criticized on the grounds that it can manipulate consumers to follow the will of the advertiser. The weight of evidence denies this ability. Instead, evidence supports the position that advertising, to be successful, must understand or anticipate basic human needs and wants and interpret available goods and services in terms of their want-satisfying abilities. This is the very opposite of manipulation.

(Charles H. Sandage)

Needs

Needs are basic inputs required to restore equilibrium to the human condition. They include physical needs such as hunger, thirst, protection from the cold, or sex; social needs such as comfort and love; and spiritual needs such as knowledge and self-enlightenment. Needs can be motivated internally or externally to the customer.

Wants

Wants are the products and services required by customers to reduce and satisfy the need requirements identified above. The customer 'wants' required, however, are culturally and psychologically generated and will vary from consumer to consumer, from region to region and from country to country.

Demand

Many people will 'want' products and services but a market will only exist when money is available to pay for that product. Many individuals would like a Mercedes or a Porsche but effective demand only exists when there is money available to purchase the product.

Decision making

The process of decision making, and all that involves, will be a major influence on buying behaviour and must be taken into account when advertising. The task that will need to be performed will depend on factors such as the degree of importance invested in the decision, who is involved in making the decision, and the decision making process itself.

The degree of importance invested in the decision

The degree of importance and the problem-solving intensity involved in the decision making will vary from product to product and customer to customer. Products of low value purchased on a regular basis (FMCG) will involve very little problem solving and will, in the main, be bought out of habit. On the other hand products bought less often and of a higher value might be either of medium or high importance and require more time, concentration and searching out before the final purchase decision (see Fig. 10.6).

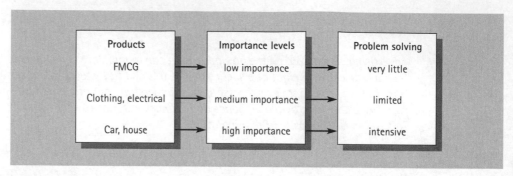

Fig. 10.6 Decision making – levels of importance

The advertising task might change in terms of the medium used and message content and intensity according to the importance level of the decision to be made.

The Decision Making Unit

There will often be more than one person involved in the decision making process and the customer is not always the same person as the consumer. In fact this might include a whole string of people often identified under the concept of the Decision Making Unit (DMU). If research shows this to be the case then the job of the advertiser becomes more complex and benefits messages might have to be aimed at more than one individual or group of individuals to achieve the end sale. In the case of a consumer product the DMU may consist of a husband and wife wanting to buy a new car; a mother, grandparents and child buying a new toy or, in a more complex scenario, parents, son and daughter-in-law, solicitor, bank manager and estate agent all involved in the purchase of a new house. With business to business products the DMU (or 'buying centre') can be extremely convoluted (see Fig. 10.7) but must be understood if the advertising is to be effective.

The Decision Making Process (DMP)

The customer will go through a decision making process when moving from unawareness of a problem to the actual purchase of a product and it is the role of advertising to facilitate and influence, whereever possible, at every stage. Decision-making models can become very elaborate as academics and practitioners try to

The Suggester:	the original person or group suggesting the product or service.
The Influencer:	any person or group that can, in any way, affect the purchasing decision.
The Decision Maker:	the person or group that has the power to make the actual purchase.
The Buyer:	the person or group that actually makes the purchase.
The End User:	the person or group that will use the product.

Fig. 10.7 The Decision Making Unit

understand both the processes involved and the factors that might have an influence as decisions are made. Figure 10.8 is a very basic model that sets it out in simple terms.

DMU members might, at any time, be at different levels of the DMP and move backward as well as forward.

Organisational buying behaviour

Advertisers need to be aware that organisational behaviour is different to consumer behaviour in the following ways:

- Products and services are bought, in the main, for rational rather emotional reasons.
- The DMU will probably involve more people and be more complex.
- The level of the buying problem will depend on whether it is a straightforward or modified re-buy, or a totally new product/service.
- The buying points will be less.
- The potential product/service order will be larger.
- The transaction will often be of a strategic nature and may involve close co-operation between buyer and seller over a long period.

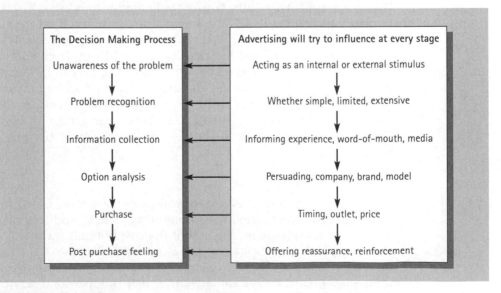

Fig. 10.8 The Decision Making Process

Market and audience segmentation

There is no such thing as national advertising. All advertising is local and personal. It's one man or woman reading one newspaper or magazine in the kitchen, watching TV in the living room or seeing a billboard from the car.

(Morris Hite)

An attempt at understanding human behaviour leads to the conclusion that people have needs and wants which seem to become ever more elaborate the more sophisticated they become. On first looking it seems that we buy products to satisfy basic functional needs, such as hunger, thirst, protection from the cold, and so on but further examination shows that needs and wants and reasons for purchase are more myriad and complex and involve an intricate mixture of the rational, emotional and instinctive, at both the conscious and subconscious level. Driving the disparate needs and wants are a multitude of factors influenced by both genetic and environmental processes. If products and services are to be purchased in the numbers necessary to sustain success then the benefits offered must match the many differing, and ever changing, needs and wants of the target market.

Segmentation, marketing and advertising

Segmentation must be seen as a process that involves marketers in many areas and at many stages in the marketing process. Marketing research will be used to identify different customer groups with different product needs and these will be translated by product developers into product benefits. Taking a simple example, a clothing manufacturer might segment the market for women's and men's clothing; they might further segment into age and social class. The advertising agency might then segment further into consumer behaviour and pyschographic groupings, honing and shaping its advertisements into customised messages that will appeal more readily to the target markets identified by the marketer. The part in the segmentation process played by the advertiser will vary from company to company and from product to product. A well-established brand, in a mature market, will have a clearly defined position and market segment and a new agency might only have to alter the approach at the edges. Conversely, a new product on the market might just have a broad segmentation outline, e.g. gender and age, and the advertising agency will need to be brought in very early in the process to add more intricate detail.

Mass advertising

In days gone by, in the developed world, companies were able to advertise to the whole market (often called the 'shotgun' approach) and lack of competition and insufficient knowledge on the part of the customer meant that economies of scale could be gained by this mass offering approach. Because of the relatively underdeveloped nature of the customers and markets it is still the way that global companies might market and advertise their products and services in developing countries with enormous populations such as China (1.25 billion), Indonesia

(210 million), Nigeria (107 million), and Brazil (164.5 million). At the risk of being bland the approach to be taken here is to try to make one advert appeal to all customers and markets.

Group segmented advertising

Because of the factors outlined above and discussed in the first part of this chapter, mass advertising is not appropriate in the more developed markets and a much more focused and audience-centred approach is necessary. For most organisations, however, it is not practical, economic or always necessary to develop individual, different, customised products and services for every single person in the market and group segmented methods are used. The market is segmented into economically viable groups of customers that have similar needs and wants so that benefits can then be more cost-effectively advertised to the group rather than to individuals.

DEFINITION	Advertising segmentation is 'Advertising product and service benefits selectively to economically viable groups of customers that have similar needs and wants'.

Advertising to the individual

The awesome development in information technology capability is beginning to make the concept of individual advertising and customised messages ever more realistic for an increasing number of industries.

Methods of segmentation

There are many ways that markets can be segmented and these will be forever changing as consumer reasons for purchase subtly change. To gain competitive advantage, advertisers, through consumer research, are continually searching for ingenious new methods that will offer more attractive and relevant audience benefits and so get their advert seen and acted upon over and above the adverts of others. Probably the first method of segmentation used, if selling in both areas, is between industrial (business to business) and consumer markets because of the strikingly different benefits demanded.

Methods of segmenting industrial markets

- Geographical location (regional, national, global).
- Size of the company (by sales, capital worth or numbers of employees).
- Density of the companies (many industries tend to cling together).
- The particular industry (retail, financial services, leisure and so on).
- Manufacturer or a service.
- Commercial, public (government) or not-for profit sector (charity).

Segmenting consumer markets

Advertising practitioners have put most effort into segmenting consumer markets, probably because of the seemingly infinite number of buying points (in theory every individual and family) available and the complex reasons for purchase when compared with business to business. Consumer markets can be segmented into many different categories.

Geographic segmentation

According to the type of selling organisation the market might be segmented according to region, town, country, continent and world trading block. The method chosen will affect both message and media choices used.

Demographics

In many cases the bottom line with advertising is the 'numbers game', how many people will have the opportunity to see the advert. In fact this is more often than not the factor that will determine the price the advertiser will pay. Demographic variables used for classification include overall size of the population, growth, densities and movement trends; and further breakdown of the population into gender, age, family size and life stage. Of particular interest to advertisers in the West are that people are living longer, less babies are being born, more couples are living together rather than getting married and one-parent households are on the increase.

Socio–economic segmentation

Demographic variables can be further sub-divided into groups based on social variables such as social class, culture and sub-culture, household type, family life stage, education and literacy levels, occupation, race, religion, nationality, leisure pursuits, club membership and so on. The audience can also be profitably divided by using socio-economic data such as disposable income, per capita income, income levels and income spread. This is crucial when advertising on a global scale.

Although any one of the variables identified here might be the basis for the advertising segmentation it is more than likely more than one will be used. So the target audience might be young married men, Afro-Caribbean origin, ABC1, university degree, enjoy adventure sports, eating out, living in the major towns. The advert content, message style and medium used would need to reflect this audience profile.

Behaviour

Advertisers also segment in terms of audience behaviour and their attitude and reactions to a company's brands.

Existing, past and new users

There are some customers more loyal than others, perhaps buying the company product for many, many years. It is argued that it can cost five times as much to obtain new customers as it costs to keep existing ones and by clear segmentation and advertising levels of loyalty can be rewarded and reinforced and customers encouraged to move up the loyalty scale. Through the use of a sophisticated marketing database and cross-referencing, loyal customers can be advertised to and cross-sold a whole range of other products from the company product portfolio. It is also often worthwhile for the advertiser to talk periodically to past users to attempt to persuade them back into the fold, and to new users to persuade them to try the product and hopefully then continue to buy it.

Heavy users

The 'Pareto' 80/20 rule, that 80 per cent of your products are used by 20 per cent of your customers, will often direct the overall thrust of the advertising. If research shows that young women between the ages of 18 and 30 drink your brand of gin and are the 'heavy' users then the benefit messages must reflect the demands of this group.

Brand switch

A great deal of advertising is concerned with seducing the consumer to switch from one brand to another. Research seems to show that customers have a repertoire of favourite brands in a product range, perhaps four or five, and they tend to switch from one to another depending on price, availability, promotional incentive, and the level of advertising used.

End use

Consumers sometimes use the product for different purposes and so benefits demanded will be different. Campbell's found that its soups were being used by some consumers as a sauce for meats and fish. This spawned a whole new product area and advertising opportunities.

Role switch and concept of self

The theory that the individual might play many roles in life, mother, daughter, wife, lover, sister, manager etc. was outlined earlier as was the idea that we may have different concepts of self, a 'core', a 'mirror' and an 'ideal'. If this is the case then the market might well have to be segmented to take account of purchase behaviour that reflects these changing role needs.

Psychographics

The biggest growth in segmentation methods has been in the use of so-called psychographics (literally the description of the mind or 'psyche' being seen as the centre of mental and emotional life, both at the conscious and unconscious level). In many cases increased affluence has rendered many of the traditional methods of segmentation, described above, outdated and unreliable. Psychographic segmentation looks at consumers' beliefs, attitudes, emotions, opinions, interests, personality traits etc. and, working on the premise that many characteristics will come together into different and separate life-view and lifestyle clusters, it attempts to identify and group like-minded people together. Research has shown that similar benefits will often be wanted by groups of consumers that have the same mental approach to life.

Group cluster change

Psychographic group clusters now abound and advertising agencies are continuously discovering more as circumstances change and consumers demand different benefits that reflect these changes. Psychographic segments are not mutually exclusive and individual consumers might be a member of many different groups depending on the products being marketed. Classifications will be constantly shifting and changing as interests, attitudes and opinions change. Very seldom will one method of segmentation be used: psychographic segments will be combined with other methods described above so as to develop customer profiles, examples of which are given later in the chapter.

Targeting

Once the bases for possible segmentation have been identified and the characteristics of each group clearly researched and established, the company must choose which segments to attack and which to ignore. By the time that the advertising agency receives the advertising brief, either marketers will already be in certain market segments or action will have been taken within the company to evaluate and analyse factors such as market size, growth, potential, cost and profit levels, levels of competition, availability of suppliers, distribution channel opportunities and so on, comparing this with internal resource capabilities and selecting market segments that they wish to enter.

The advertising agency might play a minimal part at this stage, the targeting detail being worked out by the client marketing staff, or it might have a more significant role in defining a more explicit target market if, for whatever reason, this has not been exploited in the precise way necessary for maximum effect. For example, the advertiser may want to sell to older women but may not be aware of the communicative benefits in defining and segmenting the market in more explicit terms such as behaviour, psychographics and lifestyle.

Positioning

All products (and companies), as seen by the customer, occupy some kind of 'position' in the market whether they intend it or not. This might be, for example, high price–high value, low price–low value, high price–low value, good company–not-so-good company and so on, when compared with comparable competing products and competing organisations. Most modern organisations now attempt to actively influence this position in the market by matching product and corporate benefits with the needs of clearly identified segments. The product, price and channel of distribution selected should also, if marketing managers have performed professionally, be integrated to match the identified needs of the target market.

Advertising and product positioning

Once the relevant segments have been chosen the marketer should develop brand values that reflect consumer group needs and advertising will communicate these needs and in doing so 'position' the brand in the market and, more importantly, in the mind of the relevant consumer. Again, the part that the advertising agency will play in positioning the brand will depend on the contribution by the client organisation. Some organisations are very clear about the image they want to project, whilst others are confused and uncertain. The size (and value) of the advertising task will depend on the magnitude of these problems but agencies will argue that corporate and brand positioning is crucial to the well-being of any company and so should be left to the agency professional.

Customer profiles

Messages will not be seen/read if they seem not to bear any relevance to the needs and interests of the target audience. Where applicable, detailed customer profiles should be developed for all market segments with an exact description of participants. From this advertisers can ascertain such things as age, income, class and lifestyle, enabling them to construct focused creative benefit messages exactly matching targeted group needs in terms of presentation, style and content. Customer profiles will often appear in the product positioning statement. Examples cobbled together from different agencies are given below.

General

'Go-getters': aspire after status and recognition, young, upwardly mobile, materialistic, will look for the newest and the most conspicuous product. Eat out two or three times a week, drink in pubs and clubs, will have a dozen credit cards, drive Porsches.

'Quietly comfortable': oldest of all the groups, large disposable income, confident. Like 'conservative' luxury products, dinner parties at home, three holidays a year. Drive BMWs.

'Middle of the roaders': conformist, conservative, 35–60, want safety and security, middle-income, old-fashioned values, dislike change. Will use branded products, eat out once a month, drive a Ford Mondeo and holiday in France.

'Spiritualists': inwardly driven, like to think they are non-materialistic, concerned about 'green issues'; prodigious readers, will buy own label and go to the theatre/classical music/opera on a regular basis. They will walk and cycle on a regular basis and drive a Volvo, Saab or Citroën.

The women's market

'Environmentally aware': married or living in a permanent relationship, liberal, left opinions, adopts fashionable causes, outgoing and gregarious, active in the community, works part-time.

The 'high-flyer': living in a semi-permanent relationship, 28–40 years old, doesn't want children, independent and self-centred, going places at work, affluent, high-fashion; fast-food or dines out most of the week

'Live-for-today': single, no meaningful relationship, 20–30, sensual, fun-loving, materialistic and ambitious. Out four or five times a week, clubs and pubs, high disposable income; fashion, hair, cosmetic conscious; three or four holidays a year.

'Traditionalist': married, two children over 11, reasonably affluent, believes in value for money, conservative, old-fashioned values, likes to cook at home.

The children's market

The market is predominantly segmented by age as children want different products at different ages. Unlike most other groups, children like to seem older than they are and so role models in adverts should be about one and a half years to two years older than the target market. The market is also segmented by the following:

- Power to persuade parents ('pester power'); begins around about 3 years old.
- From the age of 7 children begin to have their own disposable income.
- Future spending patterns: advertisers believe in 'catching them early' for future loyalty purchases.

Children tend to have a short attention span, like movement, colour and excitement, and develop their own language. Products must be 'cool'.

The animal market

The same concept of segmentation can also be applied to animal products markets, aimed of course at the owners, and a trip around the supermarket will reveal a plethora of products on sale for dog categories such as puppies, overweight dogs, older dogs, pedigree dogs, 'surrogate child' dogs, ill dogs and working dogs.

The segmentation process

Stage one
Market and audience segmentation

1. Identify the basis for segmentation
2. Determine the important characteristics of each segment.

Stage two
Targeting the market

3. Evaluate the marketing attractiveness of each segment.
4. Select one or more segments.

Stage three
Product positioning

5. Develop where the product will be positioned.
6. Develop an advertising approach for each targeted segment.

Segmentation and multiple benefits demanded

Consumers will buy products and services for many complex, different and shifting reasons and the task of the advertiser is to identify those that have the highest motivation. They might be classified in the following (not mutually exclusive) ways: functional and/or emotional reasons; conscious and/or subconscious reasons; role-play and 'self' concept.

Primary and/or augmented added value: primary value (value added before and at the time of the sale) includes factors such as price, convenience, perceived effectiveness, taste, shape, quality, the packaging, design and innovation, brand, associated status; feelings of security, family and social etc. Augmented added value (value added after the sale) might include after-sales service, the guarantee, the add-on benefits, delivery and installation, the returns policy etc.

Using the purchase of a watch as an example, the functional reason for purchase will be to tell the time whilst the emotional reason might be for status and recognition.

The conscious reason for purchase might also be very different from the subconscious: again taking the example of a watch, the articulated reason for the purchase may be the rational one, to tell the time, but the subconscious one may be the emotional, i.e. recognition and status. Add to this the theory of role-play and the concept of 'self' and the myriad reasons for purchase become mind-boggling.

What benefits to choose?

Any of the above can be used by the advertiser as the major benefit at the centre of the advertisement. Most products and services will have a whole raft of benefits, both functional and emotional, that the advertiser can use in the campaign. In most cases research will be used to try to identify the most effective benefit(s) to major on in the advertising campaign, however, many an advertising agency creative person has made his or her name by an 'intuitive feel' for the right benefit, usually emotional, to put into the centre of the campaign. Where multiple benefits are in evidence methods of weighting might be introduced and research used to try to subtly identify the optimum target-audience-centred approach.

The number of benefits that can be advertised at any one time will depend on the media used. TV, because of its fleeting nature, will only really accommodate one major benefit and an attempt to put over any more will dilute the overall message and risk it not being seen. On the other hand, more benefits can be offered in a newspaper ad as time can be taken in reading and absorbing the content (if seen in the first place of course.) The benefit chosen to lead with must be the most seductive and will be manifest through the product positioning statement.

Benefits of segmentation

- It helps advertising position both corporate and product brand in the marketplace.
- A product portfolio can be developed offering clear, targeted, product and service benefits tailored to meet individual and group needs.

- It enables the advertiser to focus on clearly identified group and individual needs, helping to ensure that targeted benefit messages will be read and acted upon.
- The resultant customer satisfaction should lead to greater sales and higher profit.

CONCLUSION

The times when an organisation could produce one product and market and advertise it in the same way to every market have long since passed in the sophisticated markets of the developed world. Knowledgeable and demanding audiences now insist that product and service benefits match their own needs and wants ever more closely. Unfortunately for the advertiser these 'needs and wants' are not always immediately obvious even to the target customer and the real reasons for purchase are often hidden beneath layers of complex mental and emotional mechanisms. In many cases only if social, cultural, personal and psychological influences on the customer are understood can relevant and meaningful needs be identified and productive benefits be constructed. Because it would not be practical to cater to every individual need, consumers with the same or similar benefits demands are segmented into groups of a realistic size that can then be marketed to in a profitable way. Customer benefits demanded will vary from product to product, from the simplistic to the complex, and can and will change over time. It is incumbent on the advertiser to anticipate and keep abreast of these changes if competitive advantage and message success are to be maintained.

CASE STUDY	Slicing and dicing the market

Slicing and dicing the market

Every business wants more consumers to buy more of its products or services. Unfortunately, no business can afford to splatter the market with exhaustive product variants; instead companies must come up with precisely targeted offerings every time. Here we describe two techniques that help companies to do this: market segmentation and conjoint analysis. Segmentation is the art of defining groups in a way that will be useful for marketers; conjoint analysis is a technique for optimising the products that will be offered to different segments.

Imagine you are the chief executive of a major, successful hotel chain. You operate hotels throughout the world and you are now looking for new growth opportunities. You ask yourself whether there is adequate demand for a new hotel concept in a niche in which the company does not currently operate. The concept would cater to economy-minded business and pleasure travellers. You find yourself immediately overwhelmed with questions: What would our new chain's best competitive positioning be in terms of features and amenities? What is the best location strategy? What is the best pricing strategy? What should the new hotels look like so that they will be clearly distinguishable from our other hotels? What services should we provide beyond a room for the night?

Successful Courtyard chain

Even within the room, what services are most important and what is the trade-off between a specific service and price? (For example, a lower price for the room might mean no cable movies.) What are the likely sources of new business from the competition and how much are we likely to cannibalise our own business? What should our promotional messages be?

How confident are we of our market segments and overall strategy? These are questions that the Marriott Hotel Corporation faced in the early 1980s as it sought new business opportunities. The company undertook a market-driven, customer-focused strategy as it examined opportunities. The result was its highly successful Courtyard chain, which now has more than 300 hotels, revenues in excess of $1bn and more than 15 000 employees.

Marriott based its decisions on market segmentation and conjoint analysis, two analysis methods that are widely used but whose full value is still not completely appreciated, especially by senior corporate management in other companies.

Segmentation

Market segmentation is the art and science of partitioning people or things into distinct groups. Not only will each group be distinct but ideally the groups will also be collectively exhaustive. People within each group will be more or less similar and, conversely, people across groups will be different. Segmentation can be used to find niche markets, fend off competitors and provide a base for new product design. We can create segments on the basis of different characteristics. For example, segments might be composed of individuals, households, business establishments, postal codes or cities. We can also create segments based on things that people do in purchasing products. These segments are typically composed of brands, selected product categories, use occasions, stereotyped user profiles, benefits, needs, problems to be solved or product attributes.

Conjoint analysis

Conjoint analysis is a sophisticated tool for implementing market segmentation strategies. It is used by virtually all of the Fortune 500 companies and measures the various trade-offs that consumers are willing to make when they buy a product. Its primary uses are in developing new products, repositioning old products and deciding prices. The strength of conjoint analysis is that it goes beyond simply telling us what a consumer likes about a particular product; it also helps us to understand why the consumer might choose one brand or service supplier over another. The central idea of conjoint analysis is that products and services can be described by a set of attribute levels. Purchasers attach different values to the levels of different attributes. They then choose the offering that has the highest total value, adding up all the part-worths.

Source: Paul Green and Abba Krieger, *Financial Times*, 21 September 1998. Used with permission.

Case study questions

1. Identify all the areas that Marriott Hotels would have to take into account when segmenting its market.
2. Discuss the concept of 'conjoint analysis'. What are its implications for advertising?

CHAPTER QUESTIONS

1. Discuss the many problems involved with understanding audience behaviour. How important do you think early upbringing is in affecting adult buying behaviour?
2. How can an understanding of human behaviour inform the different stages of the advertising process?

3. 'People buy products for so many different reasons and so meaningful segmentation is probably impossible.' Discuss.
4. How important do you consider corporate and product 'positioning' to be? Which is the more important?
5. Discuss from empirical observation how 'live' advertising campaigns use all the different methods of segmentation. Which do you think are the more successful?

REFERENCES

Burnett, L. *100 LEO's*; Leo Burnett Company, Chicago, Illinois.

Hite, M. (1988) *Morris Hite's Method for Winning the Ad Game*, E-Hart Press, Dallas, TX.

Sandage, C.H. (1992) 'Some institutional aspects of advertising', *Journal of Advertising*, (1993) vol. 1(1).

Smolla, A.R. 'Information, imagery, and the First Amendment: A case for expansive protection of commercial speech', 71 *Texas Law Review* 777, p. 797.

FURTHER READING

Argyle, M. 'Personality and Social Behaviour', in Harré, R. (ed.), *Personality*, Blackwell, Oxford.

Eysenk, H.J. *et al. An Encyclopedia of Psychology*, Fontana, London.

Foxhall, G. and Goldsmith, R. (1994) *Consumer Psychology for Marketing*, Routledge, London.

Gunter, B. and Furnham, A. (1992) *Consumer Profiles: An Introduction to Psychographics*, Routledge, London.

Ries, A. and Trout, J. (1980) *Positioning, 'The Battle for Your Mind'*, McGraw-Hill, New York.

Part 4 Effective audience communication

We think we will never know as much about the product as a client. After all, he sleeps and breathes his product. He's built it. He's lived with it most of his life. We couldn't possibly know as much about it as he does. By the same token, we firmly believe that he can't know as much about advertising as we do. Because we live and breath that all day.

(William Bernbach)

In the next two chapters we look at the most effective ways to communicate to different audiences, covering the strengths and weaknesses of the many media and the need for creativity in the message benefits offered.

11 The strengths and weaknesses of the various media

OBJECTIVES

By the end of this chapter the reader should be able to:

1. Identify and evaluate the strengths and weaknesses of the various media as advertising vehicles.

2. Identify and evaluate the measurement and control methods associated with each.

3. Analyse which method to use according to the advertising problem existing.

4. Outline the development of the Internet as an advertising method.

INTRODUCTION

Advertising reflects the mores of society, but it does not influence them.

(David Ogilvy)

We have looked at the communication channels available, both above and below the line, for the advertiser to select to reach the organisation's target market. The difficulty is in knowing both which individual medium to use and the best combination. Every media owner will argue that their particular medium is the most effective and should be used by the advertiser over and above any other. But to quote Mandy Rice-Davies (she of the 'Profumo Affair'), 'they would say that, wouldn't they', as they are in it for the money. The problem has become even harder with technological change and the advent of new media. In this chapter we look at the advertising services wanted from the various media and the strengths and weaknesses of each.

What advertisers want from the media

What advertisers want from the main media will vary depending on the type and size of the organisation but it is imperative for media owners to be aware of the reasons if they are to sell advertising in the global marketplace. The following will apply to a lesser or greater extent depending on these factors.

- A cost-effective way to send benefit messages that will reach their target audience.
- A flexible medium that can be adapted to meet the listening, viewing or reading needs of different customer types.
- A medium beloved by its audience so that association will enhance and add value to the product or service.
- A choice of media that will move the customer from unawareness, through awareness, to interest and to actual purchase
- A choice of options covering a range of markets from extensive through to selective and from local through to national and international.
- A medium where research can be undertaken and proof of effectiveness unequivocally obtained, preferably judged by a trusted, independent body.

Above all they want good advice and assistance based on long-term mutual needs.

The VIPS formula

David Bernstein has developed a formula and an acronym (VIPS) that succinctly and simply sums up the role that advertising might be said to play in the communication and promotion operation:

Visibility: the advertisement should be seen.
Identity: there should be no doubt whose advertisement it is or its subject.
Promise: a benefit/benefits should be offered.
Singlemindedness: it should stick to the point and not wander.

Advertising on television

ITV, Channel 4 and Channel 5

Willingness to pay will have a ceiling and I don't think it will be remotely high enough in the foreseeable future to provide secure, reliable income for entrepreneurs to take the risk of starting hundreds of expensive, high quality niche services.

(Michael Grade, Chief Executive, Channel 4, 1997)

Companies can advertise across all ITV regions or selectively across individual regions such as Anglia, London, Tyne Tees or Wales. They can also advertise on Channel 4 and Channel 5. Ninety-seven per cent of all homes within the UK own or rent a working TV able to pick up these channels and some households are able to receive more than one ITV channel. Programmes are offered 24 hours a day but peak viewing times tend to be between 18.00 and 22.30. In the UK the ITC allows an average 7 minutes per hour advertising time. Although its audiences are inexorably shrinking, ITV is still the only TV channel that can offer the sorts of mass audiences beloved by the huge global advertisers such as Procter & Gamble and Ford. Local, national and multinational businesses are currently spending more than £1.65 billion a year promoting their products and services through the ITV consortium. Channel 4 and Channel 5 have tried to differentiate themselves by the types of programmes they offer thereby inviting advertising for particular audience types.

Sophisticated viewer profiles

Sophisticated research by the independent TV broadcasting companies enables them to offer advertisers a detailed description on viewer profiles and numbers for every programme offered. They argue that this should allow the small as well as the large company to selectively advertise without efficiency loss through uninterested audience coverage.

Advantages and disadvantages of advertising on ITV, Channel 4 and Channel 5

Advantages

- Despite fragmentation it can still offer advertisers mass audiences (over 40 per cent of the population).
- Large audiences and extensive advertising revenue give economies of scale.

Disadvantages

- It is an expensive medium and prices have outstripped inflation over the last decade. Digitalisation and programme competition might well alter this situation over the coming years.
- Fear of more channel fragmentation could cause advertisers to move to other method to reach mass audiences.

Advertising on the cable network

The explosion in channel choices and station content will enable some advertisers to tightly target their audiences so that messages can be sent with little or no peripheral waste. Cable audiences are, however, considerably smaller than those of conventional television, below a million in some cases, and at the present time they tend to be very specialised. In the UK only 10 per cent of homes are connected although nearly half are bypassed and this figure will increase. This makes the medium ideally suited for small niche marketers with products or services aimed at minority, specialised and localised audiences but not for the larger mass market advertisers wanting to reach much wider audiences. Cable efficiency and targetability can provide added value to an advertising campaign, but the sheer number of channels and the microscopic audiences they typically attract make it difficult, if not impossible, to achieve mass message spread and message frequency. Soon, cable will be available in all schools, colleges and universities offering interactive, multimedia educational programmes.

Advantages of advertising on cable

- Cable is unobtrusive (being underground), needs no external aerial and can carry virtually unlimited channels.
- It can be used for multimedia and interactive activity.

Disadvantages of advertising on cable

- It is only available to those houses that it passes.
- Quality and choice of programme, crucial to advertisers, will be dependent on user companies.

Advertising on satellite

All channels and programmes offered by BSkyB are by programme, monthly or yearly subscription and tend to be aimed at a minority (a large minority with some of the sports events) selective audience and will be attractive to the same sorts of advertisers as cable and for the same reasons. The audience will, however, be widely spread because of the take-up of satellite compared with cable. Although it earned over £150 million in advertising revenue in 1997 its income from subscription is by far higher at over £1 billion and this reflects the limited attraction it has to many advertisers compared with ITV. Cable and satellite combined are now in 30 per cent of all homes and this is expected to rise to 40 per cent by the year 2001 (Mintel) but viewers will still be able to receive ITV, BBC and Channels 4 and 5. Advertising costs will vary from as little as £500 for 15 seconds on late night regional to £60 000 at peak national viewing time (detailed costs for all media in BRAD).

Station choice options already include such subjects as history, cartoons, opera, theatre, food and cooking, geographical studies, travel, a shopping channel (QVC), parliamentary activity and so on. There is almost no limit to what can be eventually offered and channels that might soon be on offer will include individual football clubs (Manchester United and Newcastle are ready to roll), videos at a time of your choice and exclusive shopping with stores such as Debenhams and Argos.

Advantages of satellite advertising

- A satellite dish has the potential to pick signals and supply programmes to anyone around the world.
- Through BSkyB it has the financial muscle to contract into major programme areas e.g. sport.
- Can deliver specific, but small audiences through pay-per-view (e.g. football, boxing matches).

Disadvantages of satellite advertising

- Not reaching a mass unified market.
- Some wastage as commercials reach non-target audiences.

Characteristics of TV

TV is at bottom a passive experience – which is its beauty.

(Viacom spokesman ,1995)

It's like going into a restaurant, having the chef point to the ingredients and saying, 'Here they are, now cook the meal yourself.' Is that what audiences want? TV audiences want to stay passive.

(Helmut Thoma, MD, RTL Plus GmbH, 1995)

- Although there have been complaints from users about the price inflation on TV advertising it still remains very cost-effective to some users when looking at cost per thousand (CPT) for reaching audiences. This is especially so in mass consumer FMCG markets.
- By utilising selected channels, stations, cable and satellite outlets and programmes, advertisers are able to provide a local, regional or national flavour to their advertising. It also enables them to reach highly selective, low number, target markets cost-effectively.
- With the advent of cable and satellite, audience numbers have started to fragment, making it more difficult for TV owners to offer mass audiences to national advertisers. This will worsen as digital permeates through the adoption curve although research shows that the masses still tend to stay with the major channels.
- It is a very flexible, adaptable and pervasive medium and almost any product or service can be advertised. Interactive multimedia offer unlimited opportunities for the future, e.g. pay-per-view, home shopping, home banking, distance learning, especially when the Internet moves from the computer to the TV in large numbers.
- Although essentially a passive medium, TV can offer the opportunity for demonstration, innovation, drama, colour, excitement and even quasi-soap-opera approaches to generate awareness and interest.
- Unlike the print media only simple benefit messages can be broadcast, and these must be expensively repeated, as the message is transient and audiences can easily forget.

Measurement and research

Advertising prices are based on audience viewing figures (TVRs) – the higher the number of viewers the higher the price to be paid for the advertising slot. This can cause problems about payment when audiences leave the room, or zip across channels when the adverts come on. BBC and the commercial channels now jointly fund the British Audience Research Bureau (BARB) to independently research and audit viewing figures. This is supplemented by other research (National Readership Survey, Target Group Index) that looks at viewing and buying habits by extensive and detailed segmentation.

Print media

Advertising in national newspapers

The new media age lowers barriers to entry. It unleashes vast energy but also potentially undermines standards of reliability, accountability, trust and accuracy.

(Michael Ovitz, President, Walt Disney Co.)

The national press is attractive to advertisers because of the range and depth of coverage available. This is especially so for the mass advertiser knowing that they can reach almost 20 million C/C1/C2 consumers by advertising in the *Sun*, the *Mirror*, the *Daily Record* and the *Daily Star*. Selective ABCs can be reached through the *Daily Telegraph*, *The Times*, and the *Independent*, women through the *Daily Mail* and individuals with liberal political leanings through the *Guardian*. Fifty-five per cent of the adult population read at least one daily newspaper and this rises to 60 per cent on a Sunday. New technology has revolutionised the approach and adverts can be designed and space obtained quickly virtually overnight. It is a well tried and tested medium and experience should guarantee safety, if not innovation, in the choice of this medium. Payment and price negotiation is with the national newspapers' own sales departments where card-rate can be discussed and argued over.

Advantages of national newspaper advertising

- National and local newspapers cover the whole of the country and are read by most of the population giving advertisers the opportunity to reach every social group both on a local and national level.
- Clear segmentation and readership profile.
- Many national newspapers have tremendous influence and respect and advertiser association can add to message impact.
- Advertising opportunities are exceedingly flexible with choice of colour or black and white, large, small, display or classified ads, many different time schedules and weekday, evening and Saturday and Sunday and other special editions.
- Many now cater for specialist groups.

Disadvantages of national press advertising

- Some newspapers have a very high advert content (over 60 per cent), even sections that consists only of ads, and this can lead to media 'clutter', reader avoidance and wasted effort and resources. Other newspapers have become so large, with so many sections that again adverts can be lost within the bulk.
- Some ad wastage for companies with skewed customer base.

Advertising in the regional and local press

The regional press is used by large, medium and small commercial and not-for profit organisations to persuade readers to buy products and services from national and local stores, come along to concerts and film shows and visit garden centres and boot sales. It is also the biggest advertising forum for selling new and second-hand cars and houses. The biggest money-spinner for the owners is the classified ads section where individuals can buy and sell anything from three piece suites and ladders to clothes and animals. According to research undertaken by the Newspaper Society, 32 million adults read classified advertising in regional newspapers – more than twice as many as any other medium.

Advantages of advertising in the local press

- It reaches local people making segmentation ideal for local advertisers.
- Will offer opportunities for classified advertising as well as display.
- In the UK it is read by the majority of the population.
- It is often referred to throughout the week giving good OTS (opportunity to see).

Disadvantages of advertising in the local press

- Very localised.
- Can create ad confusion and clutter.

Advertising in magazines

Magazines are weekly, monthly or quarterly with paid-for circulation figures that vary from *What's on TV* at 1.7 million and *Radio Times* at 1.4 million to *Practical Parenting*, 83 000, *Wedding and Home*, 43 000 and *Loaded*, 380 000. *Reader's Digest* (www.readersdigest.com) sells 1.5 million copies, and is read by 5.1 million people in the UK but has over 100 million readers and 48 editions in 19 languages around the world. There are magazines that are targeted at both the end consumer and the business market and cater for every possible interest from general men and women young and old, lower, middle and upper class, to every conceivable specialised subject – fashion and beauty, homes and gardens, practical parenting, wedding and home, photography, fishing, football, cycling, yachting, music, animals etc. The advantage for the advertiser is the tight segmentation opportunities available (identified below) in both wide and narrow markets. Consumer magazines derive most of their revenue from the cover price whilst advertising accounts for almost 80 per cent of total revenue in the case of business and the professional press. Because of the high value of some magazines, expensive-to-produce product samples (body lotion, perfume etc.) can be offered as a sales promotion with the advertiser being happy in the knowledge that it will reach the customer in an undamaged state.

Advantages of using magazines

- Magazines offer advertisers a vast number of titles (over 6500 in the UK at the last estimate) across a whole range of specialised and not so specialised areas. This allows contact with very narrow and specifically defined audiences across the whole social spectrum. This is particularly attractive to advertisers wanting to reach specific target audiences but not when attempting to reach a mass market.
- Magazines tend to have a high readership to circulation ratio and are passed on from one person to another. Some magazines hang around for weeks and months giving a high OTS.

- Many magazines are expensive to buy and expensively produced. This provides a prestige, quality environment for advertisers allowing the very latest, superb reproduction techniques to be used. Despite new techniques, however, this can lead to long lead times reducing flexibility in fast-changing markets.
- Both visual imagery and heavy copy can be used depending on the circumstances.

Disadvantages of magazine advertising

- Many thousands of magazines exist with new ones appearing and old ones disappearing on a regular basis. This can cause expensive problems if advertisers fail to keep abreast of the current situation.
- Competition can be fierce within certain industries and an advertiser may well find many competitors within the same magazine.

Advertising in business to business magazines

Business to business advertising will be one business wanting to sell industrial products to another. Both corporate and product brands will be advertised. Although visuals are used to show pictures of the product the emphasis will be on the copy informing, educating and persuading the target audience of the value of the offering. The audience, compared to that for consumer ads, will be small, specialised and probably knowledgeable, and a rational rather than emotional ad content approach will be used.

Advantages of advertising in business to business magazines

- Business to business magazines can be weekly, monthly or quarterly. They can be looked at time and time again and can offer a high OTS.
- They are often read by buyers and opinion leaders in specific industries and in many cases it is the most effective way to get to the markets.
- Many thousands exist offering an advertising medium for practically every industry and allowing precision segmentation.
- In some cases it is the only secure way of getting at particular buyers. This might especially be so if marketing abroad.

Disadvantages of advertising in business to business magazines

- So many exist that money could be wasted on advertising that gets lost amongst the clutter.
- It is an 'active' medium, has to be picked up and read, and busy managers will often either flick through or fail to read particular editions.

Advertising in customer magazines

As with free newspapers, caution is advised when advertising in customer magazines, which are relative newcomers to the advertising industry. Although some are charged for many are offered free and evidence shows that copies received free are treated much less reverently than copies paid for and so less are read. Research is being carried out by the owners on levels of readership, awareness and interest in the stories, features and adverts but concrete evidence is sketchy. Any advertising will be associated by the consumer with the proprietor of the magazine (e.g. Tesco, Safeways or Somerfield) and the products and services they sell, and this should be taken into account when considering this media form. A manufacturer might want to advertise in a customer magazine primarily to ingratiate themselves with the magazine owner rather than to necessarily reach their target market.

Advantages of advertising in customer magazines

- Many customers have great feelings of loyalty to the retail store and advertisers may glean some of this by dint of association.
- The target audience should be the wanted target audience.
- The advertiser will be able to work co-operatively with the retailer, building editorial and advertising content in a complementary way.
- It might contribute to the retailer–advertiser relationship.

Disadvantages of advertising in customer magazines

- Many, especially free ones, will not be read.
- Retailer pressure to buy advertising space may well work against best advertising practice.
- Close association with the retailer may not necessarily be advantageous.

Advertising in directories

Over 5000 directories and yearbooks are published in the UK and the number is growing. They are used by industry, by professions and by the general public.

Directories have a long life, are kept handy and are used as reference sources. There are two categories of directories – those sold or given away openly and those that have a controlled circulation – and these can be local, regional, national or international. They tend to be very specialised in the services they offer and so the advertiser can achieve extremely tight targeting certain that the readership will be highly focused. Adverts can be very cost-effective as the publication could be hanging around for long periods and, depending on usage, may be consulted on a continuous basis.

Advantages of advertising in directories

- They are kept for long periods (often for a year) and can be consulted on a regular basis.
- Many are consulted for advertising companies (e.g. *Yellow Pages*).
- Exist for both end-consumer and business to business customers.
- Different types exist for both mass and specialised markets.

Disadvantages of advertising in directories

- Many have very small readership (but could be quality if not quantity).
- Ads are sometimes left in through inertia when effectiveness has waned.
- Directories must be monitored as there is a tendency for them to 'come and go'.

Characteristics of the print media

The effectiveness of TV and print are often compared being, by far, the two major advertising methods (accounting for over 90 per cent of all revenue). Print has the following general characteristics:

- It is widespread, with the ability to reach the total population.
- A print medium exists to reach every segment in the market.
- Along with TV, it is a sophisticated medium with benefits well-proven and tested over many, many decades.
- It is an 'active' as opposed to 'passive' medium in that it has to be positively and attentively picked up and read as opposed to TV which, once switched on, stays on, and can pass superficially over an inert and indifferent audience.
- Detailed copy (as well as visual information) can be given as the reader can take time to read, put down, and read again.
- It lacks the visual and sound drama available with TV.

Measurement and research

The Audit Bureau of Circulation (www.abc.org.uk) was set up by the Association of Advertisers to independently monitor newspaper and magazine circulation and readership. With a membership of over 3000 titles globally it is the largest auditing body in the world. More detail is given about the role of the ABC and its relationship with the National Readership Survey (NRS) and the Target Group Index (TGI) in the chapter on marketing research.

Outdoor media

Outdoor media used to be seen as a support to TV and the press, reinforcing and reminding the target audience about a product that they had (hopefully) already seen advertised on the TV or read about in the newspaper. Outdoor media owners, however, insist that because of the increased sophistication in presentation, the widespread coverage they offer and the audience fragmentation of TV, outdoor advertising should be seen as a primary medium in its own right. Research has shown that solus outdoor advertisements have increased both awareness and sales on products and services – especially outdoor adverts placed around supermarkets. Companies such as Mill and Allen, Maiden and the More group now offer benefit packages aimed at particular target audiences. Outdoor sales are undertaken directly by the outdoor companies themselves.

Advantages of advertising in the outdoor media

- Because of their widespread nature outdoor media can reach every region in the UK with a relatively low cost per exposure. With the centralisation of control and national packages offered they can truly be seen as 'mass' media.
- Although it might now be seen as a primary medium in its own right it is an excellent means of supplementing other media advertising;

- It is a highly visible medium and with technological developments improving colour, lighting and movement and innovative thinking producing eye-catching creative ads.
- Although it is difficult to measure effectiveness, improvements in administration and research (POSTAR) means that more focused sites can be offered linking directly with an advertiser's target audience.
- Imaginative sites, e.g. bus shelters, seem to offer exciting new opportunities.

Disadvantages of advertising in the outdoor media

- In some areas posters proliferate and message 'clutter' is generated causing the ad not to be seen.
- Audiences can become immune to posters they see every day which then become unnoticed.
- Only a limited amount of copy can safely be used if it is to be remembered.
- There used to be complaints about badly sited, unkempt sites offered in the portfolio. (Poster owners would now argue that this is a problem of the past.)
- Some concern still exists about the environmental damage that may be caused by outdoor sites and this could encourage some not to advertise in this way.
- Flyposting can give the industry a bad name.

Measurement and effectiveness

As with the other media, accountability is of paramount importance to advertisers. They need to know that they are reaching their target audience and achieving value for money, and so this becomes just as important for the media owner. If it is proved that outdoor advertising and transport campaigns work, or if they are made to work harder, new users can be encouraged to adopt and existing users become ever more convinced. Media buyers need to know which customers pass which sites, in what numbers, walking or driving, what is the opportunity that they will see the poster and how much is remembered during and after a campaign. Reacting to customer needs the outdoor industry developed POSTAR, their own measurement and control mechanism, in which each individual site is assigned over 50 measurement characteristics; this is discussed in more detail in the chapter on marketing research. Media owners feel so confident about audience type and the number that will see a particular advertisement that they would like to charge, not by individual panel, but by total numbers of people, in the same way that TV uses TVRs. (A full description of POSTAR can be see on www.maiden.co.uk.)

Advertising on radio

The success of digital radio is far from certain. Capital is unwilling to invest substantial amounts of shareholders' money in the technology, which has no proven consumer demand.

(David Mansfield, Chief Executive, Capital Radio, UK, May 1998)

Innovative organisations will always be looking for more effective ways of communicating to target markets and as commercial radio expands, becomes more professional and specialist in the programmes it offers, more organisations are considering it as a viable option to the other media, particularly as the price of TV advertising has increased above the level of inflation over the last ten years. Because of the relatively low price of radio, a dominant share of voice can be achieved for a fraction of the money required to do so on TV; radio listening accounts for nearly a third of listeners' media consumption in a day. It allows the advertisers to influence the customers and prospects all day long, getting at them where others cannot reach – at work, out shopping or simply relaxing at home – and no other medium reaches the consumer closer to the point of purchase than radio. Half of all workers have a radio at work and nearly 90 per cent of those who drive to work listen in the car on their way. Because it is often a background medium, advertisements need to be repeated to allow a greater opportunity to hear (OTH) and should be simple and novel so as to attract attention. Radio is fighting to establish itself as a primary medium although it is still considered by most advertisers to be a secondary one, supporting TV and press advertising, reinforcing and reminding customers about the larger campaign. Digital radio is available but at the time of writing there seems to be little demand and little growth.

Advantages of radio as an advertising medium

- Radio is a personal medium, usually listened to alone and because of this, individual stations seem to generate tremendous loyalty from listeners.
- With more specialised stations and different formats developing, advertising can be selectively targeted to well-defined target audiences across the whole ABC1C2DE social range on a local, regional and national scale.
- It is an extremely mobile and flexible medium and, unlike TV, can be listened to almost any time and in any place, whether in the car, on headphones, in the home or at work.
- It is often the medium closest to the point of purchase.
- With its relatively low production costs and immediacy of implementation, radio can react quickly to changing market conditions.

Disadvantages of radio as an advertising medium

- Because of its low average audiences it is not of value to advertisers needing to reach large audiences. It also requires high advert frequency and OTH to achieve acceptable awareness numbers.
- It is often used as a 'background' medium whilst listeners are doing other things. This could cause it to lack the impact of competing media.

Measurement and effectiveness

As with all media the overriding consideration for the advertisers is the effectiveness of commercial radio in first reaching target customers in the numbers required and then facilitating listening so that clear benefit messages are both received and remembered. Radio Joint Audience Research (RAJAR, www.rajar.co.uk) is the organisation that co-ordinates the definitive measurement of radio audiences in the UK.

Funded by both commercial and BBC radio, RAJAR sets out to provide an acceptable trading currency for media owners, advertisers and their agencies. The annual sample size is in excess of 150 000 people interviewed annually.

Virgin radio (www.virginradio.co.uk) marketing managers appreciate the critical importance of good measurement and offers as part of its product portfolio a 'Premier Test package' which consists of a four-week 'heavyweight' campaign (slots at best times) at an attractive price. In addition, they will pay for the research before and after the programme.

Advertising in the cinema

Although microscopic when compared with the press and TV, cinema advertising opportunities are increasing as the industry exploits the tremendous entertainment and leisure demands that come about as society becomes more affluent. At the moment it is considered to be a narrow-cast medium attractive to companies such as Bacardi, Levi's, Fosters and Club 18–30, because its typical market is young (44 per cent under 25 years old, 74 per cent under 35 years old), with a large disposable income (67 per cent are ABC1) and enjoying conspicuous consumption of certain product categories including drinks, cosmetics, fashion and travel. But its target audience appeal is widening as the product expands.

Advantages of cinema advertising

- Creative opportunities using film, sound, colour and drama to attack all the senses.
- Clear, if narrow, target market.
- Captive audience (cinema audiences will sit through 20 minutes of adverts once settled in their seats).
- Viewers' inability to 'zap' and 'zip' through progammes as with TV and videos.
- Opportunity to show longer advertisements, 2 to 3 minutes, in attractive wide screen film format, in an entertaining environment and for some products not allowed on TV.
- Adverts can be zoned into local, regional and national areas.

Disadvantages of cinema advertising

- As with all film, TV or video media only a few simple benefits can be communicated.
- The narrow target market makes it only suitable for certain types of products. There is evidence, however, that market efforts to widen this market with improved product and service offering is beginning to work.
- Despite increased effort by cinema owners clear, reliable audience awareness measurement is still lacking.

Measurement and research

As with all other industries the cinema industry is dependent on clear, unambiguous, trusted audience research figures if it is to attract advertising away from the other media. To facilitate this process the cinema industry developed 'Cinema and Video Industry Research', 'CAVIAR' which, through primary and qualitative research, attempts to give advertisers customer information, feedback and measurement. Some information exists about the value of video advertising but it is at an embryonic and unreliable stage.

Direct response advertising

There has been an enormous growth in direct response advertising as a reaction to the fragmentation of the main media. It is seen as a way to talk directly with the end consumer and build long-term relationships. Many manufacturers and producers (e.g. Heinz) see it as a way to overcome the power of the retailer by attempting to win back customer control.

Advantages of advertising by direct response

- the ability to control the whole advertising process from message to construction, target market, measurement and evaluation of the results;
- different ad methods can be easily tested, one against the other, for effectiveness;
- marketing managers can account for ad spend effectiveness quicker;
- direct access to the consumer in his or her own home;
- allows for specific, individual targeting to both business and end consumers;
- two-way, long-term relationships can be developed;
- manufacturers can bypass the retailer and inform, persuade, make offers, and receive information back from the end consumer;
- audience information can be collected, built on, cross-fertilised in future campaigns;
- competition minimised at the point of audience contact.

Disadvantages of advertising by direct response

- it has developed an image as a 'junk media' because of the amount of material that is poorly targeted;
- complaints about intrusion of privacy and misuse of computerised data passed from one company to another (despite the Data Protection Act which was set up to rectify these problems);
- audience apathy and cynicism associated with direct response methods causing non-participation;
- 25 to 50 per cent of direct mail advertising is unread, and expensive material ends up in the junk bin;
- low response rate (1 to 5 per cent, can be improved by a creative approach);
- competition can create information overload leading to advertising effectiveness wear-out;
- lacks visual impact, sound, drama etc. associated with other media methods.

Measurement of direct response

Direct response media are the easiest of all to measure. The number of customers that respond can be compared with the original objectives. It is also a great medium for testing and comparing changes in the advertising approach.

Advertising on the Internet

The sort of application I foresee is someone watching a soccer match between, say, the US and Mexico, and a message pops up offering them the chance to buy the Mexico Strip. You could also chat with friends at the bottom of the screen during that game. Or if you were watching Seinfeld, for example, you could be automatically sent to the Seinfeld chat room at the end of the show. The advertiser who appeared during the TV show would also appear in the chat room.

(Phil Monego, President, Netchannel, US, April 1998)

Uncertainties abound when discussing advertising opportunities on the web.

Web advertising and marketing

Our strategy is simply to have Nabisco on the web. It's experimental, and we'll see where we can go with it.

(Michael Perry, Media Director, Nabisco Foods, USA)

Many companies will design and build their own site as well as advertising on the web pages of others. Interested participants have only to browse through sites to realise that many companies are uncertain about the objectives of the site, reflecting in poor design and content. When setting up a site a marketing plan should be developed in the same way as for any other company operation.

- Clear objectives should be identified.
- Statistics and methods of audience identification are continually improving but it should be axiomatic that any ad must be placed on a site that will be visited by potential customers.
- The site should be user-friendly, easy to move around and informative enough to make the viewer want to come back.
- The site selected should be easy and quick to download. Although bandwidths are improving it is extremely frustrating to wait ages whilst 'bells and whistle' perform on the screen adding nothing to the audience experience wanted.
- The advertiser should be aware of the strengths and weaknesses of the competition on-line.
- The site should be designed and produced by technical, marketing and advertising people working in consultation. Although it is a new medium, basic marketing concepts are no different.

At the present time there is some misunderstanding about the kinds of people that should be involved in the construction of adverts. Computer technicians must physically build the web site and put it together but the design of an ad should be given to a creative person who understands the relationship between the message and the receiver. Measurement and accountability are still problems with all media forms and the Internet is no exception. Although it can be shown who visits a site it is more difficult to ascertain whether the ad has been seen.

The Internet is the most important development in mass communications since the invention of the printing press.

(*New York Times*, March 1997)

Advantages of advertising on the web

- design opportunities covering film, colour, sound, movement;
- multimedia opportunities e.g. the Internet on TV, in the living room;
- unlimited potential;
- global reach with a potential market of 3 billion;
- one-to-one relationship can be developed in the home of the consumer;
- can be used to target both business to business and consumer markets;
- opportunities abound across the whole range of advertising;
- interactive possibilities.

Disadvantages of advertising on the web

- little being known about the medium; uncertainties about audience use and reaction;
- measurement methods and value for money uncertain;
- limited and uncertain knowledge about all areas of the advertising;
- confusion between conventional advertising and sponsorship;
- non-standardisation of adverts.

Measurement and research

We naturally are as anxious as anybody else to determine how effective our web advertising is and what we're getting for our money, but given the medium itself is still evolving, as is a definition of advertising on the medium, we think that patience is in order.

(Elizabeth Moore, Spokeswoman, Procter & Gamble, US)

Measurement is uncertain but improving. As with all advertising, advertisers need to know if the audience is seeing, reading and remembering its adverts. This is not a real problem with direct response because value will be reflected in audience participation i.e. buying the product advertised. However it is a problem with brand advertising. Sophisticated research can identify the number of people who click on to a web site, but cannot in most cases identify consumer profiles. Visiting businesses that have their own domain name (e.g. www.tesco.co.uk) can be identified but individuals that enter through a large web browser (e.g. raywright@mcmail.com) cannot. Many sites ask people to register, an example being www.ft.co.uk, and these members can then be identified every time they come to the site. Other factors to be considered will include the following:

- coming onto a site does not guarantee that an ad has been seen;
- clicking on ads taking the viewer onto an advertiser's site is a good indication of awareness and interest.

Conventional research can be used to partly overcome these problems.

There is no universal monitoring body but the ABC has started to audit web sites. Until there is certainty many companies will be loath to spend speculative amounts of money.

Cost/benefit analysis

Media planners attempt to allocate the advertising budget in a cost-efficient manner subject to other objectives. One of the most important and universally used indicators of media efficiency is cost per thousand. (CPM, the M representing the Roman numeral for 1000), which is the cost of reaching 1000 people. It will often be refined to represent the cost per thousand of the target market, rather than the whole market: CPM-TM. This figure is so important that all industries now insist on the auditing of the circulation/viewing figures being undertaken by an independent auditor such as Auditing Bureau of Circulation (ABC) to make certain that the figures are reliable.

CPM and CPM-TM are calculated simply by dividing the cost of an advert by the number of people in the relevant market, in thousands, that the advert will reach.

$$CPM = \frac{\text{Cost of ad}}{\text{Number of total contacts the ad will reach (circulation, viewing figures etc.)}}$$

$$CPM\text{-}TM = \frac{\text{Cost of ad}}{\text{Number of TM contacts the ad will reach (those outside the target market are waste)}}$$

It is self-evident how important the viewing/reading/listening figures are when calculating cost. It may seem horrendous to pay £50 000 for 15 seconds of TV advertising in the middle of *Coronation Street* or £25 000 for a full page in the *Sun,* but if they are reaching an audience of 18 million and 10 million respectively then the CPM comes down to pounds. However the bare statistics shown above should be treated with some caution because they are measures of efficiency, not of effectiveness. They measure CPM, not CPM-TM. In the example above all the 10 million readers of the *Sun* will probably not be in the relevant target market so more information would be needed, describing the different consumer profiles of the various *Sun* readers. Owners of the media will charge buyers on the known CPM and in this way the measure becomes the currency. Procter & Gamble has agreed to take advertising on the Internet but has insisted on paying only on a retrospective known CPM click-through rate.

Some media forms offer the audience more opportunity to see (OTS) an advert than other media forms. The *Radio Times,* for example, will be kept all week and prospective customers will pick it up to find out what is on TV perhaps many times a day, which could give an OTS rating of 20. The *Sun,* on the other hand, will last for only one day and a reader will maybe thumb through three or four times, giving an OTS of three (the figures are heavily researched).

Comparability across the media

Another problem of CPM and CPM-TM is their lack of comparability across the different media. As discussed in other chapters the various media perform different functions and are often effective in different areas. Straightforward comparisons ignore these subtleties. A lower CPM for radio does not mean it will be a better buy than a more expensive CPM for TV because so many factors have to be taken into account. In the same way the CPM for a free newspaper would not be comparable with a CPM for one that is paid for as research shows that free newspapers are read less often. CPM figures should not be used in isolation and need to be backed up by more intensive consumer research that looks at complex buying and readership habits. Use of colour, print quality, content interest, cost of the product, position and creativity of the advert as well as the attractiveness of the benefits offered will all affect whether the advert is seen and inwardly digested. TV can cause similar problems: 10 million may see an episode of *Coronation Street* but how many will remain to see the advert, or, if remaining, will be watching or be aware in the short time it is on the screen?

CONCLUSION

Effective communications will be dependent on the strengths and weaknesses of the media method chosen, the message quality and the target audience reach. Both above and below the line media have strengths and weaknesses that need to be evaluated and compared with the advertising task at hand. Individual media might be favoured by an advertiser at any one time as the primary method but normally more than one will be used. When this happens, integration across the whole campaign is crucial. This is a particular consideration with the use of the Internet because it is such a new and unknown method.

CASE STUDY

Opportunity knocks as new challenges mount

More television channels mean greater fragmentation, enhancing choice for consumers but adding to TV broadcasters' headaches. As the end of the millennium approaches, Europe's media industry, for so long characterised by limited competition and bureaucratic regulation, has begun to embrace the digital age. The results have yet to be revealed, but all the signs are that the market will undergo profound change in the next decade. The television industry, in particular, is set to change radically as digital technology introduces more channels and interactivity for consumers, and brings increased competition and higher costs for broadcasters.

'The advent of digital television is the single most important innovation to the television since it was invented', says Noah Yaskin, media analyst for Jupiter Communications, the US market research group. 'In Europe, the digital television platform offers another route by which content owners, advertisers and merchants can offer consumers interactive products and services.' Jupiter (www.jup.com) forecasts the number of households that will be interactive via their television sets will rise sharply early in the next millennium in the two markets most advanced in digital television, Britain and Sweden. In the former, the group believes the number of interactive television households will rise from 0.3 per cent in 1999, to more than 19 per cent in 2002. Sweden is forecast to increase from 0.2 per cent to 29 per cent in the same period. Elsewhere, France is expected to be at 12 per cent and Germany at just 2 per cent in four years' time.

Yet while digital television offers great opportunities for broadcasters, it also presents threats. More channels means the fragmentation of audiences and a more competitive advertising market. This, together with the high cost of embracing digital technology, will push broadcasters to look for additional sources of revenues. In Britain, for example, which is a little more than two months into the digital television era, pay-per-view and subscription-based channels have formed a significant part of the new channels launched by existing broadcasters. Bear Stearns, the US-based investment bank, forecasts that digital services will drive the growth of pay television from 27 per cent of households to 56 per cent by 2006 in the UK. 'Lower subscription prices, the TV set replacement cycle and over-the-air distribution – the ubiquitous form of TV reception in British homes – are key facilitators of this growth,' the bank concludes. Costs to the consumer are also likely to fall rapidly to aid the digital take-up. Bear Stearns predicts that interactive digital television sets will soon be no more than 10 per cent more expensive than ordinary analogue models. The gap is currently five-fold. Meanwhile, set-top boxes, which are required to process the digital signals for analogue sets, are being subsidised by operators. Thus UK consumers are paying under £200 for models, while satellite operator BSkyB is offering free installation of its digital equipment.

While the path towards digital television penetration has some obvious comparisons with earlier technological developments, the way forward for interactivity is an untried model. And although home banking and shopping will undoubtedly feature prominently in the next decade, the question remains: through which medium will interactivity be conducted?

'Interactive television has been one of the industry's dreams for a long time,' says Bill Bass, director of media and technology strategy at Forrester, the US-based IT consultancy and research group. 'The advent of digital has made convergence of the Internet and television a reality – but we believe full interactivity won't happen.' What will occur, according to Mr Bass, is 'lazy interactivity', where there will be a partial integration between the television and the Internet of particular aspects of both media.

He quotes the example of television advertising as an area 'primed for interactivity', where viewers could respond through their sets to a particular advertisement. Games shows are another example of an area likely to be a favourable platform for interactivity However, he believes that the stuff that's good on the Internet will stay there. Rather than pursuing integration, some of the biggest US media companies are viewing the Internet as another but significant arm to their business.

The reason for this has been the development of 'portal' sites. These are Internet sites which offer themselves as gateways to the web, but also have a wide variety of services and e-commerce opportunities available. Portal sites such as Yahoo!, Excite and Infoseek have become global brands. This has been achieved by enticing visitors with their content

▶

of online services and encouraging them to stay as long as possible. This then enables the portals to charge more to advertisers and sponsors, as well as take a bigger cut of any e-commerce transactions. The result has seen the portals become the most sought after destinations on the Internet. Not surprisingly, the prospect of netting such large audiences has attracted much interest from the media industry. In the most significant move, Disney last year bought a 43 per cent stake in Infoseek, one of the leading Internet portal groups. Disney is using Infoseek's experience to fashion its own portal, Go, which it will integrate into the rest of its business operations. 'In the old media world there was little point in integrating your assets,' says Mr Bass. 'In the digital age, having your business work together is vital.'

Source: Christopher Price, *Financial Times*, 13 January 1999. Used with permission.

Case study questions

1. Discuss the concept of interactive TV. What are the ways that we might want to interact with the TV and what are the implications for advertising?
2. What does Mr Bass mean by 'integrating your assets'? How will the progressive advertiser make use of the concept?

CHAPTER QUESTIONS

1. Outline the case for using TV rather than the print media for your advertising. How might the two be used together?
2. Identify the various print forms of advertising and evaluate the advantages and disadvantages of each.
3. Analyse and evaluate the worth of direct mail when compared with 'above the line' advertising. Why might direct mail now be attracting revenue from 'above the line' advertising?
4. Discuss the importance of point-of-purchase advertising. Why is it particularly important in FMCG markets?
5. Investigate the development of the Internet as a marketing and advertising tool. What might be its strengths and weaknesses?

REFERENCES

Bernbach, W. (1988), *The Art of Writing Advertising*, from Higgins, D. (ed.) *The Art of Writing Advertising*, Natl Text-books Co trade, US.

Financial Times (www.ft.co.uk)

Michael Grade, Chief Executive, Channel 4 (www.channel4.co.uk)

Independent Television (www.itv.co.uk)

Jupiter Communications (Web) (www.jup.com).

Maiden Outdoor (www.maiden.co.uk)

David Mansfield, Chief Executive, Capital Radio, UK (www.capital.co.uk)

Phil Monego, President, Netchannel, US, April 1998.

Ogilvy, D. (1985), *Ogilvy on Advertising*, Vintage Books, New York.

Michael Ovitz, President, Walt Disney Co. (www.disney.com)

Michael Perry, Media director, Nabisco foods, USA (www.nabisco.com)

Procter & Gamble, US, (www.pg.com)

Helmut Thoma, MD, RTL Plus GmbH.

FURTHER READING

Association of British Publisher Agencies (www.apa.co.uk)

Bird, D. (1994) *Common Sense Direct Marketing*, 3rd edn, NTC Business Books, London.

Corbett, M. (1995) *The 33 Rules of Ruthless Local Advertising*, Breakthru Publishers, US.

Direct Marketing Association (www.dma.org.uk)

Independent Television Commission (www.itc.co.uk)

Newspaper Society (www.newspapersoc.org.uk)

Periodical Publishers Association (www.ppa.co.uk)

Radio Advertising Bureau (www.rab.co.uk)

Rapp Collins direct marketing (www.rappcollins.com)

Rutherford, P. (1994) *The New Icons?: The Art of Television Advertising*; University of Toronto; Booknews Inc., Portland, Oregon, US.

Timmes, M. (1998) *The Power of the Poster*, Victoria and Albert Museum, London.

12 Creativity and presentation in advertising

OBJECTIVES

By the end of this chapter the reader should be able to:

1. Describe and analyse the importance of creativity in advertising.
2. Evaluate the role that understanding of consumer needs, wants, hopes and desires bring to the process.
3. Evaluate the importance of ad presentation across the various media.

INTRODUCTION

Properly practiced creativity can make one ad do the work of ten.

(William Bernbach)

All the different media have their strengths and weaknesses in communicating relevant benefit messages. In this chapter we look at the importance of innovation and creativity in breaking through the advertising clutter and reaching the target audience. This will involve both an understanding of consumer needs, wants, hopes and desires and an understanding of how advertisers are able to use various techniques to exploit the process.

Creativity in advertising

Because competition in advertising, from a multitude of sources, is so intense, advertisers are continually and incessantly looking for ways for their advertisements to be more effective then others, for their advert to be seen and remembered whilst others are ignored or seen and immediately forgotten. Advertising agencies can rise and fall on reputations built on levels of creativity, innovation and communication effectiveness. However, creativity must be linked to good research, forecasting, planning and control if risks are to be minimised and advertising campaigns are moved from development through to implementation in the most cost–effective manner.

Creativity is the ability to produce new and original ideas or to develop new ways of looking at existing ideas. Much of this tends to be associated with clever copy and imaginative artwork but creativity in advertising can offer benefits across the whole advertising planning process from new ways of thinking about the brand USP and the idea to be used for the main thrust to imaginative ways of using distribution and the media options.

There is continuous controversy about the importance of creativity in advertising and whether, on its own, it actually sells anything. It is true that it can create awareness but whether it can move the consumer to purchase the product is another matter. In fact some of the most enduring advertisements are seemingly prosaic and bland – for example, the 'hands that do dishes are as soft as your face' adverts for Fairy Liquid. 'Would you swap the new powder for your old?' (Daz) has run for over two decades in more or less the same format, as has 'eight out of ten dog breeders use Pedigree Chum'. Two women in the kitchen discussing the merits of washing powder is an enduring theme that has survived with little change for over forty years. On the other hand many agencies, using original and creative ideas in their adverts, have managed to overcome audience brand apathy and help generate increased sales. The series of ads for Levi Jeans beginning with the guy taking his jeans off in the launderette to wash them spawned a revival for the company when its fortunes were at a low ebb and the 'hello boys' ad for Wonderbra is now legendary in its effectiveness.

Creativity should be used as a way to help sell the product and not be seen as an objective in its own right. The ultimate measure must be its effectiveness in achieving agreed objectives.

Characteristics of creative ads

- Creative adverts can break through the 'clutter' of competitor advertising and draw attention to the message. Unnoticed ads are a failure no matter how intriguing the pictures and the copy.
- Creativity can build on benefits and develop brand personalities that audiences find attractive.
- To be creative and entertaining without building interest and positive attitudes about purchase will ultimately be a waste of time and money.
- Creative advertising will not work if the product fails to live up to promised expectations.

Creativity and the advertising agency

Although all agencies need to be continually looking for innovative ways to put messages over to target audiences many agencies develop a reputation for innovation, creativity and original thinking and win customers in this way. Some advertising agencies have been accused of producing creative ads to win design awards rather than to sell products although they would counter by arguing that if this was the case they would not be in business for very long.

Marketing and advertising staff will want to discuss brand positioning and message style and content as part of the strategic promotional process. Ad agencies would argue that they should be brought into this process as early as possible as their knowledge and experience can add value to the process. To have decided on an advertising strategy before calling in the ad agency staff only to have these experts telling you that it will not work in the given way can cause confusion and waste time.

It must have seemed funny at the time, but a joke in an advertisement for Audi cars has backfired, attracting more than 1000 complaints and a writ which has led to it being withdrawn. The advert, produced by creative agency Bartle, Bogle and Hegarty, showed the Duracell Bunny lying squashed on the road with its drum kit smashed. Underneath was the line: 'Audi TDI. Keeps on going. No other diesel lasts like it.' The campaign was meant as a humorous reference to the mechanical toy rabbit used in the Duracell campaigns for more than 25 years to promote long-life batteries.

Reprinted from a newspaper article – source unknown

Creativity and the agency brief

The creative advertising process begins with the agency brief. A well written, well thought through brief will provide all the information necessary to give the creative team a precise understanding of the job that they have been commissioned to undertake. It will supply the following elements:

- advertising objectives
- the type of company; values etc.
- the type of product
- the product/brand USP
- its position (or desired position in the market)
- target market and customer profiles
- message content.

Product positioning statement (PPS)

The product positioning statement will attempt to spell out to everyone's satisfaction the personality, the USP, of the brand and the creative ideas that might be used to exploit customer expectations. The PPS should also include any information that could be relevant in promoting the product, including corporate and overall product portfolio values that might have an effect on message style and content.

The corporate and/or product brand positioning statement should be available to all involved in the advertising process because it will set out all the values inherent in the brand that can have an affect on the advertising campaign, the advertising message and the media chosen. The statement refers to the company's and/or the product's position in the marketplace and in the minds of customers with reference to others in the same marketplace. It exists to protect brand values that have, in many cases, become extremely valuable assets. Many companies and company brands – Guinness, Persil, Oxo, Mars, Levi's, Yves St Laurent, Mercedes, Coca-Cola, to name but a few – have had a fortune spent on them, advertising and building brand values, often over many decades. It is crucial that this brand 'franchise' is reinforced by positive and relevant images rather than being damaged by inappropriate advertising.

A corporate/product brand positioning statement might include any of the following factors considered to be important:

- a potted history of organisational values;
- elements from the mission statement;

- customer description and benefit needs;
- both functional and emotional brand values, including
  - USP;
  - price and distribution positioning;
  - functional benefits;
  - emotional benefits (e.g. traditionalism, family orientation, safety, nostalgia with Oxo, or conversely youth, rebellion, fun, excitement with Britvic's Tango.

Brand values all contribute to build a composite brand 'personality'.

It would be unlikely that the positioning statement would be longer than one sheet of A4.

The creative team

Often the most highly paid members of the agency and the most successful, are members of the creative department. They are coveted and cosseted because of the value they can bring to the agency. They must now take the product positioning statement and translate it into a 'magical' message that will set the world alight and have the consumers panting to purchase the product.

Copywriters

These people will probably reside in a back office somewhere and, so legend has it, should not necessarily be introduced to the client because their job is not to impress with sophisticated suavity but to come up with the one piece of (usually very simple) headline copy that will set the ad alight. We only have to look at adverts that have stood the test of time and are still considered classics of their type. These might include 'A Mars a day helps you work, rest and play', 'Prolongs Active Life' (acronym of PAL dog food), 'Your Country Needs You' (first world war recruitment poster), 'Snap, Crackle and Pop' (Kellogg's Rice Krispies), 'Put a tiger in your tank' (Esso), 'Pure Gold' (Benson and Hedges) – the list is endless.

The art director

The art director will work closely with the writers and transform the copy and illustration ideas into the finished product making the whole concept come alive. The design, material used, typography, colour, illustrations etc. must all work together in bringing out and reinforcing the theme of the ad.

The broadcast director

If a broadcast medium is to be used the director has a similar responsibility to the art director taking the written script and making it work in the most effective and creative way possible on the TV, cinema or radio. This responsibility now extends to the Internet.

Creativity and the target audience

Different adverts work in different ways depending on the type of product, the advertising objectives and the intricacies of the decision-making process. As shown by the examples discussed above, well tried and tested methods work in some instances while more creative ways work in others. The need to be creative in the design and construction of adverts is driven by the way that people see and perceive adverts.

Creativity and research

We dedicated a whole section (Part 3) to the crucial need to know and understand the customer and this is never more true and never more difficult than with research needed when looking for innovative ideas. It is in this area that qualitative research comes into its own as psychological methods attempt to discover consumers' inner hopes and desires that could become the mainspring and 'big idea' of a wonderful and successful new campaign. Empirical evidence has proven that success is often a combination of good, deep, research plus the creative inspiration of the advertising team.

Haagen Dazs, the top selling premium ice cream in the world, achieved its lofty position by a series of unashamedly erotic ads featuring a man and a woman in various love-making situations using Haagen Dazs ice cream as a central theme to the campaign. The ads became the success of the year and were copied and spoofed by many other companies. Qualitative research had shown that women would sometimes indulge themselves by purchasing premium ice cream because eating it in a moment of relaxation made them feel sensual (www.haagen-dazs.com: Passion in a touch, Perfection in a cup, Summer in a Spoon).

The way advertisements are presented

Research has shown that audience perception is influenced by many different aspects in the presentation of adverts including size, position, colour, novelty, contrast, repetition and rhythm, music and tone of voice, as well as by the percipient's own wants, experiences, hopes, fears and desires. All these factors need to be taken into account when planning the presentation of an advert.

The size of adverts

As a rule of thumb the bigger the advert, the more chance there is of it being seen. Small adverts tend to get lost in a crowd whilst big adverts will have by far a greater impact. If we want double the initial impact from an advertisement the size of the adverts must increase by an amount *more than double* (Weber's Law).

The position of the advert

Possibly the most unusual advertising space in Britain could soon be available for hire – at the top of a fourteenth-century church spire. For £500 a day companies will be able to display their advertisements on scaffolding erected to help restore the spire and contribute to the cost of the repairs needed.

©Telegraph Group Limited, London 1997

The position of an advert can either increase or decrease the chances of it being seen and a small advert in the right place will be better than a large advert in the wrong place. Newspapers and magazines will sometimes charge a higher price for a position where the ad has more chance of being seen. Examples are:

- an advert on its own, away from the clutter;
- on the front or back page;
- on the left hand side rather than the right hand side – (this is where people look first);
- near the beginning rather than the end;
- if a sports connected ad, then placed within the sports section, if cooking-related, in the cooking section and so on;
- in the centrespread – the double-page spread at the centre of a magazine, which occupies one continuous sheet of paper, enjoying the double advantage both of extra size and solus position;
- beside or near editorial comment or news.

So important is position that the outdoor industry, through POSTAR, offers its advertisers the VAI ('Visibility Adjusted Impacts') system as a crucial part of its benefits service. Weighted indices on position, size, angle of approach, visibility distance, distance from the kerbside, clutter/obstruction, illumination all come together to form a net score for each and every outdoor panel (see www.maiden. co.uk/postar).

Colour

Colour is a silent form of communication. An ill-chosen colour for a product can make that product look cheap, or can make the product look luxurious. Colour will always play a crucial part in advert design because it has an emotional appeal and can mean so much to people. White can stand for purity and cleanliness; red and orange can be seen as exciting, young and sexy; blue as cool, restful and conservative; green as natural and healthy; purple as majestic and classically superior and so on. So powerful is the use of colour that it can be used in an advert, with little or no copy, and the brand it represents is recognised almost immediately by the target audience. Examples that come to mind are purple for Silk Cut, black and white for Guinness, orange for Orange mobile phones, red and white for Marlboro, green and black for Heinz, to name but a few.

You pay your money and you take your chances

The colour for the new Millennium and for advertising the Millennium Dome at Greenwich will be a vibrant yellow. 'It's bright, it's optimistic, it's pleasing to the eye; it's about the dawn of a golden age,' said a spokesperson. In France and Spain the colour is used to denote treason and according to Brewer's Dictionary of Phrase and Fable yellow tradition- ally symbolises ' jealousy, inconstancy, adultery, perfidy and cowardice'.

©Telegraph Group Limited, London 1998

Novelty and contrast

Novelty and contrast, doing something different or comparing one thing with another, can be used in many ways to cause the eyes to shift and heads to turn. Lurid colours might be used – e.g. the whole page in orange; a black and white ad instead of colour; a full page with nothing on it except the product, name or logo tucked, barely visible, in one corner; products in unusual places, e.g. a car on the top of a mountain; products of an unusual size, e.g. a giant cigarette box in the street; wacky ads, e.g. 'Pepperami, a bit of an animal'; poster ads that move; maga- zine ads that we scratch and smell; and 'teaser ads' that build day by day stimulating the curiosity. Technological progress has given ads in 3D, laser ads to project on to buildings, virtual reality ads that can be artificially projected onto TV screens and brand shapes the size of buildings.

One of the most famous poster ads of all time was the Saatchi and Saatchi ad, produced for the Health Education Council to promote the use of contraceptives, which showed a pregnant man with the headline exhorting all men with the question 'would you be more careful if it was you that got pregnant?'

Repetition and rhythm

Repetition is one of the surest ways to batter the brand image into the long-term memory. If an ad appears often enough or the catch-line is repetitive and catchy it will eventually enter into the audience consciousness (especially if taken up by broadcasters, family and peer groups) breaching all defence mechanisms except the most hardened. Famous slogans include 'Oxo gives a meal man appeal', 'Have a break, have a KitKat', 'Just do it' (Nike), 'A Mars a day helps you work, rest and play', 'A glass and a half in every pound' (Cadbury's Dairy Milk), 'We won't make a drama out of a crisis' (Commercial Union), 'We're with the Woolwich', 'I know a man that can' (the Automobile Association), 'Ariston and on and on and on' (Ariston electrical appliances), 'Don't be vague – ask for Haig' and 'Drinka Pinta Milka Day'.

Music

Music has meaning in some way or another for everybody and this is what makes it such a powerful force. Repetition used with music becomes a powerful formula indeed with jingles and tunes being remembered decades after the advertising has finished. Jingles from the past that many will still remember include 'I am going well on Shell, Shell, Shell'; 'Murray Mints, Murray Mints, the too good to hurry mints';

'Beanz Meanz Heinz' and so on. So powerful can the music in the advert be that it can both reawaken the career of forgotten singers and groups and make the career of new contenders: 'Search for the Hero' for the M people (Peugeot 406); 'We'd like to teach the world to sing' (Coca-Cola); the music for Heinz of the Ladysmith Black Mabaza; Marvin Gaye's 'I heard it on the grapevine' (Levi's). Even classical music is not safe with Delibes' 'flower song' from *Lakmé* for British Airways, and 'Coming home' from Dvořák's 'New World' Symphony ('Don't say brown, say Hovis').

Types of appeal

Hard sell

The archetypal example of this type of ad will be uncompromising in its message, 'shouting out in the marketplace' that the consumer must buy now as prices will never be cheaper, the value will never be greater, there is a limited supply and there is even a short-term incentive available. It is beloved of retailers such as Sainsbury, Comet, Thomas Cook, and B&Q.

Soft sell

This is much more subtle and is concerned with building brand awareness and desire often over the longer period. Some of the most creative and artistic ads appear with this approach and they can be just as effective as the hard sell. Cars, whisky, body fragrances and fashion will all use this type of approach. Many ads will fall between the two methods.

Through many years of extensive research advertisers are now aware of people's experiences, hopes and desires and the part that this plays in their acknowledgement and acceptance of adverts, the purchase of products and the subsequent growth of brand loyalty.

Rational or emotional appeal

Every successful ad works because it appeals in some way to the target audience. This appeal might be rational, emotional or a combination of the two, following Plato's Divided Soul theory discussed earlier. Rational appeal goes for the head whilst the emotional goes for the heart. Rational appeal will use functional benefits such as price and value for money, performance measures, features and the ability to solve the problem. Rational appeal tends to be used more in business to business advertising whilst emotional appeal is used in consumer markets.

Emotional appeal is aimed at buyer hopes, dreams, fears and desires at both the conscious and subconscious level. Every area of human emotions is used in advertisements at some time or another to induce a positive reaction from the target audience. The hope is that, if the research has been successful, the emotion used as the message theme will excite pleasant or meaningful feelings within the customer's psyche which will then come to be associated with the product or brand. The same emotive message will not work in the same way with every target market and segmentation research should expose which emotion to use and in which way.

Advertisers should be aware that the relationship between price, quality and value will vary according to product and brand usage, economic circumstance and customer perception.

Humour

'No tits but a lot of balls' was devised by the Bartle, Bogle and Hegarty (UK) advertising agency in 1987 for the *News on Sunday*, a Labour-party-supporting newspaper. The paper lasted less than a year and so the slogan was never used.

There was a time when it was argued that brands were too important to joke about and the use of humour to attract attention would devalue the brand affinities (David Ogilvy). Experience has shown this is no longer the case and humour is used continuously, especially in products for children and young adults. Many young consumers welcome the fact that brands do not take themselves too seriously, and that they use street-wise humour and make them laugh. If successful this 'feel good factor' is then transferred and associated with the product ('I feel like chicken tonight'; 'Heineken refreshes the parts other beers cannot reach'; 'I bet he drinks Carling Black Label').

Sex

The Broadcast Commission investigates, once again, complaints about the excessive use of sex both to entertain and to sell products on the broadcast media. They have asked broadcasters to voluntarily observe the 9 p.m. 'watershed' and vet more rigorously for instances of gratuitous sex. Sex (e.g. Claudia Schiffer taking her clothes off in a Citroën Xsara) and sexual innuendo (e.g. Renault Clio, 'size matters') are used incessantly in advertising to attract attention, create desire and sell products. Despite sporadic outbursts of complaints it continues to be the safest way for advertising agencies to achieve both notoriety and their advertising objectives. Sex is used to advertise everything from cars, watches and soap to ice cream, holidays and coffee.

Advertising didn't mix sex up with our daily lives. The great marketer in the skies did that.
(Barry Brookes, creative director)

Shock

A growing trend over the last twenty years has been to use the element of shock firstly to get people to look at the advert and secondly, and more importantly, to get people to talk about the campaign. The anti-fur lobby lynx 'it takes up to 40 dumb animals to make a fur coat but only one to wear it' was highly effective. So were the use of the AIDS victim, the new-born baby and the Mafia killing in the notorious Benetton adverts. Some charities have tended to use shock tactics as a compensation for small advertising budgets, looking to gain free media coverage through the ensuing publicity.

Nostalgia

Nostalgia, a sentimental longing for earlier days when summers were hotter, days were longer, food was tastier and people were friendlier, lends itself to some traditional, long-lasting brands that many consumers remember from childhood. The classic example was the series of ads for 'Hovis' brown bread with the music 'Going Home' from the ('New World' Symphony) using the images of northern country life of fifty years ago.

Fear

Fear must be used with caution by advertisers as people will switch off from uncomfortable images that have a direct effect on themselves. Images of products associated with death and illness are often shrouded in euphemisms in an attempt to get brand benefits across in as gentle a way as possible. The UK government had an advertising failure in a late-1980s campaign advertising the dangers of AIDS. The use of a graveyard and images of tombstones were said to switch the young audience off so that they were unable or unwilling to make the required association.

Parenthood and family life

At least 70 per cent of all FMCG goods are still purchased by women and, despite the structural change in family composition (in the UK, at the time of writing, one third of all households are single occupant) parenthood and family life are still important factors in product purchase. Many cleaning products (Persil, Flash), toilet products (Domestos, Andrex), food (Oxo, Bisto) have concern for family values as the central theme, often using babies, children and animals to encourage feelings of well-being and the so-called 'ah' factor ('ah, isn't the puppy cute?')

Status and ego needs

Status and the need for recognition have been the staple diet for advert content for almost as long as adverts have been produced. It seems the need to be seen to stand above others is inherent in a capitalist system and this is shown in many premium type products. ('Oh Lord won't you buy me a Mercedes Benz, my friends all have Porsches and I must make amends'; Stella Artois, 'reassuringly expensive'; L'Oréal, it may be expensive but 'I am worth it'; and 'Everything about you is different to the other guy', Audi).

Respect for authority

Despite the concern that resurfaces intermittently about the breakdown in law and order, research seems to show that people we perceive to be in authority still have an influence on our ways of thinking (see Stanley Milgram, *Obedience to Authority*). And so we see ads recommending tyres fronted by ex police chiefs, books by teachers and medical products by a scientist in a white coat.

Celebrity endorsement is very popular with advertisers working with the secure knowledge that we will buy products associated with people we admire and respect. It doesn't come cheap, however: Claudia Schiffer was reputed to have earned a six-figure sum for taking off her knickers for the Citroën ad.

Dead celebrities

TV and cinema audiences will have noticed many new and exciting methods being used in the presentation of advertising. One of the most dramatic and seemingly impossible developments has been in the use of dead actors and actresses in various scenes promoting modern products. New technology has enabled creative agencies to take old film shots of past celebrities and transpose them into modern day setting using up-to-date products. Sophisticated 'morphing' techniques allows lips and facial expressions to be manipulated so that the dead star appears to be acting in a contemporary setting. Steve McQueen, aping his role in the film Bullet, in a commercial for the Ford Puma, the late John Lennon appearing with radio and TV presenter Chris Evans and the footballer Ian Wright appearing with Martin Luther King in an advert for One-to-One mobile phones. It follows similar commercials using images of Elvis Presley and Malcolm X. The most popular seem to be Marilyn Monroe and Albert Einstein, who is regarded as a good person to promote any kind of new, high-tech product or anything to do with space. It seems that, unlike the US, very little protection exists in the UK for families of past celebrities, to stop this happening. However, a new consultancy group, The Celebrity Group, aims to halt this exploitation and is lobbying the government for more protection.

Subliminal advertising

This technique involves infiltrating the audience subconscious with surreptitious visual or whispered messages. Visually they tend to be split-second flashes that hit the audience below the level of conscious awareness. The idea is to bypass the stimulus-filtering defence mechanism of the viewer or listener. Evidence of its effectiveness is weak but it is illegal in almost all developed countries.

The use of semiotics in advertising

Advertising makes much use of the discipline known as semiotics – the study of signs and sign-using behaviour within society. The Swiss linguist Ferdinand de Saussure, writing at the end of the nineteenth century, defined semiotics as the study of 'the life signs within society'. He noted that people communicated and understood one another by many different methods other than through the use of language. This involved the use of various signals, signs and symbols communicated through the use of noises, pictures, images, shapes and colours as well as through facial and body language. These will all be used by advertisers both as a complement to and a substitute for language. So the Andrex puppy becomes a sign for caring motherhood; the Marlboro cowboy for an adventurous, vicarious, 'real-man' lifestyle; purple becomes a symbol for Silk Cut cigarettes; a white 'tick' comes to represent Nike; mountain streams represent freshness; green fields and cows, natural food products; spectacles represent intelligence; a white coat a scientific background; and an umbrella security.

Gestalt

Gestalt psychologists working in the 1930s researched the concept that animals and humans are born with in-built ways of seeing and organising the world. They argue that for our ancestors the world was a dangerous place to be born into and babies needed to assimilate as quickly as possible what was going on around them. This ability to take limited information and attempt to make sense of it has become known as 'Gestalt' or 'Closure' and it stays with us for the whole of our lives. Advertisers have taken many of the Gestalt concepts and now use them in advertising as ways of gaining our attention. Examples include closure and constancy, gestalt manipulation and the use of figure and ground.

If there are gaps we are drawn to fill them in to make a whole and advertisers will use this concept by giving us limited information hopefully causing us to pause, look and spend time seeking meaning, constancy, 'closure' and the full product picture. Examples are 'Schhh you know who' and 'tonic water by you know who' (Schweppes ads of the 1960s), 'The world's favourite airline' (BA), 'Simply years ahead' (Phillips), 'Pure Gold' (Benson and Hedges) and 'Pure Genius' (Guinness).

Churches called for the withdrawal of Christmas shop window displays bearing the slogan 'FCUK XMAS'. French Connection (United Kingdom) had previously been censured by the Advertising Standards Authority, which upheld complaints against two billboard posters (they suggested the placing of dots between the letters). They argue, however, that point-of-purchase display materials (shop window banners) do not fall within their remit and they therefore have no jurisdiction. It seems that the local Trading Standards Officer is the person to contact.

We have a basic tendency to divide what we see into figure (an object) and ground (the background or surroundings of the object). It seems impossible not to do this (try it and see). Advertisers will want their product to be the object we search out.

Attention and exposure

Advertisers must also be aware that, in the main, we look for information that reinforces our beliefs and coincides with our interests (selective attention) and conversely will avoid information which contradicts our beliefs and conflicts with our interests (selective exposure). Similarly we ignore unpleasant stimuli (discussions about death; mention of lung disease if we smoke) and we look for cognitive harmony between all beliefs and ideas (we enjoy social drinking, so it can't be seen to be bad for us).

CONCLUSION

The creative process may be summed up thus:

agency brief ⟶ positioning statement ⟶ the 'big idea' ⟶ copy ⟶ production ⟶ planning

The problem of measuring the success or otherwise of main media advertising has been discussed and touched on throughout the book. Huge amounts of money are spent by companies on advertising without any real certainty about how it works. With some advertising methods there is little or no problem in measuring results. With direct response, for example, an ad is placed in the newspaper inviting the target audience to send for more information or to buy a product and the response can be measured in an immediate and direct manner. Other ads, however, are more problematic. If an ad is placed in a newspaper or on the TV exhorting the benefits of a particular brand, research evidence seems to show that this can create awareness and interest and/or reinforce brand loyalty which might be triggered at time of purchase. This can, however, get very difficult to definitively prove. Intervening factors (see Fig. 12.1) between the advertising and eventual purchase (and re-purchase), discussed earlier, make it very difficult to relate the advertising to the rise (or fall) in eventual sales.

Consumer buying patterns and consumer mind-sets must also be taken into account, making the picture even more complex. They will include the following:

- the regularity of purchase and the regularity of use during a given period;
- the amount purchased during the same given period;
- how other brands in the same category might also affect purchase;
- how deeply entrenched ideas and purchasing habits are in consumer minds;
- the particular buying role the customer might be acting out.

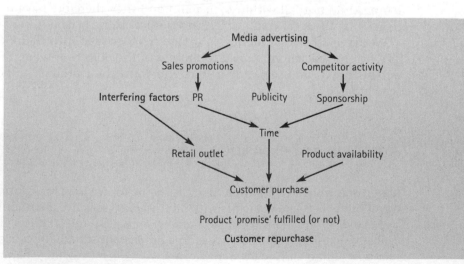

Fig. 12.1 Media advertising and intervening factors

With all these factors impinging on the buying motives, many argue that to extract the influence that advertising might have on the process is a difficult if not impossible task.

CASE
STUDY

Creativity wanes as mergers grow: to make great ads, client, agency must be willing to fail

A joke making the rounds in Canadian advertising circles is that, with all the corporate amalgamations going on, there will soon be only one client and one ad agency left – and the client, to save money, will take its account in-house. Of course, everyone chuckles at the absurdity of the notion, but then they go back to plotting their next merger.

Although no precise figures are available quantifying the pace of consolidation in the marketing and advertising sector, everyone agrees it's been heating up. Over the past few years, a succession of agency-side mergers and buyouts has practically cleared the field of mid-sized, independent ad shops, while consolidation in the media-buying industry has placed the bulk of money spent on advertising space by agency media-buying departments and independent media-buying firms into the hand of just a few massive, internationally owned players.

Client side, the pace seems to be equally frenetic. For a range of reasons readily expressed on a financial spreadsheet – including increased revenues, cost amortisation, buying clout, distribution breadth and R&D capacity – it can make eminent sense for competitors to amalgamate. But one corporate function that doesn't necessarily benefit is advertising. The art of persuading people to buy products and services isn't something that can be improved by increased size. In fact, there's a strong argument to be made that the larger an advertiser grows, the more risk-averse it becomes, and a risk-averse client winds up, inevitably, with a similar-minded agency that produces cautious, boring advertising.

Chris Staples, senior vice-president and creative director with Vancouver-based agency Palmer Jarvis DDB, puts it bluntly: 'I think we're going into the dark age of advertising.' He says this is particularly the case in the US, where there are 'all these giant agencies that have only a handful of clients, and they're all huge global advertisers.' In that kind of environment, 'agencies are afraid to take a chance,' Mr. Staples says, adding that to get surprising, break-through advertising, clients have to be willing to fail.

What this requires is for clients to feel supported inside their own organisations and to foster a sense of security within their agencies. The problem is that, increasingly, there's too much shareholder money on the line to permit risk-taking, he says. Ian Mirlin, president and creative director of Toronto-based Harrod & Mirlin/FCB, is similarly unsettled by the growing client reluctance to gamble on original ideas. He points out that a byproduct of larger advertisers and agencies is fewer people have ultimate control over what gets done. And, he says, it's become the rule, rather than the exception, for these decision-makers to subject creative ideas to research and focus-group testing. Mr Mirlin says he can appreciate that research has become a necessary part of the process, but he cautions that research itself is a gamble. 'There is a great risk when clients come to rely on research. That is the death knell for inventive, surprising work.'

Despite his concerns that creativity in advertising has begun to suffer under the weight of corporate amalgamations, Mr. Mirlin remains optimistic it will rebound. Keep in mind, he says, the hands of commerce have always been wrapped around the neck of advertising creativity. 'But creativity has always found creative ways to be more creative, if you like. Creativity is a kinetic energy that always finds ways to wriggle out.'

▶

Another potential downside of growth is that, as clients and ad agencies get larger, they can become so involved with tumbling numbers and pursuing additional growth that they neglect to nurture the corporate culture of creativity and risk-taking that got them there. Ad agency managers, in particular, ought to be rewarded not only for generating revenues but also for producing award-winning advertising. John Lee, president of Toronto ad agency Holmes Lee, says advertising-driven clients and ad agencies tend to run into problems after mergers if they let their corporate cultures drift and become undefined. But he says they can thrive if they keep creativity top of mind. 'It all comes down to corporate culture,' says Mr. Lee. 'No matter how big the agency becomes, it can still do great work if the culture is focused on creating and building brands.'

Source: Patrick Allossery, National Post, 13 November 1998.

Case study questions

1. Discuss the premise, argued above, that there is the possibility of an inherent cultural mismatch in an advertising agency between creativity and the size of the organisation.
2. How might an advertising agency, no matter the size, install a sense of innovation and creativity amongst its staff so that complacency and conservatism do not come to be the accepted norm? Why should people be 'allowed to fail'?

CHAPTER QUESTIONS

1. How important do you consider creativity in advertising to be? What are the problems that might be associated with an 'over-creative' advertising team?
2. Do you think that almost 'anything goes' with regard to advertising and the need to attract audience attention? What are the possible dangers?
3. Discuss the benefits, and dangers, of using emotions to advertise products.
4. Identify advertisements you admire and discuss why you think they are creative and the reason why you think they achieve their objectives.
5. Identify the many behavioural factors that must be considered when creating adverts. Do you think it is manipulative for advertisers to exploit many of these factors?

REFERENCES

Bartle, Bogle and Hegarty (www.bbh.co.uk)

Bernbach, W.N. (1989) *Bill Bernbach Said,* DDB Needham Worldwide.

Barry Brookes, creative director, quoted in Eric Clark, *The Want Makers: Inside the World of Advertising* (1988), Penguin Books, p.114.

Maiden Outdoor (www.maiden.co.uk/postar.htm)

Milgram, S. (1974) *Obedience to Authority,* Harper & Row, New York.

Ogilvy, D. (1983) *Ogilvy on Advertising,* Vintage Books, New York.

FURTHER READING

Bird, D. (1994) *Common Sense Direct Marketing,* 3rd edn, NTC Business Books, London.

Direct Marketing Association (www.dma.org.uk)

Direct Selling Association (www.dsa.org.uk)

Ehrenberg, A. (1988) *A.S.C. Repeat-Buying; Facts, Theory and Applications,* 2nd edn, Oxford University Press.

Financial Times (www.ft.com)

Halberg, G. and Ogilvy, D. (1995) *All Consumers Are Not Created Equal: The Differential Marketing Strategy For Brand Loyalty and Profit,* John Wiley & Sons, Chichester, UK.

Institute of Practitioners in Advertising (www.ipa.co.uk)

McDonald, C. (1966) 'How frequently should you advertise?', *Admap,* July/August.

Rees, N. (1997) *Dictionary of Slogans,* HarperCollins, Glasgow.

Russell, T.R. and Lane, R.W. (1996) *Kleppner's Advertising Procedure* (13th edn), Prentice Hall, London.

Whitman, D.E., Why Most Advertising Is Never Read (www.salesdoctors.com)

Wilson, B.K. (1973) *Subliminal Seduction,* New American Library, New York.

Wolfe, A (1994) *Primary Contact: Getting the Most From Your Marketing Spend, Financial Times,* Pitman, London.

Part 5 Planning the advertising process

1998 IPA Advertising Effectiveness Awards demonstrate power of advertising in communications wars

Two of the top awards at the 1998 IPA Advertising Effectiveness Awards have gone to two of the leading players in the communications industry. Orange wins the Charles Channon Award for the best new learning on the wider effects of advertising, for its innovative paper on measuring the effect of advertising on the City. One2One wins the ISBA Award for Best New Entrant.

The Orange paper specifically analyses advertising's contribution to the success of Orange as a FTSE 100 plc. Innovative research carried out by Orange's agency WCRS in conjunction with Lehman Bros highlights new learning in measuring the links between brand advertising and share price. The campaign created an earnings pay back in excess of six times the investment, and also increased Orange's implied value per share by £2.49, equivalent to an increased market capitalisation of £3 billion.

Bartle, Bogle and Hegarty's campaign for One2One produced a year-on-year increase of 150 per cent in the company's customer base and transformed One2One from fourth player to market leadership in a year. Through defining mobile phones as conduits for fantasy conversations, the campaign created a payback of £199.3 million from a media spend of £36.7 million. Key factors in its success included restoration of employee pride in the brand, and increased credibility with city analysts and financial journalists.

In a change to previous years, entries were invited in 1998 from advertising agencies whose campaigns most clearly expressed new learning on the manifold effects of advertising. From a total of 54 entries, a shortlist of 30 emerged in September. Top awards were given by two judging panels, from the advertising industry and from the client panel, led by Lord Marshall, Chairman of British Airways.

Institute of Practitioners in Advertising (www.ipa.co.uk)

In this section we look at the planning that goes into putting together the advert and the overall strategic planning and control that goes into the whole process.

Client: One2One, Agent: Bartle Bogle Hegarty

13 Planning, producing and scheduling advertisements

OBJECTIVES

By the end of this chapter the reader should be able to:

1. Identify and evaluate the production processes for advertisements in the different media.

2. Identify the issues involved in scheduling advertisements.

INTRODUCTION

Technological advances alone aren't enough to drive social change. At least some people have to embrace change or it won't happen. Two tendencies cause new products to be adopted over prolonged periods rather than immediately. Products evolve slowly to meet the needs of the market, and the market adapts slowly to the new opportunities. People only slowly adapt their patterns, mindsets, skills and expectations to match the opportunities afforded by a new product. It takes years for people to hear about a product, try it, get used to it, rely on it.

(Bill Gates, Chairman and CEO, Microsoft, November 1996)

There comes a time when the media have been chosen, the creative thrust has been agreed and the layout of the advert must be prepared. Many basic concepts will be the same for all media, but the approach taken will vary according to the chosen medium.

Planning layout

Factors to be considered when planning the layout of the advert will include the following:

- the objectives
- the profile of the selected target audience
- brand positioning statement
- media vehicle to be used
- message content and style
- client concerns and wants
- creative agency skills
- budget and costs.

Newspapers

Newspaper layout applies to the total appearance of the advert and it can have a variety of elements; headline, illustration, sub-heading, body copy, logotype, colour, a sales promotion, a coupon to send in, and the company name and address; these will vary tremendously from ad to ad. The ad might be in a broadsheet or tabloid newspaper, be a full page or a half page; it might be all copy and no visuals, all visuals and no copy or a combination of both. It might be in colour or black and white, white on black or colour on colour and it might be classified or display. Whatever the ad the overall demanding factor is for the ad to stand out, to be seen, to be read, to be remembered and to be acted upon by target audiences.

Designing the layout

Both the creative services department and the production department will be involved in designing the layout of the ad. Mock-ups, examples of the thinking behind the design, will be constructed and discussed with the client as the process moves forward. At this stage all possible components of the ad will be evaluated to find the best possible combination of headline, picture, copy, artwork etc. Much of this can now be put onto the computer and text, typeface, founts, typography, colour, design, illustration, size and finished layout can all be intermixed, researched and tested, both with the client and with a small customer sample, to aid the process. A standard layout scheme is shown in Fig. 13.1.

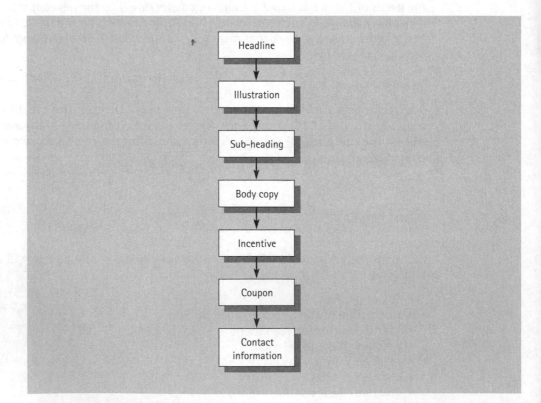

Fig. 13.1 The press advert

Copywriting

Copywriting is the writing of the text or copy for an advertisement used in newspapers, magazines, directories, posters and direct mail. This will consist of the headline, the sub-heading, the body copy, added incentives, coupons and company identification.

Copy platform

This is the theme of the advert, the 'big idea', and it is the major creative thrust coming from the product positioning statement. Examples of a copy platform are 'It's good to talk' (BT); 'Not everything in black and white makes sense' (Guinness); 'When you're only number 2, you try harder', a classic from Avis Rent-A-Car.

The headline

Attracting attention and getting noticed is the first and most important job of the advertisement and in today's global market the job is becoming ever more difficult. The most important parts of the ad are the headline and the illustration (if one is used). The headline is the first thing that people notice and it should offer a significant benefit so that interest will be aroused and the person will want to continue reading to find out more about the product being sold. If the headline isn't noticed then the reader will move on through the newspaper and the ad will be unread and wasted. There is no definitive formula for the headline but it should offer a major incentive that catches the eye and encourages the observer in to read more. Important attention-catching words include 'free', 'new', 'original', 'sale', 'introductory offer', 'half-price'.

A headline might often include 'action' words such as 'act now', 'buy now' or 'ring immediately' to encourage response.

The illustration

The right picture can be electrifying in its effect and many successful adverts have used visuals with little if any copy. Research has shown that most top-scoring ads have a picture of some sort. It's here that concepts discussed earlier such as novelty, shock, humour, sex etc. come into their own.

The sub-heading

The sub-heading, in smaller type, and sitting below the headline (or the headline and illustration) should offer more benefits, drawing the reader further into the ad.

Body copy

The body copy is the main text in an advertisement sitting below the heading, illustration and sub-heading. It is used to tell the whole story and expand on the total benefit package. Body copy can be expansive, less expansive or non-existent depending on objectives and the type of ad. An ad for hair restorer will have intricate detailed copy explaining the many benefits whilst an ad for a bottle of whisky will probably have little copy. Similarly an ad that is educational will have more copy than an ad that is concerned with brand development. It should end with a major benefit that will encourage action.

Coupon or incentive

Incentives to encourage immediate action might be included depending on the purpose of the ad and they are usually accompanied by a coupon for the prospective customer to send in to the company.

Contact information

It is surprising how many advertisements are well constructed but fail to identify the sponsoring company adequately. Name, address, phone number, fax, and e-mail address should be considered for inclusion.

Magazines

Layout of adverts for magazines will be very similar in many ways to that for newspapers, except that magazines are usually of a better quality and will be kept for longer, and so more expensive material can be used.

- Depending on the magazine the ad is more likely to be soft sell rather than hard sell.
- Space in magazines is usually sold in terms of full page and fractions of a full page (half page, quarter page, three columns, one column). Smaller ads are sold by the line.
- Right-hand pages, near the front and close to editorial appear to be an ideal position to be seen.
- Inside the front page seems to attract the most attention (the front page is not usually available) followed by the back page and then inside the back page.
- Research seems to show that a right-hand side or left-hand side ad makes little difference.
- Magazine owners will demand a higher price for a premium position.
- The use of colour will dramatically increase performance.
- Bigger ads will outperform smaller ones, but not by a proportional amount.
- Bigger ads will allow more flexibility in creativity.

It should be noted that all the above ads will often perform differently depending on the product or service being advertised. Ultimately a well thought through ad will achieve its objectives wherever it might be placed whilst with a bad ad the reverse will pertain.

Bleed pages

Bleed advertising has no margin and the ad runs all the way to the edge of the page giving the appearance of not being confined to a particular space, and so tends to attract more attention.

Posters

Poster design has become a wonderful medium for the creative designer to practise his or her artistic and creative talents. We only have to look around when travelling to see the many changing and inventive offerings. Ranging from the 4-sheet

An example of information available to advertisers about magazines

Melody Maker
The world's oldest music weekly, at the cutting edge of contemporary music
Launched: 1926
Circulation: 45 203 (ABC)
Cover price: 85p
Frequency: weekly
Adult readership: 297 000 (read, NRS)
Median age of readers: 24
Core target audience: men 15–24
ABC1 profile: 61 per cent
Opportunities to see (OTS): 10 est.
Main ad category: hi-fi audio

Colour page rate, run of paper: £4710

Woman's Own
Indulgent, inseparable companion, bubbly, fun, features, gossip, advice
Launched: 1932
Circulation: 712 494 (ABC)
Cover price: 57p
Frequency: weekly
Female readership: 3 million
Median age of readers: 39
Core target: mothers 20–45
BC1C2 profile: 65 per cent
OTS: 10 est.
Main ad categories: food, retail, toiletries and cosmetics
Colour page rate: £23 650

Source: IPC (www.ipc.co.uk)

to the 96 sheet it offers agency staff an almost limitless opportunity for new ideas and imaginative offerings. Intense copy can be used where people congregate and spend time hanging around and visuals can be used where awareness needs to be captured from a fast moving target. Design, colour, lighting, movement can all be used together to stimulate audience awareness and the future offers the prospect of computerised displays, satellite transmission to outdoor displays that can be changed centrally, and the use of fibre optics and laser technology.

We have argued that poster sites are the only true advertising form not being attached to other activity such as entertainment, transaction etc. This being the case, the following ad design factors should be considered:

- It must break through audience apathy and grab attention through its own ingenuity.
- It should be simple, as it usually has a few seconds to demand attention.
- In this short time the brand benefit has to be transmitted.
- Most poster sites will only allow for one major benefit to be communicated.
- Audience response ads have been tried with little success.
- It is the perfect medium for the use of dramatic and innovative colour and visuals.

Eva Herzigova's eye-catching Wonderbra 'Hello Boys' advertisement was included in an exhibition of the most memorable posters of the past century at the Victoria & Albert Museum. The 1994 advertisement, which overnight boosted sales of the bra by 400 per cent, was among 330 posters selected from the V&A's international collection of more than 10 000. The Czech supermodel was given pride of place at the exhibition, The Power of the Poster, among such classics of the genre as the works of Henri de Toulouse-Lautrec, Savile Lumley's 'Daddy, what did YOU do in the Great War?', Fougasse's 'Careless Talk Costs Lives' and Alfred Leete's 'Britons [Lord Kitchener] wants you' from 1914. The Wonderbra ad is also a

▶

classic which started off as a train of posters,' said Margaret Timmers, the exhibition's curator who works for the V&A's prints, drawings and paintings department. 'This is likely to become an icon'. The job of thinking up the advertisement was given in 1993 by Playtex, the company which owns the Wonderbra brand, to TWBA. Nigel Rose, the agency's art director at the time, is credited with the concept. The photograph was taken by Ellen von Unwerth. Miss Timmers said the V&A had elevated the ad to a work of art because the museum's panel of experts believed that it would stand the test of time. John Hegarty, chairman of Bartle, Bogle and Hegarty, writes: 'It was a very simple advertisement, unusual because underwear publicity had previously been confined to women's magazines. Here however it was on a huge scale and the medium was being used provocatively, challenging with slogans like "Hello Boys" and "Or are you just pleased to see me?"'

National Press

Direct-mail advertising

The bottom line is to get people to act. Whether you want people to send in a request for more information or send a nice hefty cheque, it's action that makes the advert pay off. Advertising is not journalism, it's not news reporting; sure you want them to respond intellectually and emotionally. In other words you want them to move and maybe shake them up a bit. But your primary interest is that they are well informed. Advertising on the other hand you want people to do more than just read what you write. You are not writing to entertain. You want people to do something about it – namely place an order or enquire for more information which is designed to persuade them to place an order. Hey, let's not kid each other – we advertise for one reason; to make money. Period.

(Drew Eric Whitman, *Why Most Advertising Is Never Read*, www.salesdoctors.com)

Direct-mail advertising, to both business customer and end consumer, will use many of the concepts and procedures identified above, but, because of its nature, differences exist that demand a particular attention from the advertising department.

Successful direct-mail communication

The mailing list ⟶ Being opened ⟶ Being read ⟶ Being acted upon

Mailing lists have been discussed in other chapters but it is worth repeating that the right message sent to the wrong person will be worthless and costly, giving the industry a bad name and encouraging the image of 'junk mail'. Marketing practitioners will argue that 'junk mail' would not be a problem if all correspondence was meticulously targeted.

Being opened

If we accept the efficacy of the targeting process the initial creative task for the copywriting department is to persuade the prospective customer to open the envelope (or package, depending on the communication). With so much now coming through the post this has become a major problem that if not solved can cause the letter to end up, unopened, in the waste-bin. Many creative methods can be used offering some benefit or other on the envelope to excite curiosity and encourage the envelope to be opened. Research has shown that 75 per cent of all direct mail is opened.

Being read

Once opened the task is to get the message read and the basic concepts of copywriting, heading, sub-heading, body copy and so on, identified above, will apply. Make it relevant, simple to understand and logical in the layout and there is every chance it will be read. It seems that over 50 per cent of all direct mail is read once opened.

Being acted upon

If the targeting is precise, if the product or service offers competitive, relevant benefits in an exciting and creative way, then the opportunity for it to be acted upon will be increased. A promotional incentive added will usually improve response rates quite dramatically.

The direct mailing 40-40-20 rule: 40% of success depends on the mailing list, 40% on the offer and 20% on ideas and design.

(Drayton Bird)

The broadcast media

While the construction of ads for television and cinema (and to a lesser extent radio) is similar in some ways to that for the press, and many of the concepts discussed above will apply, it is very different in other ways because of the basic differences discussed in earlier chapters between the media.

Writing the script

Writing a script for a TV ad is different from writing a press ad because of the difference between the two media forms. The reader can pause to take the press ad in, the TV ad will come and go in probably 15 to 30 seconds. This demands that the storyline is simple; the words must be easily understood and it must say, predominantly, one thing about the brand that will first attract the viewer and second press home the need for it to be considered for purchase. Due to audience attention span any attempt on the part of the advertiser to inject more than one benefit proposition is liable to end in failure. Storylines will often follow fairly predictable and stereotypical patterns proved to have been successful over many decades just allowing for subtle changes to bring them up-to-date. In this way the target audience can quickly assimilate what is going on and so give immediate attention to the message. However, imaginative storylines are used to gain attention and wider publicity. Some ads, for example those for Gold Blend, will build on the story week by week in the manner of the best romantic 'soap opera', even spawning magazine spin-offs.

Scripts for cinema can be longer, often two to three minutes, and the storyline more complex allowing the director more artistic scope. Conversely the radio scriptwriter will need to work within one-dimensional limitations and the words, sound and music will all take on an added importance attempting to 'paint' imaginative pictures in the mind.

A large advertising agency instigated research to find the most beneficial way to advertise lager to young men and to try to discover what they thought of TV advertising. A part of the finding that caused some amusement was the effect that men, in a commercial, had on audience perceptions. Traditionally beer adverts have shown young men, drinking in a pub, discussing the virtues of lager – but would it make a difference how many? Surprisingly, the answer was yes. Many respondents felt that four or more could be construed as a group having a 'booze-up', two as 'gender suspect', and one, drinking on his own, as a sad and lonely depressive. So three was felt to be the acceptable number.

Describing the visuals

The visuals in the commercial will be developed interactively with the storyline and the script and such factors as background, mood, personalities, time of day, weather etc. will be discussed and described.

The storyboard

Once the creative people have put together the script, a storyboard can be constructed. This consists of a series of drawings and words (like a comic picture story) mimicking the script and visuals of the end commercial. It becomes a valuable tool for discussing the proposed advert with the client and other agency personnel. Computers and TV monitors can now be used in creating virtual reality commercials.

Soundtrack

The value of music and its ability to communicate emotions and mood have already been discussed. Music can make or break a commercial and is every bit as important as the visual or the copy. Similarly, nuance, tone, inflection, accent and dialect are all integral parts of any spoken words, and can help to create empathy and acceptance on the part of the audience. Well-known personalities are often used, at great expense, as 'voice-overs', because experience has shown that immediate recognition often encourages immediate attention. This will apply to all broadcast media.

Producing broadcast commercials

The broadcast production manager will be responsible for overseeing the production of the commercial. The medium to be used and the value of the contract will determine which in-house and out-of house facilities will be used. The production manager must oversee the whole project, gathering, co-ordinating and organising resources, interacting between all involved and generally seeing that objectives are successfully achieved.

'Pre-production' includes, amongst other things, casting, wardrobe, set design and location selection. The more complex the advert, the longer and more expensive this process will be.

The production or shooting of the commercial is the filming or videotaping of all the scenes in the commercial. The key person is the director who is responsible for bringing the storyboard to life in the most artistic and commercially attractive way possible. He or she will cast, rehearse and direct every scene, hopefully bringing the best out of all concerned. Conflict can arise, but shouldn't, between what is 'attractive' to the director and what is 'attractive' to the client, with the former leaning toward the 'artistic' and the latter toward the 'commercial'.

'Post-production' includes film editing, arranging the shots in the order needed, bringing together sound and visuals, adding titles and presenting the finished commercial.

Producing radio commercials

Producing radio commercials is easier and cheaper, and can be undertaken by the radio company as part of the service. That is not to say, however, that care should not be taken to see that it is produced in the most effective and imaginative manner possible.

A radio advert will have the following characteristics:

- It uses sound only and so puts more emphasis on the value of the copy.
- Repetition will be necessary to create the necessary OTH.
- The quality of the sound and the music take on added importance.
- Because radio is often used as a background medium, the ad must begin with a strong introduction, hit immediately with benefits, be simple, and finish with a dramatic ending.
- It can be live or on tape.
- Celebrities can be used in the same way as in all other media.

Although radio lacks visuals – sounds, words and music brought together in the right manner can create pictures in people's minds. So exotic locations, expensive to shoot on location for TV, can be reproduced in people's minds for a fraction of the cost if the production staff are skilled enough.

Internet advertising

The Internet has the capacity to be as transforming an event as TV was to radio. We want to be second to no one in this new form of media.

(Richard Goldstein, CEO, Unilever, USA, July 1998)

Writing advertisements for the Internet is still very problematic because of its newness. Nevertheless many of the basic communication concepts, advertising objectives, target audience, measurement and control etc. discussed above will apply to all media and the Internet is no different. Because of its explosive development it is understandable that lack of knowledge, misunderstandings and disagreement exist in many areas of advertising on the net that no longer cause quite the same confusion in the more traditional media. Nevertheless enormous effort is being exerted by advertisers, agencies and media owners to rectify the situation as soon as possible. Confusion still pertains in some degree in areas such as:

- the optimum size for advertisements
- the position of the adverts
- the content of the adverts
- the role of the advert
- the style of adverts.

However, practitioners are working on the problems, and the situation is likely to improve in the near future.

When designing a web site, the following factors need to be taken into account:

- The site must both attract and keep clients in worthwhile numbers.
- The site should be easy to download. Despite broadening bandwidths some sites still take ages to download and frustration can cause the prospect to leave.
- It should be simple and attractive to the target audience.
- There should be real benefits on the site, with no unnecessary web pages.
- Avoid clutter; use novelty, good design, colour, movement.
- The design of the site should link into corporate image.
- Information and benefits on the site should mirror overall corporate benefits.

Location is important. Positioning at the top of the page is probably not as advantageous as it might first appear. Image download may be lengthy and by the time the image is displayed the viewer may have finished reading the upper part of the page and be scrolling down. Placement somewhere in the middle will probably work the best as viewer attention is held longer while the process of downloading takes place. It is recommended that the reader goes through this process his or her self so as to gain empirical data. Whether advertisers are offering services or products on their own web sites or placing advertisements on other people's, the latest technology on the web should be used to make the offering interesting and attractive.

When designing ads on own site:

- Use ads that are fixed to the screen, rather than those that scroll off the screen as the picture moves down, as the latter may easily not be noticed.
- Use movement and novelty (without undue complication that could cause delay).
- Background images are important and a company own site gives freedom to exploit this.
- The background should complement the ad in a meaningful way – e.g. a holiday company might have palm trees, sea and sun.

When designing ads on the site of other organisations:

- Ads should only be put on sites that will have meaning and attract the advertiser's customers.
- Recognise the difference between a web site ad and web site sponsorship.
- Integrate web advertising with overall advertising and promotional activity.
- Insist on adequate measurement and control mechanism; if it isn't working pull it off.

Bartle, Bogle and Hegarty, creative ad agency (www.bbh.co.uk)
LEVI'S case study

Problem Europe (1984)
- Denim in decline.
- No leadership in the market.
- Levi's jeans seen as old people's jeans, part of the Establishment.
- America associated with Reagan, Dinosaurs of Rock, Fat Tourists etc.
- In product tests consumers found Levi's 501 jeans, with their anti-fit and button fly, rather odd and unattractive.
- Client keen to launch Levi's 501 jeans in any case, as they had been successful in USA.

Solution
- Celebrate the authenticity of the original jeans.
- Focus on the fifties when Levi's 501 jeans were adopted as a badge of youth rebellion and cool.
- Develop a Mythical America far from contemporary reality.
- Capture the enduring values of youth: sex, rebellion, freedom, individuality.
- Luxuriate in product detail.

Results
- Sales of Levi's 501 jeans in the UK increased eightfold in the first year of advertising.
- In the first ten years of advertising European volume sales of Levi's 501 jeans increased by 820 per cent.
- In the same period the price premium of Levi's jeans over the average of other manufacturers' jeans increased from 4 per cent to 30 per cent.
- IPA Effectiveness Award (UK) 1988.
- 1997 Marketing Society Brand of the Year (Durables).
- IPA Effectiveness Award (Europe) 1994

Scheduling advertisements

When scheduling the advertisements, the timing, continuity, size, length and position of the ad will be determined both by the budget and by the objectives.

Cost will inevitably affect the timing, continuity and overall amount of advertising any organisation is able to contract. For all but the most wealthy, the expense involved will be a major factor in deciding the overall weight of the campaign. It will set limits on all aspects of the advertising from the media chosen through to numbers of exposures purchased.

Many argue that the advertising objectives driving the campaign should dictate the amount of media use especially if predicted end results can show worthwhile cost/benefit advantages. If it can be realistically demonstrated that high levels of brand awareness will contribute to market position gains then there should be every expectation of budget backing.

Advert timing

Research should be used to identify customer behaviour so as to time the advert correctly. Product and media trends can be analysed to try to understand the influences on target audiences of the seasons, holidays, months, days of the week, the times of the day (this will sometimes be supplied by media owners). Armed with this information the best media and the best times can be chosen to deliver the message to the specific target audience.

Depending on objectives and budget, message timings will vary according to the type of product, customer type, marketing objectives and the promotional and media interconnection.

Many products are seasonal and need to be advertised at particular times of the year. Clothes, toys, books and alcohol are advertised in the run-up to Christmas; holidays, hangover cures and new year's resolution products (e.g. nicotine patches) after Christmas; vacuum cleaners and cleaning products in spring. In many retail markets orders are traditionally placed at certain times of the year, often many months before consumer purchase, an example being spring fashion bought in the preceding autumn.

Adverts will need to reach people when they are most susceptible to the message. TV will reach young children just before and just after school time and on Saturday morning, adults between 8 p.m. and 11 p.m. and sports fans at the weekends. The press often have special days for particular areas such as cooking, travel and motoring, and associated products would best be advertised in these sections

Marketing objectives such as reversing a slowdown in sales, special events, new product launch, moving slow-moving products, reaction to competition etc. will often determine when advertising campaigns are needed.

Finally, if advertising is being used with other promotional and media tools then timings will be in some part determined by the overall objectives of the promotional campaign.

Pricing and timing

The media will charge different prices at different times depending on

- demand
- audience size
- competitive activity, and
- flexibility.

Advance (early) booking discount rate

A reduced rate for advertising booked in advance, either by a specific number of weeks or by a given date in the month preceding transmission. Usually given as a specific percentage off of card-rate.

Run of a period

Lower than card-rate prices will often be offered by media owners if the ad insertion timing is left to their discretion. Run of a period offers lower prices if the advertiser is prepared to accept ad insertion at any time during a given period in the newspaper/magazine or on TV etc. This period might be a day, a week, a month, even a year. The advantage for the media owner is the flexibility to move adverts around so as to gain optimum insertions. The advantage for the advertiser is lower prices but the disadvantage is loss of control with the danger that the ad might not reach the wanted target audience in large enough numbers.

Nearness to transmission date

The nearer the time to transmission the more discount will be offered
card-rate. Advertising space is lost once transmission is under way a
owners might even be prepared to offer loyal advertisers free advertising space
rather than transmit with space to spare.

Advert continuity

There has been much research undertaken to try to discover the most effective for-
mulae for the scheduling of a series of adverts across the period of the campaign so
that maximum advantage can be obtained. Options used include continuous
advertising, drip advertising, burst advertising and intermittent advertising.

With *continuous advertising*, the ad will run every day, every week, or every
month, without gaps. This type of advertising is used to advertise FMCG items
such as food, washing powders and soft drinks – items that are in demand all the
year round and for which brand reinforcement is continuously needed.

Drip advertising describes an advertising campaign covering a long period, perhaps 12 months, in which ads are shown 'little but often'. It is hoped that in this
way the basic brand message will eventually register in the mind of the audience
through the subconscious.

The danger with 'continuous' and 'drip' advertising – 'advertising wear-out' –
is that the audience becomes indifferent to the message due to familiarity.
Creativity and innovation in message presentation can be used to attempt to
stop this happening.

With *burst advertising*, the ads are concentrated into a short period of time, usually on the one medium. The hope is that repeated bursts with relatively long gaps
in between will avoid the problems associated with advertising wear-out. Burst
advertising is often used with the more expensive type of product (e.g. cars), in the
hope that a large amount of advertising in one hit will ensure that the message
penetrates and the brand is remembered.

Intermittent advertising is based on the concept that wear-out is caused by audiences knowing when to expect the adverts, enabling them to selectively screen
out the message. It is hoped that varying the timing, length and content of the
advert will catch the audience unaware and so overcome this perceptual defence
mechanism.

Advertising in the right place at the right time

A Scottish lawyer who believes that most of his clients end up in trouble after drinking
too much has started advertising his services on pub beer mats distributed around the
town's pubs. He argues that in a very competitive business it is important to use
imaginative promotion techniques to advertise, and reasons that, as many of his clients'
problems are caused by drinking, then the pubs must be one of the best places to
advertise his services. This advertising ploy has won the lawyer many new clients, but
the Scottish Law Society is more wary, and wants to see the beer mats, which contain a
personal photograph, the name, address and telephone number of that firm of lawyers,
before giving or denying approval.

CONCLUSION

Traditionalism and/or creativity can both be used in the construction of adverts. What is important is that the end product achieves the objective of being seen and acted upon. A deep understanding of the workings of audience perceptive processes is crucial if adverts are to be constructed in a manner that optimises their performance. Ads must then be built that consider these perceptive processes coupled with the media to be used. They must then be meticulously planned taking into account costs, timings, amounts and continuity.

CASE STUDY

In hot pursuit of the yuppie

For those who drive Porsches and are worried about the approach of their thirties, the drama series *Wonderful You* promises to be gripping stuff. Can Henry, the 29-year-old undiscovered songwriter from the north London district of Crouch End, steal the girl from his rival in love, the yuppie accountant Marshall? For advertisers, *Wonderful You* could be even more intriguing when it arrives on screens shortly in the slot to be vacated by *News at Ten*. Can the downmarket housewives' channel of ITV steal upmarket viewers from the superior BBC? Will advertisements for mobile phones and cars reach a suitable audience profile? Programmes such as *Wonderful You* and the recent *Cold Feet,* a comedy drama about twentysomethings in Didsbury – the Mancunian equivalent of Crouch End – are hardly traditional fare on ITV. It has thrived on mass entertainment, with soap operas such as *Coronation Street,* and popular quiz and game shows.

But ITV is now fighting not only to regain some of the share of the viewing audience that it lost in the early 1990s, but to shift itself upmarket. It is a tricky combination, for a mass audience is not easily combined with the closely targeted demographics that many consumer goods advertisers have come to seek. 'The ITV audience has never reflected the national average. It has always been more female, downmarket and older, and that is something to think about,' says Richard Eyre, ITV's chief executive. Just over 36 per cent of people watching television tuned into ITV in the last quarter of 1998, but its share of ABC1 adults aged between 16 and 34 was less than 31 per cent. For a long time, that did not matter too much to ITV. It was the only commercial channel until the launch of Channel 4 in 1982, and its share of viewing stood at 40 per cent in 1993. But this share has been attacked in the past five years by new channels, falling to 31.7 per cent last year. It also faced commercial threats to its dominance of the UK advertising market.

Consumer goods companies selling soap powders and household items – known among agencies as 'clean 'em and feed 'em' advertisements – became less important, and advertisements aimed at a young and more affluent audience grew. 'In the old days, advertisers were really only interested in absolute size of audience, but the growth sectors like telecoms and financial services are more targeted now, and advertisers want ITV to reflect that,' says Christine Walker of Walker Media, an advertisement buying agency. David Liddiment, ITV's network director, argues that this is more than just commercial necessity. 'We are a big channel so we need to track changes in British society. The country has become more prosperous and moved from manufacturing into services. Our programmes have to reflect that,' he says.

So comes the Blue Sky Bar in Crouch End, where the passions and rivalries of *Wonderful You* are played out, just as those of the *Friends* revolve around a coffee bar called Central

Perk. 'It is not all doom and gloom and angst. You get very involved in the characters,' says the series' producer Beryl Vertue. Yet the targeting of ITV is a delicate matter. Although *Cold Feet* has been a critical success in its Sunday evening slot, and gained a 35 per cent audience share, this is still below the 38 per cent peak-time share that ITV sought last year. The target is 39 per cent this year and 40 per cent next. The most attractive shows for ITV are the mass hits such as *Who Wants to be a Millionaire?*, a quiz show in which contestants can win cash prizes. This was watched recently by 17.5m people – 64 per cent of the peak-time audience. Blockbuster hits attract huge numbers of ABC1 viewers, whatever their precise demographic profile.

Although *Cold Feet* won a gratifyingly high share of ABC1 and 16- to 54-year-old viewers – compared with what Zenith Media, the buying agency, calls the 'dreaded DEs' and 'unwanted 55-pluses' – it is not enough. ITV would undershoot its targets if all its peak-time shows reached similar sized audiences. Indeed, the head of one advertising agency argues that ITV is placing its traditional unique selling proposition at risk with such efforts. 'A mass audience is what ITV could always give us better than anyone else. If they lose sight of mass by chasing targeting, it would be a disaster,' he says.

One problem with targeting a younger and more affluent mix of viewers is that they tend to be less loyal than the traditional ITV audience. Not only do they watch less television, but they are also less liable to revisit the same show each week. Furthermore, Mr Eyre argues that the older audience – often referred to by advertisers as 'wastage' – is more valuable than is sometimes supposed. 'I think it's a very dodgy term. Who is to say that grandma does not influence the buying patterns of the family as much as anyone?' he says.

Mr Liddiment insists ITV's new programming policy takes all these factors into account, and is aimed at a gentle 'skew' of its audience rather than abandoning its heartland. He says ITV is in a different position to US networks such as Fox and Warner Brothers, which are heavily targeted.

The WB network has made up for its relatively small audience share by aiming at younger female viewers, and Fox has taken its place alongside the 'big three' networks with shows such as *The Simpsons* that appeal to younger viewers. That has given them a disproportionate appeal to US advertisers. 'We are still a 38 per cent share channel, and that is a hell of a share. The US networks are down to 15 per cent or so, which means that newcomers like Fox and Warner can come up with their own propositions,' says Mr Liddiment. He says ITV can balance mass with more selective efforts.

Source: John Gapper, *Financial Times*, 22 January 1999. Used with permission.

Case study questions

1. Discuss the strategy of ITV discussed above. Which stakeholders should be involved in the process?
2. Demonstrate how ad design might change according to strategy adopted and audiences selected.

CHAPTER QUESTIONS

1. Identify the major differences between newspaper, magazine, TV and radio advert planning. Which is the more difficult?
2. Identify the role that research plays in the construction and planning of adverts.

3. How will the construction of adverts change as more media methods come online and existing methods fragment and contract?
4. Take a current advertisement of your choice and deconstruct and analyse the process identifying the component parts, e.g. theme, copy, illustrations, media choice, target audience etc. giving reasons and thinking behind the construction.
5. How would you approach the web advert design? What are the problems particularly associated with this media form?

REFERENCES

Bartle, Bogle, Hegarty (www.bbh.co.uk)

Financial Times (www.ft.com)

Bill Gates, Chairman and CEO, Microsoft (www.microsoft.com)

Independent Television (www.itv.co.uk)

Institute of Practitioners in Advertising (www.ipa.co.uk)

IPC Magazines (www.ipc.co.uk)

The Salesdoctor magazine (www.salesdoctors.com)

FURTHER READING

Antin, A. (1993) *Great Print Advertising: Creative Approaches, Strategy, and Tactics,* John Wiley and Sons, Chichester, UK.

Bogart, M.H. (1997) *Artists, Advertising and the Borders of Art,* University of Chicago Press, US.

Burton, P.W. (1999) *Advertising Copywriting,* NTC Publishing Group, London.

Higgins, D. (ed). (1988) *The Art of Writing Advertising: Conversations with; William Benbach, Leo Burnett, George Gribbin, David Ogilvy, Rosser Reeves,* Natl Text Book Co. Trade, U.S.

Jewler, J. (1997) *Creative Strategy in Advertising,* Wadsworth Publishing Company, Belmont, US.

Ray Wright (www.raynetmarketing.com)

14 The strategic planning process

OBJECTIVES

By the end of this chapter the reader should be able to:

1. Identify all the factors involved in the planning process.

2. Undertake a communications audit.

3. Develop an advertising strategic and tactical plan.

INTRODUCTION

Planning is at the heart of advertising; only if we all know where we are going can correct and adequate resources be integrated and made available and monitoring and measurement controls be implemented so as to ensure a satisfactory outcome.

(Account manager)

There will come a time when planning will need to take place, putting the advertising campaign on a formal footing. Planning is crucial in all areas of business and should happen at all levels of the organisation from both the top down and the bottom up. Depending on their role in the department, all members of the promotional team should be involved in the process at the strategic or tactical level, identifying relevant factors, discussing and arguing, searching for the most effective solution.

What is strategic advertising planning?

Advertising can be enormously expensive with often uncertain results sometimes taking many years before its impact can be seen to affect consumer buying behaviour. With over £10 billion being spent in 1998 on advertising in the UK alone, by more and more advertisers, it is crucial that it is planned and controlled in as effective a way as possible so that every last ounce of value is obtained. Advertising planning is the process by which all members of the advertising management team come together, discuss and analyse how the communication objectives can be achieved in the most cost-effective manner. It involves basic management practices such as

- researching for relevant information
- forecasting expected results

- organising and co-ordinating resources
- directing, communicating, motivating all team members
- implementing, monitoring, controlling and evaluating programmes.

More specifically, advertising planning will be concerned with the following tasks:

- discussing and analysing the advertising task to be undertaken (this can be quite complex if involving dialogue between the advertiser and an advertising agency);
- market research to establish the composition, behavioural readiness, and level of awareness of the target audience;
- setting clear advertising objectives;
- establishing the budget;
- selecting the relevant media;
- developing effective messages;
- implementing and monitoring the campaign;
- controlling and measuring both progress and results.

Why plan?

Planning is now seen as a crucial element of business management and it is indispensable in the advertising process.

- Planning encourages all members of the team to identify, confront, argue through the problems and agree solutions. It has often been said that the actual planning process that individuals go through can be as important as the end result.
- It helps co-ordinate and integrate advertising with all elements of the promotional mix including sales promotions, direct promotions, POP, PR, publicity, personal selling, sponsorship and exhibitions.
- Planning allows co-ordinated strategic direction to be developed for all elements of the advertising campaign working together so that optimum synergy is achieved.
- Responsibilities can be allocated within the plan so that all members of the advertising team are motivated by being clearly aware of the part that each plays in the process.
- It allows forethought to be involved in the collection, evaluation and allocation of resources.
- Planning supports the decision-making process, making as certain as possible that the risk associated with forward planning, whilst being impossible to totally eliminate, is kept to the minimum.
- It allows feedback, monitoring and control mechanisms to be implemented.
- It allows contingency arrangements to be made in case of deviations.

Formal and informal planning

Planning can take many forms depending mainly on the culture of the organisation. The more formal the organisation the more formal the planning process.

Conversely the less formal the company the less formal will be the planning process. In reality most organisations sit somewhere on a continuum between the two extremes, as shown in Fig. 14.1.

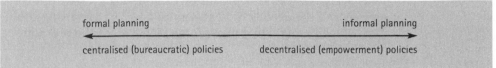

Fig. 14.1 Formal and informal planning

Formal planning involves clear head office policy statements for every division, department and unit with clear rules and pointers on what can and cannot be done in the furtherance of business. With advertising planning this will cover such issues as the media to be selected, the prices to be paid, the message themes to be adopted and the methods of control to be implemented. This form of planning tends to be associated with the larger, bureaucratic type of advertiser or advertising agency.

Informal planning, on the other hand, tends to be associated with the smaller, more flexible type of organisation often imbued with a strong entrepreneurial culture. In the extreme, as many decisions as possible are devolved down to the lowest level, empowering those in direct contact with the customer to make more immediate and customised planning decisions.

Centralised or decentralised planning

Larger companies, especially if operating on a global basis, also have the perennial problem of levels of control associated with size. How much of the advertising planning process should be controlled at the centre and how much devolved down to the various units? There appears to be no right or wrong answer and practice will vary according to company policy and business fashion. Advertisers will often choose an advertising agency because of its planning culture and ways of working and how this might fit in with its products and markets. This might be because of a reputation for innovation, creativity and flexibility or, conversely, a reputation for conservatism and tried and tested ways of advertising.

In 1995 IBM introduced the 'subtitles' advertising and marketing campaign in an attempt to improve the consistency of its international marketing and communications operations. The campaign seeks to create global imagery by using the same commercial in different countries, but including local subtitles to preserve the home cultural accent of each nation and to enhance communication by using the local vernacular. The concept underlying 'subtitles' is the universality of IBM's brand imagery. The success of the subsequent advertising and marketing campaign demonstrates that focused, singular messages can effectively be used for global advertising.

Source: Wayne R. McCullough

The advertising agency and planning

For the advertising agency advertising planning will hold centre stage for every client, every campaign being different and customised to meet individual advertiser needs. If the agency is an all-service agency advertising could well be part of a wider campaign involving many other elements of the promotional mix.

Advertising and corporate planning

All major organisations will plan in some way or other for future activity covering every aspect of operations. Advertising will play a small or larger part in the process depending on its considered importance. Corporate planning is planning at the highest level covering every division and every area of the organisation from finance and production through to human resource and marketing. Advertising planning will sit beneath marketing and promotional planning, as shown in Fig. 14.2.

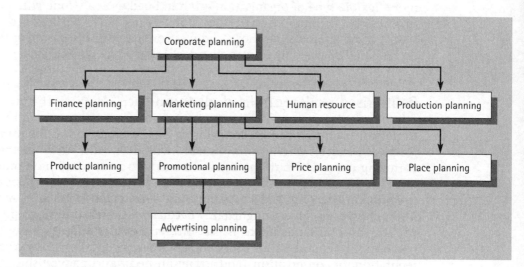

Fig. 14.2 Corporate, marketing, promotional and advertising planning

Advertising as part of promotional planning

Advertising planning can either take place on its own as a discrete campaign or, as is more likely, as part of a wider promotional campaign involving all or many of the other elements of the promotional mix, as shown in Fig. 14.3.

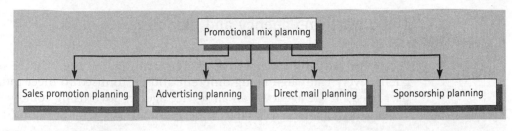

Fig. 14.3 Promotional planning

The advertising planning process

Planning at all levels of the organisation can be described as answering the following simple questions:

1. Where are we now?
2. Where do we want to go?
3. How are we going to get there?

The audit

'Where are we now?' What is known as the audit or the situational analysis can take place at every level of the organisation depending on the task in hand. All planning will begin with some form of audit (meaning an examination) as it is impossible to make realistic decisions about the future unless the present situation is understood. Corporate auditing will involve all areas of the organisation, marketing auditing will involve all areas relating to marketing, promotional auditing will be concerned with the promotional mix and advertising auditing will look at the present situation related to advertising. This is shown in Fig. 14.4.

The advertising audit might take place as part of an overall corporate audit, as part of a marketing audit, or as part of a promotional mix audit, or it might take place on its own as an advertising audit, a present situation analysis of an organisation's advertising position. The audit can be undertaken by the advertiser, the agency, or both, depending on the campaign. Whatever the circumstances surrounding the audit the basic principles involved are the same and will follow more or less the same procedure identified below.

Collection and classification of external information

Marketing research, both secondary and primary, will probably be used in the external collection of information. It is at this stage that the company information database, the marketing/advertising information system, will be used. Sources of information were discussed in Chapter 9. Any information relating to the organisation, advertising and the current situation must be collected and analysed. External information needed will include the following:

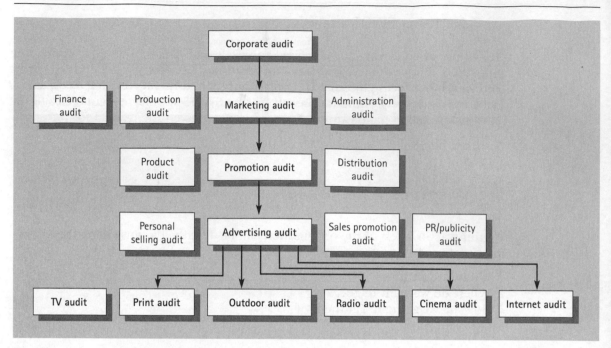

Fig. 14.4 Where the advertising audit sits within the overall corporate audit

- the current and expected future situation with regard to the media mix; TV, print, outdoor, radio and the cinema, as well as direct advertising, POP and the Internet;
- media questions including prices, target markets, readership,   audiences and circulation figures as well as timings, availability and effectiveness;
- information about the state of the target market of the brand about to be advertised, covering segmentation variables, levels of awareness, brand loyalty and buyer readiness states;
- new technologies available in creating and planning adverts – these should be researched and evaluated;
- competitor advertising activity, past, present and future.

Collection and classification of internal information

Information to be collected internally (within the organisation) will include the following:

- any current company advertising or promotional campaign that might impinge or could be integrated in some way on the campaign being developed;
- experience of past campaigns;
- current resources that might be utilised in some way by the advertising campaign under development. These might include financial, human, informational or technical resources.

An advertising SWOT analysis

The information can then be analysed and evaluated. This can often be done using the SWOT (Strengths, Weaknesses, Opportunities, Threats) model with strengths and weaknesses being internal and opportunities and threats relating to the external advertising environment. The advertising SWOT should relate directly to the advertising task in hand. An imaginary example is given in Fig. 14.5 for the advertising launch of a new product.

Fig. 14.5 An advertising SWOT analysis

It should be remembered that SWOT is merely a model to be used as a discussion and analytical tool. It can be refined and reworked as many times as needed. The art of the exercise is to get advertising team members to look at, and discuss, all relevant issues.

Once the current situation has been analysed the planning process can begin. This will involve setting clear objectives and identifying and evaluating strategic advertising options. The SWOT analysis can be used as the basis for strategic choice in answering 'Where do we want to go?'

The mission statement

All business activities will take place under the umbrella of the corporate mission and advertising is no different. Mission statements are still controversial with some practitioners arguing that they are clichéd and platitudinous and tend to be little more than an obvious high management wish-list disbelieved and often unknown by those farther down in the organisation's hierarchy. Others will argue that the mission statement can give the company long-term direction and instil a cultural sense of purpose as long as everybody in the company is involved and those at all levels are prepared to abide by its sentiments. The mission statement becomes important to advertising because it sets out issues that could affect the type and content of the advertising message at both the corporate brand and sub-brand level.

Mission statement content

The organisation 'mission statement' can appear in many forms and under many headings in company literature. This should not be a problem as long as it is understood that by mission statement we are talking about long-term corporate values covering many of the following areas:

- what business the company is in – e.g. Sara Lee Corporation's mission is 'to build leadership brands in primary packaged goods markets around the world'.
- who the customers are – e.g. purchasers of FMCG leading brands in different countries and cultures around the world;
- how long-term stockholder value will be created – e.g. ROI (return on investment), ROCE (return on capital employed), EPS (earnings per share);
- how the business will be run – e.g. in a decentralised manner, setting divisional sales and profit targets whilst empowering local employees to work in an innovative way;
- concern for environmental issues – e.g. behaving in a way that will protect rather than harm the environment;
- concern for the treatment of the staff.

In many cases corporate and product values have been historically developed over many years and customers have a distinct image concept that advertising must not damage or downgrade. Values inherent in the mission statement will often appear in the corporate or product brand positioning statement.

Objectives

All company objectives can be seen as both open and closed.

Open objectives are objectives that are not quantified in any way. To build stockholder value, to increase sales in existing markets or to create more awareness of company brands are all open objectives. They will often appear in this form in company announcements made for public consumption. However, they are insufficient if they are to be to be used as business management objectives because they lack the ability to be measured and controlled.

Closed objectives are objectives that can be quantified over time. The examples given above of open objectives could be transformed into closed objectives in the following ways:

- Stockholder value will be increased over the next five years at an average return on capital employed (ROCE) of 20 per cent.
- Sales will be increased by an average of 15 per cent a year over the next three years.
- Advertising will increase awareness of a company brand, amongst the target market, from an existing 15 per cent to 60 per cent over the six-month period of the advertising campaign.

Only if objectives are quantified over time can monitoring, measurement and control, (crucial and fundamental to planning) take place. *All* business objectives, at whatever level in the organisation, must be SMART: specific, measurable, achievable (and agreed by all involved), realistic, and time based.

Short, medium and long-term objectives

Objectives will need to be broken down into those for the short, medium and long term. What is short, medium or long term will vary according to the product, company and the industry. Long-term objectives for one area (novelty goods for Christmas) may be short-term for another (the motor car industry). The same will apply within the organisation itself and what might be short term for the organisation at corporate level, six months for example, could be considered long term at the advertising department level.

At the marketing department level the long term tends to be three to five years and so short term might be six months to a year, medium term two to three years and long term five years. In the advertising department 'long-term' can be anything from a few days to over a year. Because of the uncertainty associated with looking into the future, the longer the time period the less detailed will be the plan and conversely the shorter the period the more detail will be included.

The hierarchy of objectives

All planning will consist of a hierarchy of objectives moving from corporate, to marketing, to promotion, to advertising, to media mix, to individual programmes. The hierarchy of objectives is shown in Fig.14.6.

Corporate objectives

Corporate objectives are performance indicators for the organisation as a whole. (These can be seen to be at divisional level depending on the company size and structure.) Corporate strategies are usually defined in terms of shareholder value

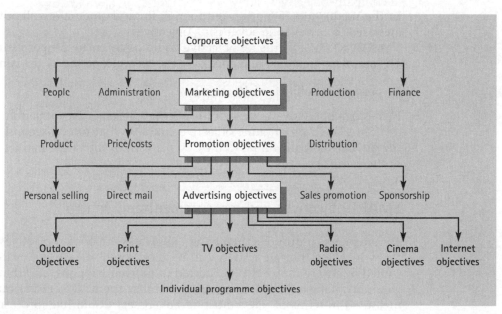

Fig. 14.6 The hierarchy of objectives

including return on investment (ROI), return on capital employed (ROCE) and earnings per share (EPS). Corporate objectives are relevant to advertising planning to show that the planners are aware that advertising planning needs to take place within the overall umbrella of corporate planning.

An example of a SMART corporate objective would be an average ROCE of 20 per cent every year over the next five years.

Marketing objectives

Marketing is a corporate strategy, along with finance, production, administration, human resource management and so on (depending on the type of organisation). As we move down the hierarchy of objectives we find that marketing objectives tend to be set in terms of sales and profit and market share.

A SMART marketing objective might be to increase sales by an average of 15 per cent a year over the next three years, while making an average net profit of 10 per cent.

Promotional objectives

Promotional objectives are the overall objectives for the promotion campaign and can be in terms of sales wanted for the length of the promotional period.

A SMART promotional objective might be to achieve sales of £100 000 over the promotional period of six weeks.

Advertising objectives

Advertising as a promotional strategy will play a part in achieving the overall promotional objective, usually by creating brand awareness, interest and loyalty.

A SMART advertising objective might be to create 60 per cent awareness amongst the target market by the end of the six-week campaign.

Media mix objectives

In the media mix, TV, print, outdoor, radio and cinema are all advertising strategies used to achieve the advertising objectives.

A SMART TV advertising objective could be to create 50 per cent awareness (on TV) amongst the target audience over the six-week period of the campaign.

TV programme objectives (tactical)

Each programme advertising spot will also have its objective (or performance indicator).

A SMART TV programme objective could be that ten 30-second adverts appearing on SKY football will be seen by 20 per cent of the target market over the period of the campaign.

SMART objectives and measurement and control

To reiterate a continuous theme that permeates the book, objectives are 'SMART' at every level, so that all activity can be monitored, measured, evaluated and controlled to ensure that what is expected to happen happens, and that the maximum value is obtained from every pound or dollar spent. Objectives cannot always be measured in terms of sales (much as advertisers would like to do so) and in many cases a lesser, surrogate alternative will have to be used, e.g. measuring whether people can recall actually having seen the advert. Market research tends to be the major method of measurement and control.

Advertising, sales objectives and intervening variables

Ideally advertisers would like to measure the success or otherwise of all advertising media in terms of sales achieved. Because of the nature of much advertising, however, this is not always possible and less attractive objectives such as awareness or recall will have to be used. This is because there are too many intervening variables between the advertising campaign, e.g. TV, and concrete purchase of the product for cause and effect to be definitively correlated. The intervening variables will include all the following confounding factors:

- The time period between exposure to the advert and the actual purchase can vary. With many products the advert may register with the consumer in a favourable way and be stored in the long-term memory, but not be acted upon for weeks, months, or even years.
- The advert may register and be stored in the mind of the consumer but be low in priority and so need some form of memory prod. In the case of a branded grocery product this could be the packaging or a sales promotion at the point of purchase.
- The advert may successfully drive the customer to the shop but they may then find that the advertised product is out of stock for some reason or other.
- The dealer staff may be untrained in product knowledge and so be unable to capitalise on the advertisement by explaining the various meaningful benefits.
- The competition may be offering better value in some way, either in brand benefits offered or through some type of sales promotion.
- The product itself may not live up to the promises made, leading to customer disappointment and non-purchase or non-repurchase.
- With an integrated promotional campaign many persuasive communicative processes will be at work and to divorce the effect of one from the other on the success or otherwise of the overall campaign can be extremely difficult.

All the above work against the linking of the advertisements directly to an increase in sales. Of course the ultimate purpose of an expensive advertising campaign is to work towards an increase in sales – there is little point in creating awareness for awareness' sake – and any manager or agency unable to achieve this will find themselves ultimately short of work.

The advertising budget

All business activity will involve a cost and advertising is no different. Advertising budgets (or advertising appropriations) are set in different ways, by different companies, and will depend on many factors including the following:

- the size and wealth of the organisation;
- the market scope of the company (regional, national, international or global);
- the mission, corporate, marketing, promotion, and advertising objectives;
- the amount and intensity of the competition in the marketplace;

- the knowledge and awareness stage of the target audience;
- the type of products being marketed e.g. FMCG, service, business to business.
- the PLC stage and position in the marketplace.
- the channel of distribution being used e.g. direct or indirect.

Organisations allocate money for advertising budgets in many different ways including the following:

- affordable (or arbitrary) method (research has shown that this tends to be the most popular method);
- the same as last year with an increase (or decrease) depending on, for example, inflation, economic or company activity;
- matching the level of the competition;
- as a percentage of past, present, or expected sales and/or profit levels;
- by task and objective; for example if 70 per cent awareness needs to be achieved over a six-week period there will need to be a budget of 'X'. Any less and these objectives could not be achieved. Ideally this must be the most sensible method but realistically the money is not always available.

Costs should always be shown as an inviolate part of SMART objectives, e.g. to create 60 per cent awareness amongst the target audience at a cost of £1 million.

Assumptions

Whenever decisions are made about future activity certain assumptions will have to be made about the expected movements in various advertising-related market factors. This might include such things as media availability, audience and competitor reaction. Of course assumptions must always be based, wherever possible, on sound research and realistic reasoning.

Strategy

Strategies are the various ways that objectives can be achieved and will appear at every level of the organisation. There will inevitably be a strategic directional choice and more than one strategy will be used. Figure 14.7 shows the relationship between objectives and strategies.

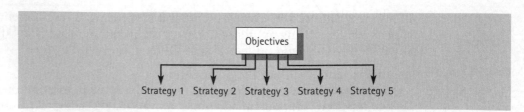

Fig. 14.7 Objectives and strategies

Strategies are long-term (within the definition of 'long-term' discussed earlier) and will co-ordinate all long-term activity. The definition of 'strategic' will change depending where the plan is coming from. At the corporate level what takes place in the advertising department would be seen as tactical whilst in the advertising department this would be seen as strategic.

- Corporate strategies are concerned with the major functions of the company, and cover finance, human resource management, production, administration, and marketing.
- Marketing strategies are concerned with ANSOFF's matrix and the marketing mix.
- Promotional strategies are concerned with the promotional mix options (advertising, sales promotions, PR, publicity, selling, sponsorship, exhibitions).

Advertising strategies

Advertising strategies involve a choice of both 'above' and 'below the line' options (TV, print, radio, cinema, outdoor, POP, direct, Internet etc.) used together in an optimum way to achieve advertising objectives (see Fig. 14.8).

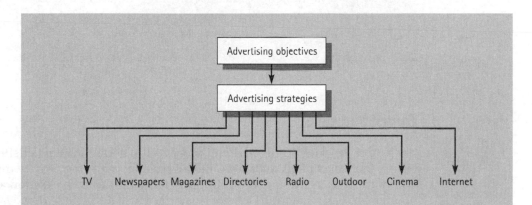

Fig. 14.8 Advertising strategies

Strategic advertising choice will depend on the following factors:

- advertising objectives
- the type of product
- target audience
- budget
- the availability and coverage of the media
- the characteristics, advantages and disadvantages of the media types
- advertiser experience and preferences
- measurement and control mechanisms.

Advertising strategic objectives (ASO)

As discussed earlier, each medium chosen – TV, newspapers, magazines etc. – will need individual SMART strategic objectives set so that outcomes can be evaluated and measured. All media chosen must integrate and work together so that synergy is achieved across the whole advertising programme (see Fig. 14.9).

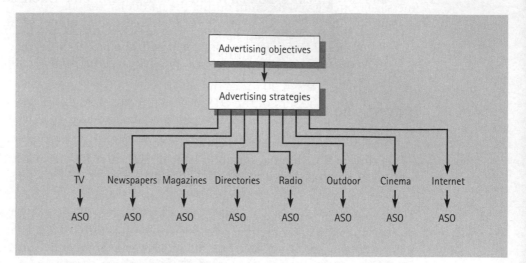

Fig. 14.9 Advertising strategic objectives (ASO)

Target audience

The whole purpose of the planning process is to communicate benefit messages to clearly identified target audiences and all strategic planning activity must have this end purpose as its driving force. Information will thus be needed on audience segmentation, behaviour and decision making. This will include demographic details such as size and geographical spread of the audience as well as gender, age and social class. The customer profile will detail audience psychographics, lifestyle, benefits sought, media watched or read, and so on, covering any information about the audience that might be of benefit in developing the advertisements. The more specific the audience description the better will be the ability to select media vehicles that effectively and efficiently reach these audiences.

Product brand positioning statement

The positioning statement is the blueprint behind the message and media chosen. It is here to justify the reasoning behind the campaign.

The message

Allowing for the advertising agency creative input, the content and style of the message will take its theme from the positioning statement and target audience detail. This should act as a guide on what should and should not be used in developing the message (message concepts and construction were examined in detail in the preceding chapter). Objectives can be set for where, when and how often messages should be sent to the target audience.

Message reach is the percentage of the target audience exposed at least once to the message from a given medium during a particular period.

Message frequency is the number of times the target audience is exposed to a message from a given medium during the particular period.

Opportunities to see (or to hear) (OTS, OTH) are the number of times a member of the target audience might be exposed to the advert. The *Radio Times,* for example, has an OTS of 20, meaning that research has shown that for the week the magazine lies about in the home the reader might pick it up perhaps 30 times, giving them an OTS of 20 to see the advert.

Gross OTS is the sum of the OTS across all media used during the campaign.

Message weight is the size of the combined target audience reached by all media vehicles during the period of a campaign.

Competitive activity

The advertising campaign can be spoilt by competitors' advertising activity before, during and after the campaign and it is very unlikely that a major competitor will stand still whilst another advertiser attempts to gain competitive advantage in some way. The reaction of competitors to the advertising campaign can be speculated about and contingency actions laid out. If competitors, media budgets, mixes and share of voice are understood effective media strategies can be constructed that take advantage of their weaknesses whilst building on the advertiser's own strengths. Rival expenditure can be gleaned from estimates published by AC Nielsen MEAL (Media Expenditure Analyses Ltd; www.acnielsen.com).

Integrating advertising with other elements of the promotional mix

An organisation can use many strategies to achieve the overall promotional objectives, including advertising, sales promotions, direct marketing, POP, PR and publicity, personal selling, sponsorship, exhibitions, and the Internet. It is very unlikely that advertising will ever be used on its own in isolation from the other elements of the promotional mix. As discussed throughout the book the great strength of advertising is its ability to create awareness and develop long-term brand values. Despite the wishes of the advertiser, whether it is able to activate the consumer to actually purchase the product is still problematic and speculative. Even where sales rise after an advertising campaign it is very difficult to make a meaningful link between the advertising and the purchase. This inevitably leads to the need to use other elements of the promotional mix with advertising to move the consumer through the decision-making process from being unaware to developing a favourable attitude to the brand and then the actual purchase behaviour (in the case of FMCG, repurchase on a regular basis). Figure 14.10 uses the AIDA model discussed in an earlier chapter to emphasise the point.

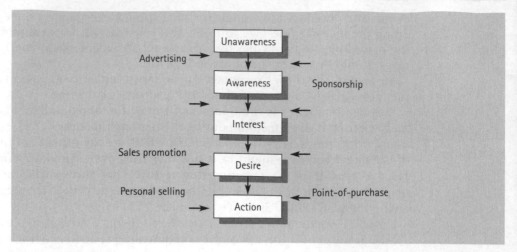

Fig. 14.10 Integrating advertising

Strategic control

Responsibility for strategic monitoring and control should be taken at senior management level in the advertising department. This will probably consist of regular meetings to ensure overall strategic direction.

Tactical planning

'How are we going to get there?' is the area of planning concerned with the tactical gathering and organisation of resources involved with the short-term implementation of the plan. It is concerned with the intricacies and detail of the strategic plan and will include the following factors:

- timings: day-by-day, week-by-week and month-by-month;
- budget breakdown;
- appointment of task co-ordinators;
- breakdown of the various tasks;
- performance indicators wherever possible for each task;
- allocation of responsibilities so that all involved are aware of individual tasks;
- continuous feedback, monitoring and control mechanisms to make certain that what is meant to happen, actually happens.

Media

Tactical planning will begin before the campaign launch when media buying personnel responsible will negotiate price and timings and book the relevant media spots.

Message development

Messages will be developed in the manner discussed in the preceding chapter. In the example shown in Fig. 14.11 this will cover all personnel involved with tactical needs associated with TV, newspaper and outdoor advert construction. This will include, among others, the creative services department (copywriters, art director etc.), the production department (print, broadcast manager etc.), the account planner (co-ordinating) and account manager (client agency consultation). Customer marketing services might be involved, linking and co-ordinating the advertising, if other elements of the promotional mix are involved.

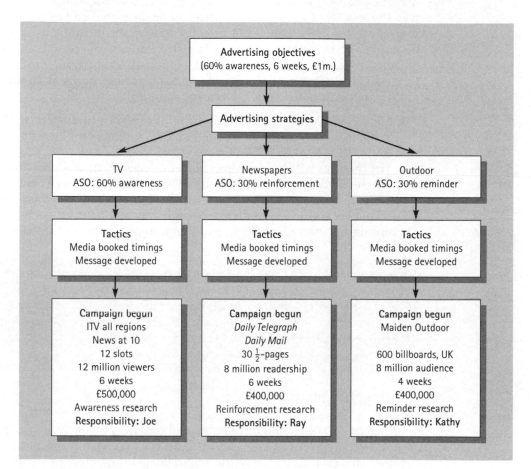

Fig. 14.11 Tactical planning

Monitoring, feedback and control

All advertising planning must have some form of monitoring, feedback and control mechanisms to ensure effectiveness and value for money. It is important that every pound or dollar spent should be accounted for in some way or another, and this must cover both internal and external spend.

Internal control methods

- Allocation of responsibilities, performance indicators, timing and report back procedures.
- Resource parameters demanding back-up confirmation.

External control methods

Every medium used – TV, radio, magazines, direct mailing, web sponsorship, outdoor billboards, POP material etc. – must have its own *individual* objective. In this way the success of each medium used can be measured and evaluated. If successful then it can be used again; if not then the money spent can be used through a more effective and profitable medium. Holistic evaluation consists of looking at the advertising campaign as a whole whilst atomistic evaluation consists of looking at the individual elements. Monitoring and control mechanisms should be involved at every relevant level of the advertising campaign.

- Media owners will offer advertisers independently audited (e.g. ABC) audience/readership/user figures in quite complex and intricate detail (see BARB, NRS, RAJAR, POSTAR etc.).
- The problem with readership or audience viewing figures is that they will not tell the advertiser whether the advert has actually been seen. We may know that 18 million people watch *Coronation Street* but we don't know how many remember seeing any particular adverts shown. Market research is used, before, during and after a campaign, to attempt to overcome this problem.

Newspaper tycoon Sally Aw Sian is alleged to have approved a plot to deceive advertisers by inflating circulation figures of the *Hong Kong* and *Sunday Standard*, a court heard. 'The *Hong Kong Standard* used these figures to boost its own position and as a sales toll to dupe advertisers into taking advertising space in her newspapers', the state prosecutor claimed in his opening address.

Source: *The South China Morning Post*, Hong Kong, 27 November 1998.

Contingency plans

Contingency plans should be outlined and resources made available (perhaps 10 per cent of overall advertising budget) to adjust the approach if specific audience targets are not being met. Examples of this might be spending more in a particular medium, or readjusting message elements if awareness objectives are not being met.

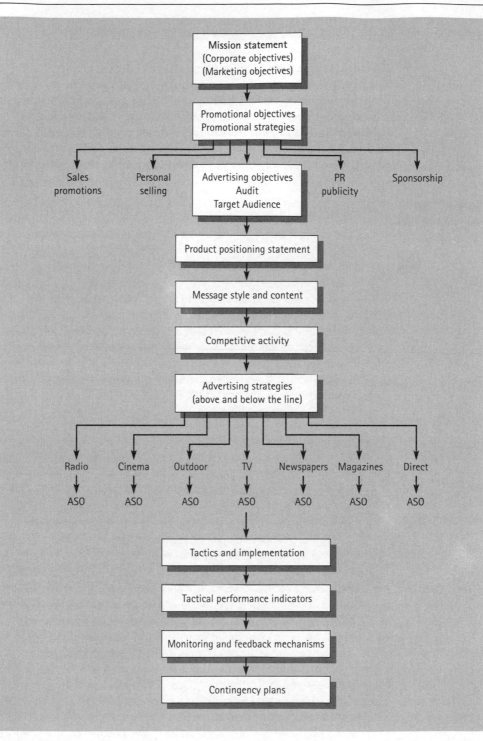

Fig. 14.12 The advertising plan

CONCLUSION

Planning is an essential ingredient in the building of advertising campaigns. Its initial purpose is to involve all relevant personnel in the advertising process so that major issues involved with the advertising campaign in hand are identified, discussed and argued over in a constructive and objective manner. Solutions can then be mooted and strategic choices made based on analysed and evaluated investigation and research. Planning forces all personnel to address problems in a logical and objective way. The advertising planning process is summed up in Fig. 14.12.

CASE STUDY

Accidental advertising campaigns

Intel, the world's leading chipmaker, and Yahoo!, a start-up that has become the leading Internet media group, stumbled into the business of building global brands almost by accident. For Intel, the lights went on in 1989. An advertising campaign aimed at urging computer manufacturers to switch to its latest microprocessor, the 386, had the surprising side-effect of persuading consumers to ask for 386-based computers. At the time, says Dennis Carter, Intel vice-president and director of marketing, 'I didn't really know what a brand was. But it became evident that we had created a brand and that it made a difference in consumers' purchase plans.' The next step was to brand not merely one product but the whole range, using the now-familiar 'Intel inside' logo. Intel launched the campaign in 1991 with its first 'co-operative advertising' programme, offering to share the costs of advertising with computer manufacturers that used Intel chips. Soon after came the first 'Intel inside' TV commercial – a journey through the innards of a personal computer, ending up at the microprocessor stamped with Intel's logo. It had become the first semiconductor company to hawk its product to consumers as though it were a new cola.

Intel initially tailored its advertising to different markets. In Japan, for example, the logo read 'Intel in it', but this was abandoned when the company found the 'Intel inside' brand was recognised because of information from the US. 'This really drove home the homogeneity of the global PC market,' says Mr Carter. Since then, its logo has appeared in more than $3.4bn (£2.1bn) worth of advertising – including spending by PC manufacturers – according to Intel.

In comparison, Yahoo!'s marketing resources are meagre. But the web navigation service has made full use of the global reach of the Internet to build its name, relying heavily on users to spread the word. Yahoo! grew out of a list of favourite web sites maintained by two Stanford University students. Although theirs was one of hundreds of similar hobbyist web guides at the time, it drew followers with its contemporary style and catchy name.

'A big portion of what has got Yahoo! on the map is just great word of mouth,' says Karen Edwards, director of brand management. In particular, Yahoo! built a grassroots following among the many newcomers to the Internet who regarded the service as a friendly 'home base' among the confusion of the web. Yahoo! also attracted users at minimal cost through strategically placed 'hyperlinks' on other web sites, such as the home page of Netscape Communications, the leading supplier of web browser software.

The start-up company demonstrated the potential of the Internet for building global brands, a lesson that has not been lost on bigger companies. Even before Yahoo! spent money on traditional advertising, it was attracting users worldwide. Last year it began advertising on television and radio in an attempt to encourage 'near surfers' – people not yet online but who are interested in taking the plunge – to use its services.

'When we went out and advertised on television early last year, it was every last penny we had; Ms Edwards recalls. But the move paid off by helping Yahoo! to differentiate itself from a growing band of competitors by achieving broader brand recognition. Recently, the group launched its initial public offering providing extra funds for more advertising and expansion of its services. Yahoo! is the most highly valued Internet media company, with a market capitalisation of $2.3bn. An estimated average of 5m computer users go to Yahoo!'s web pages every day.

About 30 per cent of visitors to Yahoo!'s web site are from outside the US and the company has also established web guides aimed at international markets. Even as Yahoo! is making more use of 'old media' to promote its brand name, Intel is moving on to the web. The semiconductor company is among the biggest spenders on the 'banner ads' that adorn many web pages.

Source: Louise Kehoe and Nick Denton, *Financial Times*, 17 October 1997. Used with permission.

Case study questions

Intel is an example of a business-to-business organisation that has managed to use a classic combination of a 'push' and 'pull' promotional campaign to advertise its products. It is now using the web to advertise its products. Yahoo! began by selling its service first through word of mouth and then through the use of web page advertising.

1. Using Intel as an example develop a full business to business and consumer advertising campaign over a one-year period using the Internet as the main media.
2. At the time of writing Yahoo! is the largest Internet search engine on the web but its position is being continually threatened by competitors and so it cannot afford to stand still. It needs to attract new users from those not yet using the Internet. Develop an advertising campaign in the UK aimed at a new user group using 'above the line' traditional media.

Try to base the audit on actual information about the company selected for the advertising plan. Other information – target audience, budget, objectives, strategies, monitoring and control mechanisms – can be artificial (reflecting the difficulties of getting at relevant 'live' information) but should mirror reality as closely as possible. Reasons should be given for decisions and choices made.

CHAPTER QUESTIONS

1. Identify all the factors that are included in the advertising planning process. Why is planning so important?
2. Discuss the proposition 'advertising on its own is unable to sell products'. What are the implications of this for the advertising planning process?
3. Analyse the importance of monitoring, feedback, control and evaluation of the advertising planning process. Identify some of the commercial companies involved in the process and evaluate their product/service offerings.
4. How important is research in the advertising planning process? What kinds of information are needed before, during and after a campaign?
5. Why is it important that SMART objectives be set for every part of the advertising campaign? Discuss the argument that in some creative areas of advertising it is unrealistic to set quantifiable objectives and it is much better to go on intuition and experience.

REFERENCES

Sara Lee (www.saralee.com)

McCullough, W.R., 'Global advertising which acts locally: the IBM subtitles campaign', *Journal of Advertising Research*, May–June 1996, p. 11.

The Media Measurement Task Force (www.iab.net/advertise/content)

ACNielsen MEAL (www.acnielsen.com)

The South China Morning Post, Hong Kong, 27 November 1998.

FURTHER READING

Aaker, D.A. and Stayman, D.M. (1990) 'Measuring audience perceptions of commercials and relating them to ad impact', *Journal of Advertising Research*, 30(4), pp. 7–17.

Ambler, T. (1995) *Marketing from Advertising to Zen, A FT Guide*. Pitman, London.

Argenti, J. (1992) *Practical Corporate Planning*, Routledge, London.

Johnson and Johnson (www.johnsonandjohnson.com)

Kiger, E., 'Media and measurement technologies' (Backer Spielvogel Bates Inc. report, part one of two), *Direct Marketing*, March 1991, p. 25.

McDonald, M. (1995) *Marketing Plans*, Heinemann, London.

Morley, K. (1995) *Integrated Marketing Communications*, Heinemann, London.

Neal, W.D. and Bathe, S. (1997) `Using the value equation to evaluate campaign effectiveness', *Journal of Advertising Research*, 37(3), pp. 80–6.

Reid, A. (1995) 'Can hi-tech help the quest for precise effective frequency?', *Campaign*, 12 May, 1995 p. 27(1).

Part 6 Advertising into the future and on the world stage

15 Global advertising and change

FT

Net spreads to the mainstream

The phase 'Internet time' refers to the tendency to change faster on the net than on the 24-hour clock. Now, even Internet time seems to be speeding up. Thanks to a frenzied series of mergers, the net has seen as much change in a few weeks as most industries see in months or years. This week Yahoo!, which runs the second most popular Internet site, bought Geocites, which operates the third largest. The week before, Excite, a leading competitor of Yahoo!, was bought by @home Network, the leading supplier of Internet connections through cable television connections. Last year American Online, the largest Internet company, bought Netscape, the Internet software pioneer which operates the fifth most popular site on the net. A change in the nature of the Internet audience lies behind these moves. Nearly one in three Americans uses it.

As more and more people move onto the net, users are becoming increasingly mainstream. A telling indicator came last week when the Pew Research Center found that the weather had overtaken technology as the subject of most interest to Internet users. Newcomers are not the teenage geeks who first adopted it. The Pew report found that most new users were female, and most were aged between 30 and 45. These are people less interested in exploring the Internet for its own sake and more interested in finding somewhere quick and easy they can go to check news, send mail and shop.

The big Internet sites – called portals – aim to be just that. The leaders Yahoo! and AOL.com are used by roughly half of all Internet users. AOL.com attracts 30m visitors each month. The most successful of all retailers, Amazon, is seen by only 7.8 million visitors a month. Also web research analyst, Jupiter, found that they were both trusted and used more widely than specialist news sites such as CNN.com or FT.com.

Portals have two great weaknesses however. The first is that people spend on average only 10 minutes before moving on to other web pages on the Internet. Though more and more services are being made available – e-mail, shopping, entertainment and weather – searching the Internet remains overwhelmingly the main use. Second, all portals offer more or less the same information. This explains the rush of mergers. In time, no doubt, as the Internet grows and users become more experienced, the undifferentiated offerings of the leading portals will come under attack from niche sites that will be able to attract particular markets. And that could happen tomorrow. After all, we are dealing in Internet time.

Source: Financial Times, 30 January 1999. Used with permission.

15 Global advertising and change

OBJECTIVES

By the end of this chapter the reader should be able to:

1. Describe and evaluate the part that advertising plays on a global scale.

2. Describe the pace of change affecting future advertising and media developments.

3. Identify and speculate where future developments might happen.

INTRODUCTION

If we know what the future is, we aren't looking far enough ahead.

(Tim Berner-Lee, inventor of the World Wide Web, July 1997)

The biggest challenge facing advertisers, advertising agencies and media owners is the monumental pace of change taking place in the communication industry on both a national and global scale. The world is truly becoming a global marketplace and any advertiser can now talk to existing and potential customers on any continent and in any country from the US to China and Russia to Australia.

Future change

The pace of change is now moving at such a pace that researching future media statistics becomes so problematic as to be almost meaningless. Advertising around the world by the year 2002 could be worth anything between $300 billion and $400 billion, Internet users anything between $200 million and $500 million, advertising on the net, $10 billion to $20 billion, while sales could reach $500 billion. Marketing and advertising departments and organisations working in this brave new world must now take into account many different and changing factors if they are to communicate successfully and satisfy customer needs and wants in whichever corner of the world they might be. These will include the following:

- diverse global markets
- customer demands
- communication structure, media mix and media usage in differing countries
- global or indigenous advertising agencies
- the technological change driving media developments.

Diverse global markets

The data superhighway is the most important marketplace of the twenty-first century.

(Al Gore, Vice-President, USA, May 1993)

The largest advertiser in the world, Procter & Gamble, will be advertising in almost every country in the world and it must take into account both changing circumstances at the present time and future predictions, if markets are to be worth attacking and if its promotional campaigns are to be successful. The following factors will all have an influence on the type, amount and method of advertising an advertiser might use.

Industry infrastructure

Public and private sector sizes and growth, services and manufacturing size, growth, types and advertising spending patterns will dictate both business to business and consumer advertising spend.

Demographic factors

Population growth, age and sex structure, geographical movement, life expectancy and levels of literacy will indicate the availability of various market segments, levels of well-being and the future market potential. Comparisons are enlightening.

Afghanistan (1998 est.)
Population size: 24.792 million
Life expectancy at birth: 46.34
Infant mortality rate: 146.7 deaths/1000
Literacy levels: 31.5% (15 and over)
GDP levels: $19.3 billion
Per capita income: $800

USA (1997)
Population size: 270.311 million
Life expectancy at birth: 76.13
Infant mortality rate: 6.44/1000
Literacy levels: 97%
GDP levels: $8.083
Per capita income: $30.200

UK (1998 est.)
Population size: 58 million
Life expectancy at birth: 77.25
Infant mortality rate: 6 deaths/1000
Literacy levels: 99%
GDP levels: $1.242 trillion
Per capita income: $21.200

China (1997)
Population size: 1,236 .9 billion
Life expectancy at birth: 69.59
Infant mortality rate: 45.46/1000
Literacy levels: 81.5 %
GDP levels: $4.25 trillion
Per capita income: $ 3.460

Source: odci.gov/cia/publications/factbook

Economic developments

Size and annual growth in gross domestic product (GDP), per capita income, disposable income and income spread differences will give an indication of present and future demand for different products and services (measurements used here accord with the Purchasing Power Parity (PPP) method).

Legal considerations

Censorship on the Internet

Saying that a federal Internet censorship law would restrict free speech in the 'marketplace of ideas', a Philadelphia court recently blocked Congress's second attempt to censor the Internet. The American Civil Liberties Union, which filed the lawsuit along with the Electronic Privacy Information Center (EPIC) and Electronic Frontier Foundation (EFF), hailed the decision as a significant victory in 'round two' of their fight against federal online censorship. In granting a preliminary injunction against the 'Child Online Protection Act,' Judge Lowell A. Reed, Jr., held that the groups are likely to succeed in their claim that the law 'imposes a burden on speech that is protected for adults.' The ruling came after a six-day hearing at which the ACLU presented testimony from website operators who provide free information about fine art, news, gay and lesbian issues and sexual health for women and the disabled, and who all fear that the law will force them to shut down their websites.

Jupiter Communications (www.jup.com)

Despite attempts by trade associations, national bodies and governments to harmonise international law and regulations on media use there are still vast differences between countries on what can and cannot be advertised on the different media. In some cases, because of differing religions and culture there never will be this coming together because fundamental values are different. In many other areas, however, progress has been made, not least within trading areas such as the European Union.

The World Intellectual Property Organization (WIPO) (www.wipo.int) has a membership of over 170 independent countries. It is one of 16 specialised agencies of the United Nations. It is responsible for the promotion of the protection of intellectual property through co-operation amongst states, and for the administration of various multilateral treaties dealing with legal and administrative aspects of intellectual property. Intellectual property comprises two main areas:

- industrial property: inventions, trademarks, industrial designs, and original names;
- copyright: literary, musical, artisitic, photographic and audiovisual works.

A substantial part of the activities and the resources of the WIPO is devoted to development co-operation between developing countries.

Other legal problems with the growth of the global media include the question of where web sites, advertising and retail activities should be controlled. Should this be at the point of user/customer contact? This could be very difficult, even impossible, according to the level of co-operation. Should it be the home base of the operation? This is easier to control, but operations can easily be mirrored or moved from country to country at a moment's notice. Or should it be a combination of both?

Payment of taxes is also a real conundrum for governments to sort out. Products and services can now be sent electronically around the world and may be impossible to trace. There is a problem concerning which country will have prior claim on tax revenues.

President Clinton has vowed to make cyberspace a 'global free-trade zone' without new taxes or tariffs, and with a minimum of government intrusion. He was reacting to US industry leaders who say the White House has been slow to realise that places such as the World Wide Web are becoming key to the future of commerce. The thinking is that the global electronic network will develop into a business generating up to $1 trillion by 2010. But without firm protection against copyright and credit card theft, as well as breaches of privacy, many US companies are reluctant to push on-line transactions. He directed his administration to develop basic consumer and copyright protections to be adopted within the next year. This is to happen while the White House is negotiating international agreements to ensure that US Internet products and services are not subject to tariffs imposed by other countries. The Commerce Department is also being instructed to develop codes of conduct and technology tools to protect on-line privacy. The President said he was sending a delegation to Europe later this month to outline his vision for international electronic trade.

(National press, July 1997)

Customer demands

Both business to business and end consumer advertising needs will probably be different according to both cultural and national factors. Intercultural advertising is advertising that crosses cultural boundaries whilst international advertising is advertising that crosses national boundaries. The difference between the two is that intercultural advertising can take place both within a country and across national boundaries.

Intercultural advertising

Intercultural advertising within a country

There is a need in many countries for intercultural advertising within the country because of the diverse nature of the population. This need will probably increase into the future – certainly within the European Union, with the breakdown of national frontiers and the free movement of all EU citizens. The various groups will often be the basis for large niche markets e.g. ethnic foods, cosmetics, music, clothes. In countries such as the USA, minority cultural groups have substantial buying power and advertisers must continually research to identify ever-changing wants and needs. Companies such as Procter & Gamble, Toys 'Я' Us, Coca-Cola and Wal-Mart have learned that they can increase their market share by segmenting and targeting particular ethnic and cultural groups.

UK cultural groups

Ethnic groups: 81.5% English, 9.6% Scots, 2.4% Irish, 1.9% Welsh, 1.8% Ulster, 2.8% West Indian, Indian, Pakistani and other.

Religions: 27 million Anglicans, 9 million Roman Catholics, 1 million Muslims, 400 000 Sikhs, 350 000 Hindus, 300 000 Jews.

Afghanistan cultural groups

Ethnic groups: Pashtun 38%, Tajik 25%, Uzbek 6%, Hazara 19%, minor ethnic groups (Aimaks, Turkmen, Baloch, and others)

Religions: Sunni Muslim 84%, Shi'a Muslim 15%, other 1%

Languages: Pashtu 35%, Afghan Persian (Dari) 50%, Turkic languages (primarily Uzbek and Turkmen) 11%, 30 minor languages (primarily Balochi and Pashai) 4%.

Chinese cultural groups

Ethnic groups: Han Chinese 91.9%, Zhuang, Uygur, Hui, Yi, Tibetan, Miao, Manchu, Mongol, Buyi, Korean, and other nationalities 8.1%

Religions: Taoism, Buddhism, Muslim 2%–3%, Christian 1% (est.) (officially atheist, but traditionally pragmatic and eclectic)

Languages: Standard Chinese or Mandarin (Putonghua, based on the Beijing dialect), Yue (Cantonese), Wu (Shanghaiese), Minbei (Fuzhou), Minnan (Hokkien-Taiwanese), Xiang, Gan, Hakka dialects, minority languages.

US cultural groups

Ethnic groups: white 83.4%, black 12.4%, Asian 3.3%, Amerindian 0.8% (1992)

Religions: Protestant 56%, Roman Catholic 28%, Jewish 2%, other 4%, none 10% (1989)

Languages: English, Spanish (spoken by a sizable minority)

Source: odci.gov/cia/publications/factbook

Intercultural advertising on a global scale

I don't know the rules of grammar; if you are trying to persuade people to do something, or buy something, it seems to me that you should use their language, the language they use every day, the language they think in. We must try to write in the vernacular.

(1990)

(David Ogilvy)

The problem of intercultural advertising gets more daunting when approached on a global level. It is difficult enough at home where information and statistics are reasonably easy to obtain but the problem is magnified many times when advertising around the world because of the difficulty of getting hold of solid, reliable, up-to-date information about markets, customer segments and media worth and availability.

Race, language and cultural values

Once the audience has been identified there are still many hurdles for the advertising agency and the creative staff to overcome. Cultural differences must be respected if they are important to the audience. Advertisers have sometimes been accused of ethnocentrism, the belief that one's own culture is superior to others, and of ignorance and lack of understanding and putting out adverts unchanged from the home offering. This can work if the products and messages have a universal appeal but will lead to wastage if cultural factors are important. A few global companies, such as Coca-Cola, have been able to create universal appeal for brands and have then been able to gain economies of scale by creating one advertising strategy (with perhaps minor adjustments) for every country. Most companies will not be able to do this and will thus employ customised offerings for each country.

Factors to consider if preparing different advertising strategies for different countries include the following:

- the cultural values of others will probably be different from one's own;
- cultural values may differ from one region to another;
- language and dialects may be different from region to region (over 300 dialects in China);
- the use of religion, sex, humour, animals etc. might well vary in meaning and potential effects should be well researched;
- laws and regulations will vary and what is allowed in one country may well not be allowed in another.

> The growing trend of using religion to promote anything from jeans to beer can cause offence with religious groups around the world. Examples include Diesel Jeans using nuns, images of the Pope to advertise condoms, a paper manufacturer using slogans such as 'Behold the King of paper is born.' In a survey undertaken by the ASA in the UK, 80 per cent of respondents said that disrespectful references to any religion, race or culture should never be allowed.

Communications infrastructure

It is self-evident that advertisers need to be aware of the communications structure, size, growth, and price in a country they intend advertising to. This will include knowledge on all above and below the line advertising media, the distribution and ownership of newspapers, magazines and directories, TV ownership and channel choice, radio stations available, the situation with the outdoor media and the adoption level of the outdoor media. They will also need to have reliable statistics on viewer and readership numbers and behaviour. Table 15.1 shows comparisons that, despite global advances, give a stark indication of the still vast differences around the world in telephony, TV and radio coverage and ownership.

Communication technology: adoption rates around the world

The Internet is the most important marketing medium in history. As marketers we really don't know how to use it effectively.

(Denis Beausejour, VC, Advertising Worldwide, Procter & Gamble, July 1998)

Although the take-up of new media changes, digital TV and the Internet, has been breathtaking in the US and only slightly less so in Europe statistics for other parts of the world are more difficult to come by. There is no doubt that it will be accepted in the same way that it has been in the developed world; the only question is how long it will take.

Table 15.1 Communications infrastructure in Afghanistan, China, the UK and the US

Afghanistan communications
Telephones: 31 200 (1983 est.); very limited telephone and telegraph service
Radios: 1.8 million (1996 est.); about 60% of families own a radio
Television broadcast stations: NA
Televisions: 100 000 (1993 est.)

Chinese communications
Telephones: 89 million (1997 est.); 2.5 telephones per 100 urban population and 7.2 telephones per 100 total population, unevenly distributed.
Radios: 216.5 million (1992 est.)
Television broadcast stations: 202
Televisions: 75 million

UK communications
Telephones: 29.5 million (1987 est.)
Telephone system: technologically advanced domestic and international system
Radios: 70 million
Television broadcast stations: 207
Televisions: 20 million

US communications
Telephones: 182.558 million (1987 est.) a large system of fibre–optic cable, microwave radio relay, coaxial cable, and domestic satellites carries conventional telephone traffic; a rapidly growing cellular system carries mobile telephone traffic throughout the country
Radios: 540.5 million (1992 est.)
Television broadcast stations: 1092 (in addition, there are about 9000 cable TV systems)
Televisions: 215 million (1993 est.)

Source: odci.gov/cia/publications/factbook

In a recent study a team of researchers at Morgan Stanley, management consultants in the US, examined the adoption rate of the web and compared it to the adoption rate of radio and TV. As the measure they used the amount of time it took for each medium to attract 50 million users.

- Radio took 38 years to reach 50 million users.
- TV took 13 years to reach 50 million users.
- The Internet has taken just 5 years to reach 50 million users.

The Internet has to prove its value to advertisers

We are as anxious as anybody else to determine how effective our web advertising is and what we're getting for our money, but given that the medium itself is still evolving, as is the definition of advertising on the medium, we think that patience is in order.

(Elizabeth Moore, Spokeswoman, Procter & Gamble, US)

Despite the herd-like action on the part of both individuals and organisations to buy into new media share companies, pushing values to vertiginous heights, many large advertisers refuse to be sucked into the 'Klondike'-like rush to accept new media methods in a meaningful manner until certain conditions can be satisfied. These are that

- the new medium will reach wanted target markets;
- it has been tried and tested;
- it will be able to be measured in a reliable and independent way;
- it can be shown to achieve corporate objectives, e.g. brand awareness and sales;
- it will work in conjunction with other media methods;
- it will 'fit' with overall corporate mission and objectives;
- the price is right.

Global and indigenous advertising agencies

I think there is going to be two kinds of agencies in 10 years' time: digital agencies and dinosaur agencies.

(Denis Beausejour, VC, Advertising Worldwide, Procter & Gamble, July 1998)

The last decade has seen a rationalisation in the advertising business with the demise of the smaller agency and the growth in corporate agency giants operating around the world. These companies are multi-billion-dollar operations with offices in practically every country in the world. However, many agencies still stay firmly rooted in their country of origin. Which to choose will depend on the task that is to be executed but it is a strategically important decision that would need to be decided at the highest level within the organisation. If the advertising is on a local or national scale then it could be argued that the task is simpler than if it is a global problem because the risks involved are more quantifiable although it will depend on the country or countries where the advertising campaign is to take place.

An indigenous national agency

The benefits of choosing an agency in the country of export rest on the premise that indigenous agency staff will understand audience needs much better than somebody coming in from outside. Social and cultural differences still abound from country to country and region to region, though these differences may be lessening, especially with the internationalisation of travel, communications and global advertising and branding. As well as differences in audience needs, in many cases media ownership and media uses are different, and subtle nuances may not be understood by non-native agencies. These differences become more intense at the regional and local level. Local knowledge is the major benefit that a small local agency is likely to have over its larger brother.

Difficulties

In spite of the fact that English now tends to be the lingua franca of the business world there could well be problems with translation, interpretation and the eventual understanding of the part of the agency of what the advertiser wants to achieve. It might also mean the advertiser having to deal with different agencies in different countries and this will mean expensive trips, in terms of cost and time, travelling out to see foreign agency staff.

The global agency

The news that the UK's largest advertising agency, Abbott Mead Vickers is to be taken over by the US conglomerate Omnicom shows the changing nature of the agency business. To be a top 30 UK agency is, of itself, no longer enough. To survive UK ad agencies now have to be part of larger international groups, and that increasingly points them in the direction of the US.

(National press)

The global agency staff would want to argue that they can solve the problem by offering a one-stop service covering the whole of the globe. McCann Erickson has overseas agencies in over 120 countries offering either a tailored package geared to each individual country or a more or less standardised approach to the whole of the commercial world. They will use expatriates as well as local people thus obtaining the benefits from strategic centralised control with tactical peripheral flexibility. Their size also enables them to gain scale benefits which can be passed on to the client. As with all areas of advertising there is no real answer and the solution will depend on many different product and market circumstances. The argument about whether it is possible to use a standardised global advertising approach or to allow for national and regional differences is very much a 'live' issue and of great concern to global marketers.

The global agency can be a 'one-stop' agency for the client, saving time and money by centralised dealings. It can offer economies of scale and savings based on experience. Central strategic planning and control can allow for overall integration and accountability to be co-ordinated from one central contact point. However, the personal touch may be lost.

The national agency offers local knowledge and skills and the possibility of personal attention, but there may be problems with co-ordination, and it may be unable to optimise scale economies.

Voluntary agencies and international partnerships

Many independent national agencies around the world have come together to form voluntary agency associations pooling localised skills, experiences and knowledge in the hope of fighting the global agencies by offering similar co-ordinated services through a networking process of agency partners in major towns and cities around the world. This method is also an exceedingly quick and relatively inexpensive way of expanding the business. The global agency might operate the same concept using an umbrella holding company.

Holding companies and individual corporate brands

Many of the world's largest communications and advertising companies operate individual company brands under the overall umbrella of a corporate holding company.

- Agencies are often acquired by merger and takeover and, as with many companies, the brand name is too valuable, in terms of the values it represents to clients, to discard. In fact this is often the reason for the takeover.
- By operating as a cluster of competing agencies within a holding company advertising subsidiaries are able to serve rival clients, without competitive conflict, while using the resources and worldwide connections of the parent.
- The agency brand might have developed a reputation for proficiencies in certain areas and the parent company will not want to diminish this.
- National agencies might be well known and holding companies not.

Omnicom, the biggest agency in the world, owns BBDO, DDB Needham, GGT group, TBWA International Network, Diversifed Agency Services (DAS) and many more.
WPP Group plc, No. 2, owns J. Walter Thompson, Ogilvy & Mather, Millward Brown, BMRD, Kantar Media Research, and more.
The Interpublic Group of Companies, No. 3, owns McCann Erickson, Ammirati Puris Lintas, The Lowe Group and Western International Media.
Dentsu Inc, No. 4, is a Japanese company.
Young & Rubican Inc, No. 5, owns Burson-Marsteller.

Advertising agencies or management consultants

A battle of words has broken out between the advertising agency and the management consultant agency. Management consultants such as Mckinsey, Bain and Anderson argue that strategic brand development will involve all organisational resources both technical and human and only they have the necessary range of skills to encompass all management needs. Conversely advertising agencies such as Ogilvy & Mather and JWT argue that brands are about creative ideas that can transform a company's business (BA 'the World's Favourite Airline'; the AA 'the Fourth Emergency Service') and only they have skills and experience in this area. The answer probably lies somewhere in the middle with both sides needing to recognise the strategic limitations of the services they offer.

The technological change driving media developments

Digital TV has destroyed the 'convergence theory'. For many years now, the word 'convergence' has gone side-by-side with digital, a convenient way of explaining how TVs and PCs will get married and live together happily ever after. Well, I'm sorry to be the bearer of bad news, but there's been a divorce. It's increasingly clear that people's use of the TV and the PC are hugely different experiences. TV will continue to be the dominant medium for lean-back leisure rather than lean-forward interaction.

(Elizabeth Murdoch, General Manager, Sky Television, UK, August 1998)

Digital technology and the development of the World Wide Web have truly revolutionised the communications industry in a way commensurate with the invention and use of the printing press. Due to digitalisation the TV set now has the potential to receive many hundreds of TV channels including telephony, video and of course the Internet. The great leap forward will happen if and when the following developments happen:

- digital TV channels offer real perceived value and the customer is prepared to adopt;
- the Internet on the desktop computer, the TV and the telephone combine in the living room;
- the multimedia methods come together in a user-friendly manner;
- the early and late majority target markets accept the concept of interaction and are prepared to participate.

Bubble.com: Rupert Murdoch says Internet stocks are overvalued

You could call it sour grapes. Rupert Murdoch's global media empire has embraced many communications technologies but he has not so far embraced the Internet with any enthusiasm – and that medium is the hottest thing on Wall Street. Mr Murdoch [recently] lashed out at the stock market's passion for the Internet. Many Internet companies are heavily overvalued and will not produce the profits to justify the exuberance, he said. For good measure, he added that the net will eventually 'destroy more businesses than it creates'. It is not surprising that the naturalised American media baron was feeling curmudgeonly. His own News Corporation, which took a lifetime of wheeling and dealing to build, is worth about $24bn (£14.5bn). On the day he spoke, Yahoo!, the Internet's version of a media company, reached a stock market value of $40bn.

Source: Richard Waters, *Financial Times*, 16 January 1999. Used with permission.

Fight for customer control

The Internet, once the preserve of computer nerds, early adopters and academics, has become a business battleground. A fierce struggle is developing between Internet service providers, Yahoo!, Freeserve, AOL, Compuserve, Demon, Tesco, for the control of the gateway, the portal, to the most powerful media communication tool on the planet. Control of the portal will offer the winner the following benefits:

- access to potential consumers, in the case of AOL over 30 million in the US and one million in the UK;
- having first access gives the portal owner the ability to direct the user deeper into the web site;
- this allows exposure to advertising, costed at approx. £15 to £20 (CPM) per thousand visitors;
- it also allows exposure to retail sites with the opportunity to sell products online, with retailers being charged rent for the web-site space or a web-site link;
- ownership of the most powerful media form the world has ever known.

Some Internet service providers charge for the service, e-mail post room facilities and web-site space (mcmail £7 a month) whilst others offer the service free (freeserve). All ISPs will charge for a monthly service cover at prices of around £8 to £12 a month.

The future of retail

There really is a whole new world in retailing and banking just around the corner. Retailers will be able to reach huge audiences for less than the cost of opening a store. Companies will be able to run their businesses far more efficiently. Interactive TV is genuinely going to revolutionise the way we do business.

(Chris Townsend, Commercial Director, British Interactive Broadcasting, July 1997)

If anything is certain about the new multimedia it is the fact of retail opportunity. With retail companies already successfully selling products as diverse as computers, books and grocery, it seems that anything can be sold on-line. Both business customers and end consumers will use the convenience of shopping from the place of work or from home; of this there is no doubt. Whether conventional methods will be abandoned by large numbers is more problematic. People shop conventionally for many reasons including social interaction, to alleviate boredom and depression, to get out of the house, for enjoyment, for choice and to see and touch real products. It is very doubtful if this will really ever change.

A recent study conducted by Netsmart Research found that the web plays a significant part in the purchasing decisions of Internet shoppers. Among the findings were that 62 per cent of respondents said that information found on-line directly influenced their retail purchases, and that 93 per cent of big-ticket buyers use the web to help them decide which brand to buy.

Other uses of the net include bill-paying and making travel bookings. According to Jupiter Communications, by the year 2002, 15 million households in the US will be paying their bills on-line.

The Travel Industry Association of America has found that 6.7 million American adults (9 per cent of Internet users) have used the Internet to make travel reservations in the past year.

The future of advertising

The future for advertising seems safe whatever the changes that might happen. People will always need information about products, services and brands wherever they might be and there is little or no sign that this is changing. Change however might very well alter the role and relationship between the major players, the advertisers, the advertising agencies and the media owners. Whatever might happen, the following basic fundamentals will not alter.

- Know and understand the customer and audience segment.
- Set clear objectives.
- Identify benefits needed.
- Select a proven appropriate medium or media.
- Integrate all media used in the most effective way.
- Communicate these benefits in an effective customer-sensitive manner.
- Research, monitor, control and evaluate the results.

CONCLUSION

Five of the most valuable companies in the world top twenty are now new media, new technology companies. The largest, Microsoft, is worth a cool $50 billion making its owner, Bill Gates, the wealthiest person on the planet. Never can media and advertising participants be living in such exciting and changing times with global media opportunities seeming to be unlimited. Whether the spectacular development hyped by media, commentators, journalists, businesspeople and academics for digitalisation and the World Wide Web will ever reach the cataclysmic levels predicted only the passing of time will tell. Whether customers will be content to sit in the living room and interact with the TV, telephone and Internet to buy products and services, to garner information, to be entertained, or to talk to one another, in the numbers that some speculate about, is the multi-billion-dollar question. And finally, how the multimedia revolution will alter the way advertisers use the press, TV, outdoor, radio, cinema, merchandise and home viewing on a global scale is the holy grail for all that work in the advertising business.

CASE STUDY

FT

Consumer revolution

If you are ever in any doubt that China is in the throes of a consumer revolution, take a walk down Nanjing Road. Shanghai's premier shopping street has been carved in two by Pepsi and Coca-Cola, who have commandeered every lamppost to hang neon advertisements for their soft drinks. Buses are plastered with ads for haircare products from Unilever and Procter & Gamble, who have also gobbled up hoardings, bus shelters and rooftops across the city. 'It is a chaotic outdoor media environment. Essentially, everything, everywhere is for sale', says Soames Hines, former managing director of J. Walter Thompson in Shanghai, the largest advertising agency in China.

But behind the advertising bonanza lie some awkward challenges – and Hines, who oversaw JWT's rapid expansion during his four years at the helm in Shanghai, knows how 'the marketer's dream in China can quickly become a nightmare'. The scramble for the Chinese consumer has prompted an explosion in advertising.

In Shanghai spending on advertising multiplied 16 times between 1990 and 1994. China's advertising spend, valued at Yn45bn ($3.2bn) last year, is forecast to grow to Yn200bn by 2000. Nevertheless, Hines puts advertising in its place. Most international companies in China 'are pushing packaged goods when their first concern should be getting a decent distribution system in place', he says. Pricing, too, is critical. Customers, generally on monthly incomes of around $100 (£59), remain highly price sensitive.

Nor is the nature of the advertisement the determining factor, in Hines' judgement: 'Everyone likes to think that there is some mystique about China, but the Chinese consumer actually behaves much like any other. The key to getting it right is the advertising strategy, not the execution of the advertising.' By this he means primarily understanding the needs of the market, and cites the example of S.C. Johnson's Toilet Duck. Toilet Duck, with its hooked neck designed to reach beneath the toilet' s rim, positions itself in developed markets as a more convenient way to clean parts other products cannot reach. It was planned to launch in China with a Hong Kong advertisement that stressed these benefits.

However, even those Chinese who have modern toilets tend to use washing up water to clean them and so the Toilet Duck proposition would have been wasted. S.C. Johnson did some market research and 'avoided a very expensive mistake'. Hines, who left China last month, has been 'consistently amazed' at how companies fail to spend time and money to understand the market before launching inappropriate products. Given that China's increasingly sophisticated consumers are leapfrogging conventional product cycles – jumping from no telephone to a cellular phone – he sees little point in bringing to China anything other than the most up-to-date product.

Companies must also be prepared to tailor, or be seen to tailor, their products to Chinese tastes. Once the strategy is in place, though, advertising can quickly build a brand's reputation. The ad needs to be lively, entertaining and 'impactful'. JWT China calculates that the average person in Shanghai watches 650 commercials a week, double the number in the UK and more than anywhere else in Europe. A commercial break tends to be 10–15 minutes long, but some last half an hour and include 100 advertisements, says Hines. Clients must be prepared to pay more for less air time, as media inflation is forecast to run at 25 per cent per year to 2000.

Advertising content naturally depends on the product, but Hines offers a few guiding principles. Young people are not cynical, but optimistic, he says, counting themselves the lucky generation that knows they will be more prosperous than their parents. Despite modernisation, there is a fondness for what are perceived to be Chinese traditions, making family values a powerful selling point even among the young. The only categorical advice is not to press an international brand's superiority over its Chinese counterpart: 'Consumers know the international product is better, but don't want a foreigner rubbing it in.'

If would-be advertisers have a difficult route to navigate in China, then so too do agencies.

JWT has been losing money in China. The rise in revenue from Yn4m in 1992 to Yn45m has been outstripped by the increase in costs driven by the expansion in personnel over the same period from 10 to 125 people, including a large proportion of expensive expats. Hines expects the agency to break even in Shanghai this year, but doggedly defends the losses as part of the investment in people that will ultimately determine the success or otherwise of any agency in China. Not all agencies agree with Hines. They say agencies can expand organically in line with billings, thereby remaining profitable. The hiring of expats is also controversial – some suggest it cultivates international clients, but deters the growing numbers of potential Chinese clients. Hines has been succeeded by David Ma from Taiwan, who has been brought in to ensure profitability and cultivate local customers.

Source: James Harding, *Financial Times*, 14 July 1997. Used with permission.

Case study questions

1. Identify and discuss the problems encountered by the advertising agency working in China. Do you think that these problems are specific to China, or are they more general when advertising on a global scale?
2. What factors would need to be taken into account if the new media were to be adopted as an advertising and marketing tool?

CHAPTER QUESTIONS

1. What major differences might face an advertiser advertising in global markets?
2. Discuss the future direction of advertising and the media; what major changes might shape future activity?

3. Would you consider that the Internet will ever supplant the other main media? What might its advantages be.
4. How might TV and the Internet be used by advertisers in a meaningful and effective manner? Are consumers ready for interactive TV?
5. Speculate on what advertising methods might be available in the future. What role might governments and legal authorities play?

REFERENCES

Advertising Standards Authority (www.asa.org.uk)

Central Intelligence Agency World Factbook (www.odci.gov/cia/publications/factbook)

CNN (www.cnn.com)

Dentsu (Japan) (www.dentsu.co.jp)

Interpublic Group (US) (www.interpublic.com) includes McCann-Erickson Worldgroup; Ammirati Puris Lintas; The Lowe Group; Western International Media.

Jupiter Communications (www.jup.com)

Ogilvy, D. (1990), quoted in Dennis Higgins, *The Art of Writing Advertising: Conversations with the Master of the Craft*, NTC Business Books, Lincolnwood, IL, p. 70.

Ogilvy and Mather (www.ogilvy.com)

Omnicom (US) (www.omnicomny.com) agencies include BBDO Worldwide, TBWA International Network, and Diversified Agency Services (DAS).

Procter & Gamble, US (www.pg.com)

World Factbook (www.odci.gov/cia/publications/factbook)

World Intellectual Property Organization (WIPO) (www.wipo.int)

WPP group (UK) (www.wpp.com) J. Walter Thompson; Ogilvy & Mather; Millward Brown, BMRD, Kantar Media Research.

Young & Rubican (UK) (www.yr.com) owns Burson-Marsteller.

FURTHER READING

Advertising Association (www.adassoc.org.uk)

Bovée, C.L. *et al.* (1995) *Advertising Excellence*, McGraw-Hill, London.

The Institute of Practitioners in Advertising (IPA) (www.ipa.co.uk) The IPA is the industry body and Institute for UK advertising agencies.

International Advertising Association (www.iaaglobal.org)

Marketing Week (www.marketingweek.co.uk)

Mooij, M.K. de (1997) *Global Marketing and Advertising: Understanding Cultural Paradoxes*, Sage Publications, London.

Index